The Origins and Rise of Dissident Irish Republicanism

NEW DIRECTIONS IN TERRORISM STUDIES

A series edited by

Max Taylor

Professor in International Relations (retired), University of St Andrews, Scotland where he was formerly Director of the Centre for the Study of Terrorism and Political Violence

P. M. Currie

Senior Visiting Fellow at the School of International Relations at the University of St Andrews, Scotland

John Horgan

Professor of Security Studies at the University of Massachusetts Lowell and Director of the Center for Terrorism & Security Studies.

New Directions in Terrorism Studies aims to introduce new and innovative approaches to understanding terrorism and the terrorist. It does this by bringing forward innovative ideas and concepts to assist the practitioner, analyst and academic to better understand and respond to the threat of terrorism, challenging existing assumptions and moving the debate forward into new areas.

The approach is characterized by an emphasis on intellectual quality and rigour, interdisciplinary perspectives, and a drawing together of theory and practice. The key qualities of the series are contemporary relevance, accessibility and innovation.

The Origins and Rise of Dissident Irish Republicanism

The role and impact of organizational splits

JOHN F. MORRISON

B L O O M S B U R Y

NEW YORK • LONDON • NEW DELHI • SYDNEY

Bloomsbury Academic

An imprint of Bloomsbury Publishing Inc

1385 Broadway	50 Bedford Square
New York	London
NY 10018	WC1B 3DP
USA	UK

www.bloomsbury.com

Bloomsbury is a registered trademark of Bloomsbury Publishing Plc

First published 2013

© John F. Morrison, 2013

ISBN: HB: 978-1-6235-6844-3
ePub: 978-1-6235-6009-6
ePDF: 978-1-6235-6677-7

Library of Congress Cataloging-in-Publication Data
Morrison, John F.
The origins and rise of dissident Irish republicanism : the role and impact of organizational splits / by John F. Morrison.
p. cm.
Includes bibliographical references and index.
ISBN 978-1-62356-844-3 (hardback)
1. Irish Republican Army–History. 2. Provisional IRA–History. 3. Real IRA–History.
4. Sinn Fein–History. 5. Republicanism–Ireland–History–20th century.
6. Republicanism–Northern Ireland–History–20th century. 7. Ireland–Politics and government–1949- 8. Northern Ireland–Politics and government–1969–1994.
9. Northern Ireland–Politics and government–1994- I. Title.
DA963.M59 2013
322.4'209415–dc23
2013029985

Typeset by Newgen Knowledge Works (P) Ltd., Chennai, India

For Mom and Dad.

*For believing in me, and supporting me
every step of the way.*

Contents

Foreword

Irish poet and playwright Brendan Behan joined the Irish Republican Army's (IRA's) youth wing when he was 14 years old. In retrospect, his subsequent involvement in 'adult' IRA was hardly surprising. His experiences in the youth wing, *na Fianna Eireann*, were steeped in lessons about Irish mythology, history and tradition. These were lessons Behan would first embrace and ultimately question. Behan quickly became fluent in the Irish language, before graduating to fully-fledged membership of the IRA. An astute observer of human behaviour, Behan is now synonymous with his apparently off-hand quip that one could always count on 'the split' to be the first item on the agenda at just about all IRA meetings. In fact, so inevitable was the tendency for all Irish Republican militant groups to splinter, factionalize and break apart that for his PhD thesis at the University of St Andrews, John Morrison asked whether the development of Irish Republicanism could best be characterized as 'the affirmation of Behan?'

In this carefully researched and meticulously detailed book, John Morrison cautiously navigates the alphabet soup of 'spoiler' groups that have arisen both before and since the Northern Irish accords finally offered a pathway to stability and a future for a community long denied it and still dealing with the legacy of decades of ethnic violence. If that was all this book did, John would already be providing a valuable service to those who seek to understand the recalcitrant nature of terrorism in Ireland.

Yet *Origins and Rise of Dissident Irish Republicanism* offers so much more than that. John's analysis is also informed by his thousands of hours of interviews with participants in this activity. Not content with relying on second-hand information or event-driven data, John went to the source – the dissidents themselves – carefully asking them questions about the nature of their continued struggle both to discredit the existing peace process and to themselves alone offer their (admittedly obscure) alternative to peace and prosperity in this region. It is his interviews with leaders and followers alike, both north and south of the Border, that distinguish his ability to decipher the difficult question of just who precisely are today's Irish Republicans in an era where just about everyone safely assumes – *I thought Ireland's terrorism problems were over?*

Today's dissidents are small, seemingly disorganized and apparently lacking in both vision and organizational acuity such that the dissident Republican scene is as chaotic as it is diverse. The affirmation of Behan? Definitely. A threat to peace and prosperity in the region? Possibly. They may be small, without much support, but just as the Provisional IRA itself proclaimed on the steps of a Dublin house in 1970, today's dissident Republican groups take their inspiration from the past. They maintain the capacity to choreograph attention in Northern Ireland through selective assassinations and characteristic disruption through low-level attacks, hoaxes and threats. They see themselves as nothing less than representing the true fundamentals of Irish Republicanism while Sinn Fein and the IRA leadership have, in the dissidents' eyes, sold out. Attempting to understand the dissidents' position is as much a challenge of understanding the psychology of betrayal as it is history. As the hundredth anniversary of the 1916 Easter Rebellion is almost upon us, those who would seek to dismiss the dissidents as irrelevant would be wise to avoid premature speculation.

It is fortunate then that this book provides the answers to the multitude of questions that arise from any attempt to make sense of these groups. John Morrison has done something extraordinary. He has presented us with nothing less than the definitive account of the origins and evolution of dissident Irish Republicanism.

Professor John Horgan
Series Co-Editor
New Directions in Terrorism Studies

Acknowledgements

This project started as a doctoral dissertation back in 2005. There was no way that I would have been able to make it through it without the help, friendship and support of so many amazing people. I would first of all like to thank Dr John Horgan for encouraging me to move over to St Andrews, and then to Pennsylvania, and for his constant support when things weren't running so smoothly at the beginning. Without you I wouldn't have a career. Thank you for showing faith in me all along the way. Similarly I would like to give the warmest thanks to Dr Michael Boyle for his insightful, thorough and often times witty supervision at the end of the project. I have the utmost respect for any man who can calmly tackle what was initially a 150 page theory chapter on organizations and split, and come out the either side laughing and joking while still pointing me in the right direction. Without either of these men I would never have been able to finish this. I would also like to thank Max Taylor, P. M. Currie and John Horgan, and all at Bloomsbury and Continuum, for inviting me to be part of the exciting New Directions in Terrorism Studies Series. It is an honour to be a part of this series.

I would similarly like to thank all those who were not officially affiliated with the project but yet gave me academic guidance and support, as well as their friendship throughout. I would especially like to thank all the staff within the School of International Relations, St Andrews and the librarians at the Northern Irish Political Collection in the Linen Hall Library, Belfast, as well as my colleagues at the ICST in Pennsylvania and the School of Law and Social Sciences at the University of East London. While I won't name you all I would especially like to thank Andrew Silke, Anthony Richards, P. M. Currie, Max Taylor, Paul Gill, Mia Bloom, Jim Piazza, James Windle, Daniel Briggs, Barry Heard, Fiona Fairweather, Nick Rennger, Trudy Fraser, Torsten Michel, Sean Elliott, Kimo Quaintance, Faye Donnelly, Alison Careless, Aleko Kupatadze, Adham Saouli, Joel Busher, Su Dutta, Kurt Braddock, Machelle Seiner, Bryan Carter, Patricia Berwick and Sharon Senner. You have all contributed to the completion of this project. For that I give you thanks. To my friends, flatmates and colleagues both past and present in St Andrews, Edinburgh, Sligo, Dublin, Belfast, London and all around the globe. I am very lucky to have met each and every one of you. I thank you all for your friendship, support, humour and interest in my work. There truly are too many of you to mention. But I hope that you all know how much your friendship means to me.

To everyone who agreed to give up their time to meet or be interviewed by me I will forever be grateful. There would be no book without you. Similarly I am forever indebted to all those who helped arrange interviews and meetings for me. In this regard I would especially like to thank Tommie Gorman of RTE for both welcoming me to Belfast and allowing me to 'use his name' in my attempts to meet with numerous people. This opened so many doors for me, doors which would have stayed shut without you.

I have the most amazing family, both immediate and extended, and they have excelled themselves in support and love throughout these years. This is especially true of my three siblings Una, Kevin and Brendan. You are more than my brothers and sister, you are my best friends. Also to my late Grandma, Ita Stephens, you always showed nothing but love and support to me in this and all of my endeavours down through the years. *Gra Mor.* And to Dianna, I am so lucky to have met you. Thank you for supporting me through the final stages of this process, and more importantly thank you for being you. However, above all others who have been mentioned I don't know how to thank my amazing parents Barbara and Peter Morrison enough. You have gone beyond the call of parenting in your support of me throughout these years. I love you both so much, and will never forget what you have done for me.

I would finally like to acknowledge the pain and suffering which so many people in Northern Ireland, Great Britain and the Republic of Ireland have endured throughout the years, be it at the hands of paramilitaries, security forces or governments. Nothing is worth the death, injury and permanent trauma which has been endured. It is up to us all to make sure that we never return to those days.

John F. Morrison,
Stoke Newington, London
June 12, 2013

1

Towards 2016

The fifteenth anniversary of the signing of the Good Friday Agreement has inevitably warranted a retrospective analysis of the historic, and at times fraught, peace process which brought about its naissance. There is no questioning that this process has succeeded in bringing a stable political culture to the region. Tourism is gradually increasing, and inward investment is starting to come to Northern Ireland's shores. However, just beneath the surface remains the spectre of paramilitary violence. While the end of 2012 was defined by the Loyalist 'flags protests' the most persistent threat still comes from violent dissident Republican groups. These groups have been responsible for some of the worst atrocities in a post-Good Friday Northern Ireland. From the Omagh bombing of August 1998 to the murder of prison officer David Black in November 2012 their violent actions have consistently attempted to wreak further havoc. Their tactics and targets may have evolved over time but their message has remained constant; they are committed to the maintenance of an armed campaign in order to achieve a united Ireland. The tragic evidence is there for all to see that the threat they pose should be of real concern to people both north and south of the border. Their violent acts, and threats of violence, have aimed to disrupt the normalization of a politically maturing region. While they have failed in destabilizing the political process they have succeeded in bringing a growing realization that while the peace process has prospered organized paramilitarism still survives, and will continue to survive. The Northern Irish Secretary Theresa Villiers admitted as much in a 2013 interview with *The Independent* newspaper.

The threat is severe and is likely to continue to be so in the years to come. I'm afraid to say there isn't an imminent prospect of these terrorist attacks coming to an end.[1]

This growing realization that the threat is not going away emphasizes the necessity of understanding. Academics and policy makers alike must strive to understand the purposes, aims and origins of these groups, while also recognizing why people may join or support them. Without this broader understanding in place the job of countering and silencing is all the more difficult. This understanding and appreciation of the groups and the threat they pose is not tantamount to approval. It is instead the essential starting point we must reach if we are ever to eliminate this threat, a starting point we are still largely seeking.

The debates continue about whether the term 'dissidents'[2] or 'ultras'[3] is the most appropriate to describe them. Throughout this book they are consistently referred to as dissidents. This phrase is used as it my belief that their most defining characteristic is their dissent from 'mainstream' Republicanism.[4] However, I do respect the argument of Jonathan Tonge and believe that it is also viable to refer to these groups as 'ultras' due to their persistence with armed Republicanism in deliberate ignorance of the wishes of the vast majority of the republican and nationalist populations of Ireland. However, the threat we are facing does not come from dissident Republicanism. There is clearly nothing wrong with disagreeing with the direction taken, and decisions made, by the Sinn Fein leadership. It actually promotes democratic voice within republican and nationalist communities. It allows for these communities to question this direction. However, it is when this dissidence is manifested in violent, threatening and paramilitary activity that there is a real problem to deal with. Therefore it is *violent* dissident republicanism specifically that we must be aiming to counter, and we must be supportive of the right to question all political parties through peaceful means.

With all this considered the purpose of this book is to add to our growing understanding. It aims to present and analyse the origins of these groups and the threats they pose. However, parallel to this it provides an analysis

---

[1] David McKittrick, 'Threat of Terrorism in Northern Ireland "will last for years"', *The Independent*, www.independent.co.uk/news/uk/politics/threat-of-terrorism-in-northern-ireland-will-last-for-years-8644668.html (Last Accessed, 9 June 2013).

[2] John Horgan and John F. Morrison, 'Here to Stay? The Rising Threat of Violent Dissident Republicanism in Northern Ireland', *Terrorism and Political Violence*, 23(4) (2011), 642–69.

[3] Jonathon Tonge, '"They Haven't Gone Away, You Know." Irish Republican Dissidents and Armed Struggle', *Terrorism and Political Violence*, 16(3) (2004).

[4] Horgan and Morrison, 'Here to Stay?', 671–93.

of how the Provisional Republican leadership brought the majority of their movement away from sustained paramilitary activity. This has been through the gradual politicization process which has seen them take their seats in Dail Eireann and Stormont and accept and support the legitimacy of the Police Service of Northern Ireland. It has similarly seen the former Provisional IRA leader, Martin McGuinness, move away from his paramilitary past to a political existence in which he, as deputy First Minister, has referred to violent dissident Republicans collectively as 'conflict junkies', 'stupid and selfish' and most vehemently of all as 'traitors to the island of Ireland'. In his eyes they are waging a 'useless war against peace'. In order to assess all of this the book analyses the process which preceded these parallel results. It asks the question how did we get to where we are today? How did we get to a place where the former leadership of the Provisional IRA is committed to upholding the peace, and pursuing their goals, through democratic and political means while the remnants of paramilitary Republicanism are still engaged in a never ending 'war'? These questions will be answered through the analysis of one of the most persistent phenomena in Irish republicanism, the split.

The power of a split extends far beyond the simple division of an organization. It is the culmination of a process of internal conflict and significant change. While a cursory analysis of division will justifiably signal them as the birthplace of the dissidents their effect is much wider than this. It is argued here that an analysis of the politicization of Provisional Irish Republicanism necessitates an analysis of the splits. It has been through splits that the Provisional leadership has been able to politicize. It has provided them with a platform to enable their gradual move away from paramilitary activity. However, at the same time it has similarly provided the impetus for sustained violent activity on both sides of the divide.

The continued success of the peace process is reliant on the commitment of the leaders of the various Northern Irish organizations, both violent and non-violent, to the utilization and promotion of peaceful politics.[5] However, what is more important is that the majority of their organizational membership similarly ascribe to the power of politics as opposed to the employment of the gun and the bomb. A leadership promoting peaceful politics is only constructive if they convince their internal membership and support of its benefits. It has been the ability of the leadership of the modern day Provisional IRA and Sinn Fein to successfully convince the majority of its membership of these benefits which has ensured their continued involvement in the enduring peace process.

---

[5] Paul Dixon, 'Political Skills or Lying and Manipulation? The Choreography of the Northern Ireland Peace Process', *Political Studies*, 50 (2002) 725–41.

This has been a slow gradual process. In order to fully understand it one must assess Irish Republicanism from as far back as the early 1960s. In doing so there are four key splits analysed throughout this book. Each of the four splits can, to a degree, be regarded as a result of the leadership of the time aiming to bring a stronger political emphasis on the movement. The level of politicization within each of the splits was different, as was the resulting strength of the parent and dissident organizations. Therefore one of the most important parts of the research here is to assess why one leadership was more successful than the other in convincing the majority of their membership to support their politicization process.

The four main splits analysed here are:

- **1969/70:** The IRA and Sinn Fein splits to form Official Sinn Fein and the Official IRA on one side and Provisional Sinn Fein and the Provisional IRA on the other side of the split.

- **1974:** The Official Republican Movement[6] splits which sees the creation of the Irish Republican Socialist Movement consisting of the Irish National Liberation Army and the Irish Republican Socialist Party.

- **1986:** A split in the Provisional Irish Republican Movement where a group led by Ruairi O'Bradaigh and Daithi O'Conaill, among others, leave to form Republican Sinn Fein and the Continuity IRA.[7] And,

- **1997:** The Provisional Republican Movement splits which sees the formation of the 32 County Sovereignty Committee[8] and the Real IRA.[9]

These splits are not regarded as separate entities. They are intrinsically linked within the macro-process of Irish Republican involvement in the 'Troubles'. The '69/70, '86 and '97 splits are contained within the Provisional process while the '69/70 and '74 splits can be considered part of the Official process.

The start date of the analysis, 1969, is resonant within Irish Republicanism for a number of different reasons, one being the failure of the Goulding leadership of the IRA and Sinn Fein to bring the Irish Republican Movement away from violence and towards the acceptance of parliamentary politics, resulting in a dramatic split in the movement, a split which continues to effect both Irish and

---

[6] Official IRA and Official Sinn Fein.
[7] While Republican Sinn Fein to this day deny any formal affiliation with the Continuity IRA, it is credible to mention the two groups as being affiliated.
[8] This group is now known as the 32 County Sovereignty Movement.
[9] 32 County Sovereignty Movement deny any official affiliation with the Real IRA. However it is widely acknowledged that 32 CSM acts as the political wing of the Real IRA.

British society and security to this day. Alternatively the end date of 1997 can be regarded as being the point in time where the Provisional Irish Republican Movement, then the largest grouping of Irish Republican paramilitaries, ultimately moved to reject the further dominant use of violence in order to achieve their goals, and accepted a peaceful political approach.[10] Consequently the choice of these four specific splits has provided an opportunity uncommon among much previous research on organizational splits. The four splits can be viewed as a continuum, with each interconnected.

The research analyses the splits from both an organizational and an individual perspective. Unlike much of the terrorism[11] literature the book does not automatically class the splits as a form of 'end of terrorism'. Not all splits are analogous to the end of the terrorist group and some can be more accurately regarded as the naissance of a terrorist organization. The '69/70 split which saw the birth of the Provisional IRA is a clear example of this.

While fundamentally analysing why and how the splits took place this research additionally allows one to see how and why the Provisional leadership of the late '90s was able to succeed where the Goulding leadership had failed. They managed to convince the majority of Irish Republicans to accept the use of peaceful politics, as opposed to the dominant use of violence, to achieve their aims and goals.[12] Therefore while the research at first glance is analysing splits in Irish Republicanism and the origins of the dissidents it is also at a deeper level assessing how the leadership of the Republican Movement

---

[10] This is not to say that there was no Provisional violence after this date. However the events leading up to and during this split can be regarded as vital in the process of the Provisionals ultimately announcing their permanent ceasefire and the decommissioning of their weapons.

[11] For the purpose of this book there will not be an extensive discussion outlining the ins and outs of the debate. Any use of the word 'terrorism' refers to the employment of violence or the threat of repeated violence by the individual or group intent on bringing about a social or political effect. The aim of this action is to bring about a state of fear in a wider audience than the direct physical victims of the initial act or threat of violence. A terrorist incident should be defined by the use of violence or the threat of violence to bring about social or political change, not by the specific motive of the perpetrators. Therefore terrorism is a tactic which can be employed by any individual or group, whether they are state or non-state actors. See, for example, Alex P. Schmid and Arthur J. Jongman, *Political Terrorism: A New Guide to Actors, Authors, Concepts, Data Bases, Theories and Literature.* (New Brunswick, NJ: Transaction, 2005), 1–38; Louise Richardson, *What Terrorists Want.* (London: John Murray, 2007), 19–39; John Horgan, *The Psychology of Terrorism.* (London: Routledge, 2005), 1–47; Bruce Hoffman, *Inside Terrorism.* (New York: Columbia University Press, 2006), 1–41; Leonard Weinberg, Ami Pedahzur and Sivan Hirsch-Hoefler, 'The Challenges of Conceptualising Terrorism', *Terrorism and Political Violence*, 16(4) (2004), 777–4; Andrew Silke, 'Terrorism and the Blind Man's Elephant', *Terrorism and Political Violence*, 8(3) (1996), 12–28; Richard English, *Terrorism How to Respond.* (New York: Oxford University Press, 2009), 1–26.

[12] While this is only referring to the 1969/70 and 1997 splits, the 1974 and 1986 splits also play a vital role in the process and need to be analysed in order to gain the most comprehensive understanding possible.

has successfully moved the majority away from a long campaign of terrorist violence and into the arena of peaceful politics. It provides an opportunity to assess why certain groups and individuals deemed it necessary to move away from this politicization process at certain points in time. In essence the research is not only looking to the reasoning for the splits but also to their functionality in allowing for Republican involvement in the peace process.[13]

The chosen splits can, and will, be looked at in two separate ways. They are analysed as individual stand-alone case studies of organizational splits. However, they are similarly analysed together as a series of intertwined splits within the one movement. They are presented in the book as four stage-based micro-processes within the macro-process of Republican involvement in the Troubles. This analysis is achieved by comparing and contrasting the two sides within each of the splits, as well as comparing the results of each of the individual divisions. Throughout the research there is the acknowledgement that the tactics of the Irish Republican Movement are not, and rarely have been, solely reliant on the use of terrorism and other violent tactics. It is a movement which has often times had armed and political wings working parallel to, and often times with, each other. This relationship between the use of paramilitarism and politics[14] is a theme which is acknowledged by many to have played a central role in each of the splits. In order to appreciate the aims and achievements of modern day 'mainstream' republicanism, and the continued actions of the dissidents, it is important to first of all understand and contrast the actions and attitudes of the movement today with that of the vast majority of republicans in the late '60s and '70s.[15] The present study utilizes the cases of the splits to achieve this understanding. In order to carry out this the analysis has aimed to answer three core questions.

1   Why did each of the splits take place when they did?

2   How did each of the splits take place?

3   What were the effects of the splits?

---

[13] This is distinct from the peace process literature which focuses on the success from a counter-terrorism perspective and looks at the actions taken in policy and legislation. This research looks to how one of the groups of illegal actors internally brought their membership away from the application of terrorism as a tactic and towards the acceptance of peaceful politics. See, Adrian Guelke, 'The Northern Ireland Peace Process and the War Against Terrorism: Conflicting Conceptions?', *Government and Opposition*, 42(3) (2007), 272–91.

[14] See, Leonard Weinberg and Ami Pedahzur, *Political Parties and Terrorist Groups*. (London: Routledge, 2003).

[15] Rogelio Alonso, 'Pathways Out of Terrorism in Northern Ireland and the Basque Country: The Misrepresentation of the Irish Model', *Terrorism and Political Violence*, 16(4) (2004), 695–713.

A decade of centenaries:
A decade of violence?

In 2012 the people of Ireland entered into what can be regarded as a decade of centenaries. One hundred years previous to this Ireland was going through some of the most defining events of its history. Change was afoot. The Irish Home Rule Movement born in the 1870s was gaining momentum in their demands for self-government and the repeal of the Act of Union of 1800. However, just as progress was being made, and the Government of Ireland Act of 1914 was placed on the statute books with Royal Assent, the First World War took centre-stage and redirected the focus of the United Kingdom and the rest of Europe. Under the flag of the United Kingdom tens of thousands of Irishmen lost their lives in battle. Back in Ireland in 1913, under the auspices of protecting the threatened Union of Great Britain and Ireland, an armed militia known as the Ulster Volunteers was established. They were rivalled by an Irish nationalist equivalent going under the name of the Irish Volunteers, a group supported by the Irish Republican Brotherhood, an organization dedicated to the establishment of an independent Ireland. It was their aim to pressurize the British government, and to ensure that the promise of Home Rule was seen through, while securing and maintaining the liberties of the people of Ireland. With tensions mounting and the desire for Irish independence intensifying the Irish Republican Brotherhood began to plan a rising, plans which came to the fore in Easter week of 1916, and made folk heroes of the likes of Padraig Pearse and James Connolly. Although it was to only last six days in that short time, the rebels managed to seize key locations across Dublin and proclaimed an Irish Republic independent of British rule.

While the Rising's leaders were court martialled and executed, they had succeeded in reviving the tradition of physical force republicanism. They inspired their own generation and continue to be called upon today to legitimize modern day physical force republicanism. The years after the Easter Rising saw the growing popularity of the Arthur Griffith led Sinn Fein, a party which was newly established at the turn of the twentieth century. In the 1918 general election they won the vast majority of the seats on offer in Ireland, 73 out of a possible 105. However, they refused to take their seats in a British Parliament which failed to recognize an independent Ireland. Theirs was a policy of abstentionism, a policy which has proved to be divisive throughout their now lengthy history. While the abstentionist Sinn Fein MPs failed to take their seats in the British parliament they did establish the First Dail Eireann (an Irish House of Representatives). One of their first acts was to declare the formal establishment of the Irish Republic, a move both the British and

Ulster Unionists rejected. This declaration and the British rejection sparked yet more violent conflict with the birth of the Irish War of Independence which engulfed the country between 1919 and 1921. This war was largely fought by the Irish Republican Army, a guerrilla organization descending from the Irish Volunteers of 1916. They targeted and attacked the personnel and symbols of the British presence in Ireland, from the armed police force of the Royal Irish Constabulary (RIC) to British Army patrols and barracks across the island. In turn the British fought back by bolstering the RIC ranks with the, at times brutal, auxiliary unit known colloquially as the Black and Tans. The violence of the war was brought to a close when the British government and representatives of the Irish secessionists met in 1921 entering into negotiations and ultimately signing the Anglo-Irish Treaty. The terms of the Treaty stated that the British would withdraw from the majority of Ireland, but that the British monarch would remain as head of the newly formed Irish Free State. However, it similarly declared that Northern Ireland,[16] an entity which the year previously had come into existence under the Government of Ireland Act, could opt out of the Free State if they so wished. As expected in December 1922 the Parliament of Northern Ireland declared their intention to remain part of the United Kingdom. The Treaty was only narrowly ratified when put to Dail Eireann due to the contentious issues, some of which are presented above. In the eyes of many the Treaty negotiators had fallen too far short of Irish independence. This in turn led to a split in both the IRA and Sinn Fein between the pro and anti-Treaty sides, a split which saw the dawn of the Irish Civil War (1922–3). This was won by the pro-Treaty side, the official armed forces of the newly formed Free State supported by the United Kingdom, and lost by the IRA. However, history has shown that this was far from the end of armed Irish Republicanism. From this war and the splintering Republican movement saw the emergence of Fianna Fail (1926) from the anti-Treaty side and Fine Gael (1933) from the pro-Treaty side. To this day, even with the recent 'collapse' of Fianna Fail, they remain the dominant forces in the political life of the Republic of Ireland.

While many moved away from armed force republicanism the IRA maintained the paramilitary struggle, stating that while there is still any form of British presence on the island of Ireland that there will be Irish men and women willing to take up arms. The dissident Republicans of today still hold on to this history to legitimize their armed campaigns. Through names such as the Continuity and the Real IRA they present a belief that they are

---

[16] Northern Ireland constituted the six counties of Down, Armagh, Derry, Fermanagh, Tyrone and Antrim. They are six of the nine counties in the province of Ulster. This was a provisional border ratified by the Boundary Commission of 1924–5.

the true republicans, the true heirs to 1916. While we are in the midst of the centenaries of these historic events it is my belief that the modern day dissidents will use this as an opportunity to intensify their paramilitary activity and reaffirm their belief in the legitimacy of armed republicanism. They will not only use it to target the British presence in Northern Ireland, they will continue to question the parties of the Republic of Ireland and the republicanism of the modern day Sinn Fein party; their comrades turned adversaries. While the vast majority of the people of Ireland, both north and south of the border, unionist and nationalist, republican and loyalist, show no support for paramilitary activity these 'micro-groups' still insist on the utility of violence. They will be targeting 2016 as a chance to reiterate their connection to the past, a reiteration which will only show their failure to respect the wishes of the people they claim to represent. Therefore while the main body of the book analyses the four core splits highlighted above the final chapter analyses the actions of post-Good Friday Agreement dissident Republicans and their push towards 2016.

Methodology

This research has been carried out predominantly through the utilization of semi-structured interviews with Irish Republicans who were involved across the splits. This interview process started in late 2007 and culminated in mid-2013. So as to gain as complete an understanding as possible the participants spoken to represent both leadership and rank and file members of Irish republicanism on each sides of the relevant splits.[17] Some of these participants were interviewed on multiple occasions and others were interviewed only once. While the interview data provided the main body of the analysis the results were validated, where necessary and possible, through the use of primary and secondary sources. However, central to the analysis was an appreciation for the fact that the decisions made at the time of the splits were not always based on a factually accurate interpretation of the context of the time. Therefore it is more important to understand why decisions were made, and why splits took place, due to individual and organizational interpretation of context rather than assessing whether this interpretation was factually accurate. The decisions could only be made utilizing an individual's knowledge at the time. As many of the participants are public figures they were given the option of having their name used

---

[17] For a full list of interviewees see Appendix A.

or anonymized. As will be seen throughout the process the majority of participants chose to have their name used. It is believed that this is due to the fact that the research was for the large part discussing a legal activity, within an illegal organization.

A variation of interpretative phenomenological analysis (IPA) was employed as the methodological tool to analyse the primary data generated from this series of interviews. IPA is a qualitative research technique which has predominantly been used in health psychology. However, recently academics from outside of health psychology have utilized it in their research. IPA has recently been applied to terrorism research. In their 2007 paper Mark Burgess and colleagues interviewed both former members of the IRA and peaceful civil rights activists to assess how they interpreted the social conditions in a post-Good Friday Agreement Northern Ireland. The researchers deemed IPA to be the appropriate methodological tool for their project as it provided them with an appropriate tool to analyse complex issues that directly impact on the lives of individual participants and their decision-making process.[18] This methodology allowed for them to gain an insight into how individuals make sense of their social circumstances. Their justification for the method is reflected here.

The nature of many previous IPA studies has led the researchers regarding 'traditional criteria' for evaluating research quality, such as reliability, as inappropriate in assessing their work.[19] While this may have been the case in previous research the political and historical relevance of the issue at hand and the nature of the participant group assembled have enabled the research results here to be assessed under the 'traditional' headings of both reliability and validity. While still maintaining the focus of the research on the individual participants' views and perceptions the availability and prevalence of secondary and tertiary sources such as speeches and policy papers from the time of the splits have provided the author with further valuable resources to strengthen the analysis.

IPA projects are principally concerned with issues which affect the individual actor, the decisions which they make and how this affects their life. One of the central research questions of the current project is 'why and how did the splits take place in the Irish Republican Movement?' At first glance

---

[18] Mark Burgess, Neil Ferguson and Ian Hollywood, 'Rebels' Perspectives of the Legacy of Past Violence and the Current Peace in Post-Agreement Northern Ireland: An Interpretative Phenomenological Analysis', *Political Psychology*, 28(1) (2007), 69–88.

[19] See, for example, Esther H. Riggs and Adrian Coyle, 'Young People's Accounts of Homelessness: A case study analysis of psychological well-being and identity', *Counselling Psychology Review*, 17(3) (2002), 5–15.

IPA may be deemed an inappropriate technique for answering this question. However, while this question is dealing with a group action[20] the application of IPA has gone on to ascertain what the important factors in splits are in the opinion of individual actors on either side of the divide and at different levels within the groups. Therefore in dealing with the questions of the research IPA has enabled the researcher to establish why and how the splits took place in the opinion of different groups of individuals. This is keeping with the philosophical origins of the technique as the researcher is concentrating on individual perceptions and opinions.

This book should not be regarded as a history of Irish Republicanism, or even a history of dissident Irish Republicanism. This is an analysis of the internal dynamics of one of the longest lasting terrorist movements the world has ever seen. It acknowledges the atrocities that were carried out in the name of Irish men and women, yet it does not focus on them. This should not be seen as an ignorance of the brutality. However, it is not the purpose of the book to focus on the terrorist elements of this movement. These acts of terrorist illegality are peaks within the overall existence of a terrorist organization. It is proposed here that it is only when we understand a group's continued existence within the troughs away from the illegal activity that we will fully understand what it really means to be a terrorist or a terrorist organization. Within these troughs are the internal debates and factionalisms analysed here.

---

[20] The split.

2

The affirmation of Behan?

The history of the Irish Republican Movement is beset by splits, from the aftermath of the Treaty of 1921 right up until the modern day. For many observers this prevalence of division may be regarded as the defining feature of Irish Republicanism. The oft-quoted line by Brendan Behan is regularly cited in reference to their historical frequency.

> Brendan Behan famously said 'the first thing on the Republican agenda is the split.'[1]

This nod to Behan is frequently used as a reflection not only of the predominance of splits within the Irish Republican Movement but as an illustration of how this regularity sets the movement aside from other organizations. However, while this can, and should, be regarded as a defining characteristic of the history of Irish Republicanism this does not mark it out as unique. A more accurate reflection of the situation would suggest that the incidence of splits is reflective of the situations experienced in all human organizations, rather than as a unique trait of Irish Republicanism. This assertion is supported by Richard McAuley, a senior advisor to Gerry Adams within Sinn Fein, and a former Republican prisoner and member of the Provisional IRA.

> The reality is that in almost any political party, any political organisation, any political movement you care to think of in the history of humanity somebody has disagreed with the leadership at some point and gone off and done their own thing, and sometimes more than once. So Republicans are no different than anybody else. God help us it is almost part of the human condition. We like to disagree.[2]

---

[1] Interview by the author with Gerry Adams.
[2] Interview by the author with Richard McAuley.

This dispelling of the uniqueness of the Irish Republican propensity to split allows one to analyse their occurrence in a more constructive and pragmatic manner. It allows the research to move away from looking for any unique feature of the movement which may leave it susceptible to split and instead analyses the normality of this organizational occurrence.

The present research classes each of the four main case studies, from 1969 to 1997, as occurrences of splits. This is not in line with the assessment by the current leadership of Sinn Fein. While acknowledging the presence of organizational division they are averse to refer to 1986 and 1997 as instances of 'splits'.

> You see you need to be careful about using the word 'split'. When you consider what happened in 1986, what happened at the beginning of all of this was a fairly major split between the Official Republican Movement and the Provisional Republican Movement. But in the aftermath of all of that we had all sorts of situations with for example the formation of the INLA and the IPLO, which really were offshoots from the Official Republican Movement. But in terms of what was known as the Provisional IRA right through there were two big situations that had to be dealt with, which were the 1986 situation and I think that clearly there was a split but it wasn't a 50/50 split, it wasn't even a 60/40 split, it wasn't even a 70/30 split. So be careful with the use of the word split. In terms of the situation in the aftermath of the Good Friday Agreement, even lesser so again, with probably only less than five percent of people deciding that this was not the way to go. So I wouldn't have regarded that as a split, so if you like those people tried to cause a split and it was fended off, it was defeated by the strategy put in place by the leadership of Republicanism of Sinn Fein, and indeed the leadership of the IRA were hugely supportive of the process of drawing the Unionists in, and the British government into peace negotiations.[3]

The aversion to the use of the word, which for many is regarded as analogous to failure, is a method utilized so as to protect and enhance this leadership's legacy. It is with great pride that they define their leadership as one which has successfully avoided splits, where others have failed to do so.

> . . . the ability of this leadership not to have splits is I think probably the real part of it which is unprecedented in Republican history.[4]

---

[3] Interview by the author with Martin McGuinness.
[4] Interview by the author with Gerry Kelly.

In the present research each of the case studies is individually, and collectively, analysed as instances of organizational split. However, it is recognized that the outcome of each is considerably different. The case of 1969/70 is regarded as a close to even divide. With respect to 1986 and 1997 in particular the results of these are significantly weighted in the favour of the Provisionals. Rather than ignoring these situations the present research has analysed them as cases of split so as to observe why and how there was such a distinct difference in the results of each case. While the current Provisional leadership may wish to be acknowledged as the only leadership to have avoided split they would be more accurately described as a leadership who successfully lessened the impact of two splits in 1986 and 1997. This provides the researcher with the opportunity to interpret how they managed to be as successful in attracting such significant levels of membership and support for their position, and why and how the Goulding leadership for example was unsuccessful in this regard in 1969/70.

By allowing oneself not to look at this regularity of splits as Irish Republican trait, but as a trait common to all human organizations it opens the research up to drawing our understanding of splits from a variety of theoretical sources. With this in mind the purpose of the present chapter is to provide a theoretical foundation on which the splits in Irish Republicanism will be analysed throughout the book. Throughout there is the acknowledgement that the tactics of the Irish Republican Movement are not, and rarely have been, solely reliant on the use of terrorism. It is a movement which has often times had armed and political wings working parallel to, and often times with, each other. This relationship between the use of armed struggle and politics[5] is a theme which is acknowledged by many to have played a central role in each of the splits. However, there is no getting away from the fact that for sustained periods of time throughout the Troubles and right up until the present day this movement has been one of the most consistent and persistent perpetrators of terrorism. Therefore it is a necessity to analyse these for what they are, splits in a terrorist movement.

To split is not to end: Splits in terrorist organizations

In recent times there has been an undoubted proliferation of academic interest in the tactic of terrorism, and the organizations which utilize it. However, even

---

[5] See Leonard Weinberg and Ami Pedahzur, *Political Parties and Terrorist Groups*. (London: Routledge, 2003), 105–18.

with the abundance of research there are still too many significant gaps in the literature. One of the fundamental areas often ignored is that of the internal conflicts within the terrorist groups. While the work carried out on internal organizational conflicts and splits in terrorist groups is sparse, this is not to say that it is completely non-existent.[6] However, terrorism researchers are still decades behind their contemporaries analysing economic, religious and social-movement organizations. In order to gain a greater understanding of splits in the Irish Republican Movement this chapter first proposes the application of political organizational and social-movement organizational theory to the analysis of splits in terrorist organizations and ultimately towards the development of a theoretical framework and a process model. In doing so the chapter critically analyses the current and historic thinking in the terrorism literature with respect to splits, as well utilizing a multi-disciplinary viewpoint in the development of a stage-based process model of splits in terrorist organizations.

In their 2008 study Jones and Libicki noted that of the 648 terrorist organizations they analysed 130 splintered, including 26 of the 45 religious terrorist groups in their sample.[7] While their statistical analysis may prove enlightening their viewpoint on the nature of splits must be considered significantly flawed. Throughout their analysis of the splintering of terrorist organizations they continuously refer to it as a way in which a terrorist group ends.[8] This fails to acknowledge the complete process of a terrorist split. A split need not constitute the end of the parent organization, as by definition it is only a section of the membership which is leaving, and therefore the parent organization can, and often does, still remain in existence. It can prove more accurate to describe an organizational split as a way for a new terrorist organization to form, or the end of an organization as a unified movement.[9] This is therefore the antithesis to the end of terrorism. While the parent organization may change in membership levels, and possibly strategy, tactics and goals, the organizational split does not necessarily constitute the end of

---

[6] See Ronald D. Crelinsten, 'The Internal Dynamics of the FLQ During the October Crisis of 1970', in David C. Rapoport ed., *Inside Terrorist Organisations*. (London: Frank Cass, 2001) (originally published in 1987), 58–89; Cynthia L. Irvin, *Militant Nationalism: Between Movement and Party in Ireland and the Basque Country*. (Minneapolis, MN: Minnesota University Press, 1999); Assaf Moghadam and Brian Fishman, *Fault Lines in Global Jihad: Organizational, Strategic, and Ideological Fissures*. (London: Routledge, 2011); Ethan Bueno de Mesquita, 'Terrorist Factions', *Quarterly Journal of Political Science*, 3 (2008), 399–418.
[7] Seth G. Jones and Martin C. Libicki, *How Terrorist Groups End: Lessons for Countering al Qa'ida*. (Pittsburgh: Rand Corporation, 2008), 35–6.
[8] Ibid., 10, 13, 36.
[9] Kent Layne Oots, 'Organisational Perspectives on the Formation and Disintegration of Terrorist Groups', *Terrorism*, 12 (1989), 139–52.

this group. The viewpoint taken by Jones and Libicki is much too narrow to constitute an accurate description of all forms of splits.

Terrorist groups are 'not monolithic entities that remain constant over time'.[10] Similar to all social organizations they adapt to their changing environment, an adaptation which may at times result in the splintering of the group.[11] Few terrorist organizations have successfully evaded the effect of organizational split in some shape or form. The Popular Front for the Liberation of Palestine (PFLP), the Democratic Front for the Liberation of Palestine (DFLP) and the Popular Front for the Liberation of Palestine-General Command (PFLP-GC) can all trace their roots to splits within the Palestine Liberation Organisation (PLO) nominally over the issue of the Israeli-Palestinian peace process.[12] Similarly between 1965 and 1975 the Basque separatist movement saw the development of numerous splinter groups breaking away from ETA, among these were ETA-berri, ETA-VI, ETA (politico-militar) and ETA-Zutik, each group claiming to be the true representatives of the movement.[13] While not always leading to organizational split the Islamist movements in Afghanistan, Egypt, Jordan, Lebanon, Pakistan, Iran and Sudan were all brought into serious crisis due to factionalism up to the late 1990s.[14] Recent times have also seen the splintering of sections of the Al-Qaeda movement. However, what may be considered as a splintering in Al-Qaeda would sometimes more accurately be described as the fragmentation of a terrorist coalition, as opposed to splits in a terrorist group. This was illustrated in 2009 by groups such as the Libyan Islamic Fighting Group (LIFG) leaving the Al-Qaeda movement which it had joined two years previously.[15] As this organization was an autonomous group prior to joining Al-Qaeda their movement away from the group must be considered in a different light to the formation of a completely new breakaway organization.

As can be seen by analysing any terrorist movement in-depth no single split is identical, even within an individual terrorist organization or movement like the Irish Republican Movement. While there may be similarities there

---

[10] Crelinsten, 'The Internal Dynamics of the FLQ', 61.

[11] Ibid.

[12] Audrey Kurth Cronin, *How Terrorism Ends: Understanding The Decline and Demise of Terrorist Campaigns*. (Princeton, NJ: Princeton University Press, 2009).

[13] Cyrus Ernesto Zirakzadeh, 'From Revolutionary Dreams to Organisational Fragmentation: Disputes over Violence within ETA and Sendero Luminoso', *Terrorism and Political Violence*, 14(4) (2002), 66–92.

[14] Fawaz A. Gerges 'The Decline of Revolutionary Islam in Algeria and Egypt', *Survival*, 41(1) (1999), 113–25.

[15] David Blair 'Extremist Group Announces Split from Al-Qaeda' (9 July 2009). www.telegraph.co.uk/news/worldnews/asia/5788302/Extremist-group-announces-split-from-al-Qaeda.html (Last accessed, 22 October 2012).

are individual unique contributing factors. In the lead up to splits in a terrorist organization, as with the splits in all other human organizations, the groups divide into at least two distinct factions. These factions develop due to an internal conflict and/or disagreement. Historically one of the most common divides is between the militant and the political factions, ostensibly those who wish to continue the terrorist activity and those who believe, or at least propose, that it would be more productive to advance their goals through non-violent political means.[16] However, the partition is not always this uniform in nature. While there may be political and armed factions in an organization, and an overlap between the two, this does not suggest that either of these wings is united themselves. Crelinsten in an analysis of the internal dynamics of the FLQ outlines that the most divisive factions within the organization were not strategic between politicos and militants but ideological between Trotskyites and Maoists.[17] Similarly the divide may have its origins in a leadership struggle[18] with the membership aligning behind either the potential or actual leadership.[19] This division may be portrayed by the sub-groups as being based on organizational strategy. However, the membership's decisions of who to support may be similarly based on a number of other more diverse factors such as personality, regionalism and loyalty.[20] These are all themes which will appear throughout the book.

While the reasoning for the factionalism may vary across organizations, and across time periods, it is clear that factionalism is not at all uncommon among terrorist organizations.[21] This can be more common within larger organizations[22] as there is greater diversity of opinion there is likely to be with regards the organizational objectives.[23] Crenshaw has proposed that the proliferation of factionalism in these organizations may be largely due to the terrorist group's aversion to internal dissent, or to borrow the parlance of Albert Hirschman they are averse to 'voice', and often regard it as more

---

[16] Kevin Siqueira, 'Political and Militant Wings within Dissident Movements and Organisations', *Journal of Conflict Resolution*, 49(2) (2005), 218–36.

[17] Crelinsten, 'The Internal Dynamics of the FLQ', 60.

[18] Oots noted that a leadership struggle may be initially motivated by the significant material benefits, prestige and other psychological rewards gained by leaders of political organizations.

[19] Oots, 'Organisational Perspectives', 149.

[20] John Morrison, 'Why Do People Become Dissident Irish Republicans?', in P. M. Currie and Max Taylor eds. *Dissident Irish Republicanism*. (New York: Continuum, 2011).

[21] Martha Crenshaw, 'An Organisational Approach to the Analysis of Political Terrorism'. *Orbis*, (1985), 465–89.

[22] This is consistent with Bruno Dyck and Frederick A. Starke, 'The Formation of Breakaway Organisations: Observations and a Process Model', *Administrative Science Quarterly*, 44(4) (1999), 792–822.

[23] Oots, 'Organisational Perspectives', 149.

detrimental than exit.[24] Therefore the organizations may promote separately functioning sub-groups so as to resolve intra-organizational conflict.[25] While not always destructive for the organization this can at times be extremely debilitating for the group in the pursuit of their goals, especially when there is a significant proportion of membership discontent. Therefore it is proposed here that the most successful and long lasting terrorist organizations have other mechanisms to deal with their most divisive internal conflicts, mechanisms which may be best explained by looking to the work of Albert Hirschman. However, before it is possible to look at the reasons for success or failure in a split it is first of all necessary to lay the foundations of understanding by first analysing why and how splits take place.

Why and how terrorist organizations split?

Before one can look in-depth at splits in terrorist organizations specifically it is necessary to first outline why and how all organizations split, and to gain a general understanding of the process preceding and following this division. Splits in human organizations are the result of internal debate, disagreement and/or conflict which ultimately results in one faction deeming it necessary to move away from the parent organization in order to establish a new group more in line with the viewpoints and expectations of that section of the membership. With this basic understanding splits are therefore the result of specific intra-organizational dynamics. Consequently in order to fully understand why and how a split takes place, and the resultant choices made by members, we must first appreciate organizational purpose, aims and function. This is not to say that the importance of external factors is diminished. As no split is completely unaffected by external forces one must always be aware of the environment in which splits take place and how certain external actors and actions can affect the internal dynamics of organizations.[26] However, in order to effectively assess the influence which external and environmental factors may have on an organization it is the organization itself which must first be clearly understood.

In agreement with Crenshaw, Oots and others it is proposed that terrorist organizations should be analysed and appreciated as a form of political interest

---

[24] Albert O. Hirschman, *Exit, Voice and Loyalty: Responses to Decline in Firms, Organisations and States*. (New York: Columbia University Press, 1970).

[25] Crenshaw, 'An Organisational Approach', 484.

[26] Deborah B. Balser, 'The Impact of Environmental Factors on Factionalism and Schism in Social Movement Organisations', *Social Forces*, 76(1) (1997), 199–228; Narayan Khadka, 'Factionalism in the Communist Movement in Nepal', *Pacific Affairs*, 68(1) (1995), 55–76.

group.[27] Similar to 'regular' political organizations the terrorist group aims to achieve collective values, which involve bringing about change in specific political and social conditions.[28] The key difference between a terrorist organization and other political organizations is clearly the reliance on violence and the threat of violence as a tactic.[29] As with all political organizations the goals of a terrorist organization can evolve over time. This may occur due to a number of internal and external factors. These changes and evolutions in goals are generally initiated by the leadership of an organization, or other influential members or groupings. It is more likely that they will be successfully brought about, especially if the changes are in any way controversial, when the leadership, individuals or groups wishing to implement the change, are at a moment of strength and have the support of the membership and the relevant external actors. If this is attempted at a time of weakness for the leadership the change is less likely to be successful and may, in extreme circumstances, lead to intra-organizational conflict, factionalism and ultimately split.

By focusing on the terrorist organizations, rather than the terrorist acts or motives, as a determining factor, significant advances can and have been made in our theoretical understanding of comparisons of terrorist groups.[30] By analysing the organizational process of the group one can integrate multiple aspects such as ideology, social conditions and individual motivations.[31] If the terrorist group is to be regarded as a political organization it is clear that the researcher must also recognize the dilemmas and recommendations faced by those researching non-violent political organizations.

At the centre of all organizational theory is the immediate goal of organizational survival. If a political organization is to have any chance of realizing the purposive goal of achieving a specified public good it is essential that they first maintain the survival of the organization. This is as true for violent political organizations such as the IRA as it is for peaceful democratic political organizations.[32] However, much of the organizational literature has looked at organizational survival at the basic level solely of maintenance of a unified membership. In reality this is not always beneficial for the progress of the organization to their desired goal. The maintenance of organizational numbers can at times be damaging, and unity can hold a group back from making their desired advances. A unified membership in name only should

---

[27] Crenshaw, 'An Organisational Approach'; Oots, 'Organisational Perspectives', 139.

[28] Martha Crenshaw, 'Theories of Terrorism: Instrumental and Organisational Approaches', in David C. Rapoport ed., *Inside Terrorist Organisations*. (London: Frank Cass, 2001) (originally published in 1987), 13–31.

[29] Crenshaw, 'An Organisational Approach', 465.

[30] Ibid., 465–6.

[31] Ibid., 472.

[32] Oots, 'Organisational Perspectives', 144.

be considered as a form of 'false survival'. Bueno De Mesquita outlines that in the case of split that the original leader's payoffs are equal to the sum of the potential membership and support that they can achieve.[33] However, this sum should not just be assessed by physical numbers, but by the intention of the membership. Therefore it has been deemed more accurate to hypothesize that the immediate goal for each sub-group at the time of split is organizational survival in a form which they respect and recognize. It is the addendum of 'in a form which they respect and recognize' to the traditional survival hypothesis which more accurately describes the immediate goal of an organization, especially at a time of split or intra-organizational conflict. Within these conflicts both sub-groups are not aiming for the survival of the organization just for the sake of survival. They wish that if the organization was to survive that the basis of the surviving organization would be in a form which they respected and recognized. It is deemed that there is no point in remaining within the organization if it is not at least deemed to be moving in the direction they aspired to. Therefore if the survival of the organization at a basic level of maintenance of a unified membership is stunting the desired progress of the leadership, or a rival sub-group, a split may prove beneficial in this regard as it rids the parent or breakaway organization of the internal detractors deemed to be holding the organization back.[34]

With respect to organizational splits it is necessary to understand the overall purpose of a political organization, the acquisition of specific public goods, before it is possible to fully appreciate the reasoning for the split. The most comprehensive evaluation of this must also analyse the intra-organizational conflicts which precede the formal division of the organization. However, only in extreme circumstances of conflict do actual splits occur. Throughout their existence human organizations, both violent and non-violent, invariably become involved in some form of intra-organizational conflict. It is believed that those conflicts which do result in split are deemed to be threatening to the organizational identity by at least one of the conflicting sub-groups.[35] While clearly assessing the existence and development of tensions and factions within the organization the study of intra-organizational conflict can demonstrate the capacity of conflict research to detail a wide variety of organizational behaviour due to the dynamic nature of the conflict process.[36]

---

[33] Bueno de Mesquita, 'Terrorist Factions'.
[34] Balser, 'The Impact', 226.
[35] See Fabio Sani and Steve Reicher, 'Identity, Argument and Schism: Two Longitudinal Studies of the Split in the Church of England over the Ordination of Women in the Priesthood', *Group Processes of Intergroup Relations*, 2(3) (1999), 279–300.
[36] Louis R. Pondy, 'Organisational Conflict: Concepts and Models', *Administrative Science Quarterly*, 12(2) (1967), 296–320.

Process model of split in terrorist organizations

Within the wider organizational literature stage-based process models have been developed in order to understand the origins, act and aftermath of split and/or intra-organizational conflict. I believe that a similar model would be beneficial in understanding the process of splits in terrorist organizations in general, and within the Irish Republican Movement specifically. Therefore what follows is the introduction to the proposed models developed for the purpose of this research. These have been developed through the analysis and consideration of various models of intra-organizational conflict and split, as well as the extended research from the organizational and terrorism literature.

Two separate models for splits have been developed in order to accommodate for the fact that not all splits are even in nature. The aftermath of some splits sees one side significantly more dominant than the other. In turn the processes for both of these forms of split vary in nature. The model for uneven split does not stipulate which side, the parent organization or the dissidents, is more dominant in the aftermath. While the first two models outline the processes of two separate forms of split the third outlines a model of split avoidance. This has been included as in order to attain the most comprehensive understanding of how and why splits take place it is necessary that one also understands how and why these organizational divisions are avoided. Unlike Bueno de Mesquita[37] these models are applicable for those splits where the dissidents are more extreme than the parent organization as well as those with more moderate dissidents.

Even split

Stage 1: The origins of split

Stage 2: Factional development

Stage 3: Inevitability of and preparation for split

Stage 4: Organizational exit and breakaway group formation

Stage 5: Aftermath of split: Inter-organizational competition and re-organization

---

[37] Bueno de Mesquita, 'Terrorist Factions'.

Uneven split

Stage 1: The origins of split

Stage 2: Factional development

Stage 3: Successful application of voice *and* inevitability of and preparation for split

Stage 4: Organizational change ormaintenance of status quo *and* organizational exit and breakaway group formation

Stage 5: Aftermath of split: Inter-organizational competition and re-organization

Split avoidance

Stage 1: The origins of conflict

Stage 2: Factional development

Stage 3: Successful application of voice

Stage 4: Organizational change ormaintenance of status quo

Stage 5: Aftermath of conflict: Re-organization

As is displayed above each of the three processes are identical for the opening two stages with the origins of split or conflict which may date back a significant length of time. It is proposed that it is the actions which take place within stage 3 which determine whether the conflict is resolved or results in split. If one of the developing sub-groups accentuates their position by actively preparing for split, due to what they deem an irreconcilable conflict, perceived to be threatening to organizational identity, then the third stage brings about the inevitability of split. However, if one or both of the sub-groups successfully apply compromise and voice then a split is avoided through either the maintenance of the status quo or the successfully supported implementation of organizational change. In the case of split avoidance this organizational change may at times be less extreme than the originally proposed change which may have caused the conflict, as compromise may have been needed.

In the aftermath of an even split there is competition for both membership and support with each organization trying to justify and legitimize their position. Both the parent organization and the breakaway group need to organize or re-organize in some way. During split avoidance the organization has to similarly re-organize as if there is not an adequate re-organization in the aftermath of conflict the residue may lead to further conflict and possibly split; thus beginning the process again.

The majority of intra-organizational conflicts are resolved during the third stage through the successful application of 'voice'.[38] Hirschman states that when one is dissatisfied with the quality of product produced by an organization and wishes to enhance this quality, rather than exit the organization, they will voice their concerns in order to change and improve the product. While the language used in this statement may be regarded as overly economic this can be modified so as to prove relevant in a discussion of political organizations; terrorist groups included. A similar statement may read that if a member, or group of members, disagree with the policies, strategies, outputs or goals of the organization they may articulate their concerns in order to bring about what they deem to be requisite changes within the organization. In Hirschman's terms this represents the members utilizing the option of 'voice'. This can be regarded as any attempt to bring about change rather than exiting the organization, either collectively or individually, at a time of decline. It must be noted that throughout his 1970 study Hirschman constantly refers to a drop or decline in 'quality' as being the impetus for the utilization of exit or voice. The 'quality' of product, strategy or policy is particularly subjective in nature. It would be more accurate to state that those who in their opinion perceive a significant deterioration in the quality of product, policy or organization will choose to utilize the options of either exit or voice. This provides the grounding for one explanation as to why some members will not utilize either voice or exit during a period of what by some may be perceived as deterioration. Those who neither exit nor voice concerns may believe that the output or product provided has not deteriorated in quality and may have improved in their eyes. With this understanding a potential split is avoided when 'voice' is successfully applied. There is no finite time by which this stage takes place. A resolution to the factionalism may be attempted over a prolonged period of time, one which can theoretically continue for the entire existence of a group.

Hirschman proposed that those members who care most about the quality of a product, or in the case of political organizations a policy, strategy or goal are the most active agents of voice within an organization. Consequently they will be the most likely to exit when there is what they perceive to be a significant deterioration in quality.[39] With this rapid exit at a time of perceived quality deterioration the organization is also deprived of its strongest voice.[40] If voice

---

[38] See, Hirschman, *Exit, Voice and Loyalty*.
[39] Ibid., 47.
[40] Ibid., 51.

is to have a significant impact, while these individuals are still present, the individuals utilizing it must be placed significantly within the organization.[41] It is much easier for leadership figures to ignore or dismiss the grievances of an ordinary member than a fellow member of the leadership, or other influential individuals. Similarly the type of organization may also prove relevant when assessing the influence of voice.[42] It has been identified that within terrorist organizations specifically voice may be regarded as a more serious threat than exit. Within many of these organizations voice can be regarded as an act of mutiny.[43] Crenshaw proposes that this may be due to the belief that terrorist organizations are founded as groups who prefer to utilize action rather than discussion as a tool. Consequently the leadership may see any form of voice as a questioning of their legitimacy.[44] While this may be true it is proposed that if the leadership is to be most successful in implementing, and gaining support for, any form of significant organizational or strategic change that they must be prepared to actively engage with voice. If they can successfully convince the majority of the membership, and perhaps convert some if not all of the agents of voice, in the necessity of change they will have a stronger and more robust organization. This is central to ones understanding of the determination of the result of a split.

Throughout Hirschman's discussion voice is predominantly referred to as a tool for the rank and file speaking out against the leadership. However, it should also be considered as a tool of the leadership. In order to successfully implement any significant proposed changes the leadership must gain support both internally and externally. The achievement of sufficient support will maintain and progress the organization in a form deemed acceptable to the leadership. Therefore similar to those rank and file members who wish to show their disagreement with the organization a leadership seeking reform must actively voice why they deem it necessary to implement such change. Through this form of voice the leadership is, similar to rank and file detractors, denouncing the structure, strategies or goals of the organization in its current appearance and in turn are calling for reform. When voice is utilized as a tool of protest against the leadership the remonstrated against may wish to defend their position. When voice is used as a tool of the leadership to call for organizational change the defence may come from the rank and file membership. This defence of the organization in its current form generally comes from those traditionalist members who do not approve of proposed

---

[41] Ibid., 70–1.
[42] Ibid., 74.
[43] Ibid., 121; Crenshaw, 'An Organisational Approach', 484.
[44] Ibid.

change. For some the preservation of the 'traditional values' can in extreme circumstances be more important than the preservation of a numerically strong membership. Connected to this may be a desire to form allegiances only with those who share similarly strongly held beliefs. Therefore the positioning of the group can at times be ostensibly more important to some members of the group than numerical strength. As stated earlier this is contrary to the traditional 'survival' of organizational theory, as well as Bueno de Mesquita assertion that the payoffs are 'the sum of the proportion of potential supporters that join her faction'.[45] This will be emphasized specifically in the case of the 1986 split between the Provisionals and the Continuity IRA and Republican Sinn Fein.

It is proposed here that voice should not be considered as a one-sided event. In order to produce the best analysis possible voice must be considered a two-sided dynamic process. This enables the analysis of the original action of voice as well as the subsequent responses. Dyck and Starke propose that the nature of voice is dependent upon the reception which it receives from the target audience and have suggested that dependent on the reaction voice may exist in one of three forms; *tolerated, resisted* and *militant* voice.[46] This ascribes to the notion of voice as a dynamic process.

When 'voice' has been unsuccessfully applied, or at times not even attempted, and at least one faction believes that they have no future within the organization, this leads to the inevitability of and preparation for a split. Within this vital stage of the process at least one of the factions are preparing for the inevitable split by reaffirming their opposition to their rivals on the central and peripheral issues. They attempt to court and firm up support both internally among the membership and externally among organizational supporters. This is no longer just to gain support for their beliefs but now also for the need of a new autonomous organization. In order to be successful in gaining sufficient levels of support each of the factions may target influential individuals and groups within the organization who in turn may bring with them their own support base. This can influence undecided members and supporters. As the rationale for a split can be multi-layered at this point, or even from the beginning, supporters can at times be convinced on a range of different issues. At times the decisions of allegiance may be solely made due to the presence of specific trusted individuals siding with one faction over another.[47] Within terrorist groups the preparation may also involve the acquisition, or securing of, sufficient weaponry and finances for the successful implementation and

---

[45] Bueno de Mesquita, 'Terrorist Factions', 402.
[46] Dyck and Starke, 'The Formation of Breakaway Organisations', 817.
[47] Morrison, 'Why Do People', 25.

continuation of a terrorist campaign. Not only is this important for the post-split survival and activity of the group, but it also can be utilized to display the capabilities of a group in achieving their aims. At times it is not enough for potential membership or supporters to agree with the group on the issues. They must also believe in the capabilities of the new group and agree that the issue(s) at hand are significantly threatening to the organizational identity to warrant this extreme organizational change.

The event of organizational exit and split takes place when one of the factions deems their presence within the terrorist organization no longer tenable and that they are ready to move away from the parent organization. This may be brought on by the completion of a satisfactory preparation for split whereby the dissidents believe that their future organization has sufficient levels to support, membership and resources to both survive and be successful in their aims. However, the split may also be prompted or enforced by their opposition in one of two ways. They may either force the hand of the dissidents by making their membership of the organization no longer tenable by implementing significant changes deemed threatening to the overall organizational identity of the group. Alternatively the leadership of the parent organization may expel their internal detractors. If the dissidents are expelled prior to the completion of their preparation this can have a detrimental effect on the survival of their new organization. It can have the result of a smaller membership and support, a lack of resources and an incomplete organizational identity and strategy. In these instances when the organizational identity and strategy has to be forged as an autonomous organization it can have a damaging impact on the possibility of gaining new membership and support, as they will find it difficult to ultimately survive and provide a strong argument for them as a viable alternative to the parent organization.

The final stage of the process is that of inter-organizational competition and re-organization. Any analysis of an organizational split should not end with the split itself but must continue by looking to the aftermath of the event and what takes place in the months and years subsequent and the consequences, both organizational and otherwise. This allows one to assess the effect and possible functionality of the split. While the intra-organizational competition for membership and support is a distinguishing feature of the lead up to a split this competition, in its new *inter*-organizational form, intensifies in the aftermath when there are two distinct organizations vying within the same populations for membership and support.[48] The decision as to which faction to side with may have been made by many in the lead up to the split but

---

[48] Oots, 'Organisational Perspectives', 147.

a number of individual members and supporters may remain undecided, or may even have been unaware of the developing factionalism within their organization. It is only when the division is no longer internal, and there exist two autonomous organizations, that many members and supporters will make the decision as to which group to side with.

The competition between organizations so close in origins and objectives requires the leadership of each group to be responsive so as to distinguish their organization from their competitor's and therefore make membership and support more attractive. This can often lead to a shift in goals or strategies employed by the organizations, which can move closer towards the centre, or alternatively towards the extremes.[49] The direction of the movement is often times dependent on the positioning of their competitor and how best to distinguish their group. The movement in position is not always one sided in nature and Della Porta and Diani have noted that the 'institutionalisation of one organisation can go along with the radicalisation of another'.[50]

Due to the parallel origins of both organizations this distinction and competition will not be for the purposive objectives but for the immediate goals, strategies and tactics. This competition can often times distract the organizations from the pursuit of their purposive objectives with an over-proportionate amount of time and energy being spent on competition between two groups who to many external observers may be regarded as indistinguishable in nature. As the conflict intensifies purposive goals are often times displaced by the aspiration to harm and inflict injury on the rival organization. This can lead to growing animosity between the two groups,[51] and may lead to a redefinition of 'enemy' in the eyes of some members. No longer are these former allies merely rivals, they can become enemies, irrespective of their closeness in goals. Invariably both groups share a common enemy, be it organizational, governmental or societal. However, they can be distracted by the perceived necessity to undermine former comrades, and therefore may concentrate more on the developing competition.

The level and degree of inter-organizational competition is often times reliant on the span of the divide. In a situation where there is one organization in the aftermath of the split which is significantly larger than the other, they will

---

[49] Mayer N. Zald and Roberta Ash, 'Social Movement Organisations: Growth, Decay and Change', *Social Forces*, 44(3) (1966), 332.

[50] Donnatella Della Porta and Mario Diani, *Social Movements: An Introduction* (second edn). (Oxford: Blackwell Publishing, 2008), 151.

[51] Leonard Weinberg and Louise Richardson, 'Conflict Theory and the Trajectory of Terrorist Campaigns in Western Europe', in Andrew Silke ed. *Research on Terrorism: Trends, Achievements and Failures*. (London: Frank Cass, 2004), 138–60.

not see as much of a need to compare and justify their positions against those of their competitors. Due to their dominance they will tend not to perceive their former allies as a threat to their position, and can consequently pay more attention to moving the organization forward in the pursuit of their purposive goals. Conversely their rivals will be in too weak a position to effectively challenge the stronger party's position. However, if there is a relatively even split the competitive situation is accentuated. Both sides will perceive the other as a threat to their position, or their potential dominance within the relevant communities. This can result in a near disregard for their ultimate objectives and an over-zealous concentration on demeaning their movement competitors.[52] As will be seen later this disparity of post-split competition can be observed in the aftermath of two of the most significant splits in Irish Republicanism. In the aftermath of the 1969/70 split the divide was relatively even. Consequently both groups perceived the other as a threat and entered into a violent feud. In contrast the aftermath of the subsequent 1986 split the divide was uneven. The Provisional IRA and Sinn Fein remained dominant, retaining the vast majority of the membership. As a result they were able to continue with their long-term strategy without showing any acute concern about the threat which the newly formed groups posed to their membership, recruitment and legitimacy. In contrast the Continuity IRA and Republican Sinn Fein were not strong enough to mount a significant campaign against the Provisionals. The majority of their focus had to be on the establishment, and ultimately, the survival of this new movement.

Competition can result in the mutual enticement of members or supporters over from one group to the other,[53] or alternatively can demoralize people to the consequence of them moving away from the movement completely. For those organizations, such as Irish Republican groups, reliant on a very specific population for membership and support the level of competition can become intensified due to the finite potential communities which they can draw from. Therefore for ethno-nationalist organizations the existence of a competing group can be particularly threatening.[54] Within such a situation if a group can assemble a package of both purposive and selective incentives which is perceived to be better than those of the competing organization, it will be able to entice new and rival members to join their group faster than their

---

[52] In Barabara Ryan, 'Ideological Purity and Feminism: The US Woman's Movement from 1966 to 1975', *Gender and Society*, 3(2) (1989). The author witnessed this while researching American feminist organizations of the 1960s and 70s. Within the feminist movement there was a considerable level of 'painful personal attacks' against inter-organizational competitors. This climate of competition had a significant debilitating effect on the movement as a whole.
[53] Hirschman, *Exit, Voice and Loyalty*, 28.
[54] Irvin, *Militant Nationalism*, 40.

competitor can. With respect to those individuals willing to move from one organization to another in such a competitive situation they will be most likely to be those who choose organizational affiliation mainly due to the selective incentives on offer. Therefore competitive organizations will often find the need to increase the supply of these selective incentives.[55]

The resulting competition for support, membership and resources can result in a significant variation in organizational behaviour.[56] This change of behaviour can result in a significant rise in the intensity of violence.[57] Due to the fact that terrorist organizations by definition are committed to the application of violence as a tactic to achieve their political targets one of the principal competitive arenas becomes terrorist activity.[58] This can be witnessed in an escalation of violence in the pursuit of organizational membership and support, or alternatively competition can result in the naissance of inter-organizational violent feuds between the former allies. Violent acts are often times utilized to display the potential, capabilities and dominance of the perpetrator in comparison to their rivals. Therefore the main purpose of the act may in actual fact be an attempt to undermine competitors and prove the strength of the organization to their members and supporters, as well as potential future recruits on each of these fronts. Schiller outlines that the purpose of the simultaneous attacks by Abu-Nidal on El-Al ticket counters in Rome and Vienna airports in December 1987 was not linked to their pursuit of an independent Palestine but instead was an act designed to humiliate Yasser Arafat in the eyes of the sympathetic Italians and Austrians.[59] It has also been indicated in reference to those groups utilizing the tactic of suicide bombing that in the presence of multiple insurgent organizations, each competing for public support, there can be an increase in the scope and quantity of suicide bombings as a show of strength from each of the particular organizations.[60] Such violent actions in a competitive environment can similarly be conceived in order to attract the necessary financial resources from external supporters in order to maintain the organization activity, as well as providing the ability for the organization to develop the supply of the selective incentives necessary to attract and maintain membership.[61]

---

[55] Oots, 'Organisational Perspectives', 148.

[56] Ibid., Hirschman. *Exit, Voice and Loyalty,* 44; Crenshaw, 'An Organisational Approach', 473, 483.

[57] Crenshaw, 'An Organisational Approach', 486.

[58] Irvin, *Militant Nationalism,* 41.

[59] David S. Schiller, 'A Battlegroup Divided: The Palestinian Fedayeen', in David C. Rapoport ed., *Inside Terrorist Organisations.* (London: Frank Cass, 2001) (originally published in 1987), 90–108.

[60] Mia Bloom, *Dying to Kill: The Allure of Suicide Terror.* (New York: Columbia University Press, 2005), 78.

[61] Ibid., Oots, 'Organisational Perspectives', 148.

External sponsors will be hesitant to support an organization financially, or otherwise, in any significant way unless it believes that it has the ability to act on and achieve its stated aims. Often times the only way to display this ability for action in a competitive environment is by mounting extensive violent actions or campaigns of violence. In this competitive situation, with the heightened threat of exit of personnel due to the existence of a new close alternative, the leadership of the organization must continually attempt to distinguish their organization from that of their competitors in order to prevent the defection of the membership, support and sponsorship to their rivals. If the membership perceive the alternative grouping to be more actively pursuing their objectives they will be more likely to defect.[62] Therefore the increase in violent activity in a competitive arena can be a display of strength and the greater potential to achieve the targeted objectives.[63]

As has been suggested above the stages during splits are not necessarily uniform, and during each individual process the length of time to move from one stage to another varies. Even though there may appear to be a uniformity of themes an in-depth reading of the analysis will show that these factors can carry different degrees of importance and consequence across cases. It is this variation in influence of different factors which can prove most significant in the outcome of the split.

While the presentation of the analysis within this book may suggest that each of the splits analysed should be regarded as independent case studies the three 'Provisional' splits should be looked upon as three separate stages of Provisional evolution and ultimately politicization. Similarly the 1974 and post-Good Friday Agreement splits are part of the overall Republican evolution. One can gain a greater understanding of the causes, results and consequences of the cases by simultaneously analysing each individual split as a micro-process within the macro-process of Irish Republican evolution rather than looking at each as an independent case study.[64]

In other studies the comparison of unrelated splits may present the analysis of each equivalent stage side by side. However, due to the interconnected nature of these splits it has been deemed beneficial and informative to present them splits chronologically so as to examine the macro-process of Irish Republican involvement in the 'Troubles'. Therefore rather than viewing the splits as individual entities they are assessed and presented as processes which had a significant effect on each other. This is signified in the fact that

---

[62] Crenshaw, 'An Organisational Approach', 486.

[63] Jones and Libicki, *How Terrorist Groups End,* 13.

[64] This is a belief shared by the Republican groups themselves. See, IRSP, 'Brief History of the IRSP' in *IRSP Information Sheets.* (Date Unknown)

the micro-process of 1969/70 split in general, and the split aftermath in particular, must also be regarded as the opening stage for both the 1974 split in the Official Republican Movement and the 1986 split in the Provisionals.

'Success' and the functionality of splits

While the process models presented above outline the stages which an organization goes through in the lead up to and aftermath of a split they also provide an introduction to how one faction may be more 'successful' than the other. In order to fully understand an organizational split we must look beyond why and how a split takes place. We must attempt to grasp an understanding of how a faction achieves significant levels of support in the face of the other faction's difficulty to gain traction. Hirschman describes how one of the competing parties may achieve such a success. The situation outlined refers to the ideological division being positioned along a finite linear scale from left to right. If the parties initially place themselves at the midpoints of their respective right and left halves this can prove the ideal situation for the voters as it will be clear for the majority of them where their allegiances lie as ideological distance between them and the parties' policies will be minimized.

However, the situation changes if and when one of the parties, for argument's sake the one on the left-hand side of the scale, is able to shift its location without incurring any negative cost while the party on the right-hand side feels ideologically or otherwise tied to their existing position on the scale. In such a situation a vote-maximizing party will invariably move their position towards the right of the scale. As long as their position remains towards the left of the other party they should retain a hold on their far-left voters while stealing new voters from the 'right-wing' by moving in towards their terrain.[65] The advancing group must be careful in such a situation not to move too far towards the right as their party's position may become indistinguishable from their competitions's and this may result in the emergence of a third party maximizing on left-wing voter discontent and disillusionment.[66]

It is hypothesized that a similar model may be applied to factionalism within terrorist organizations. Consider the previously referred to factionalism between those in support of militant strategies and those advocating political

---

[65] Hirschman, *Exit, Voice and Loyalty,* 66–7.

[66] Just because this description describes the parties as being left-wing or right-wing this does not automatically translate as the parties' having left-wing and right-wing political view but merely refers to the positioning of the parties along a non-specified linear scale.

strategies. If the political advocates see themselves as being tied to their proposed strategies and would not advocate any move along the linear scale towards the militants but the militants regard their position as more flexible this then provides a distinct opportunity on which the militant leadership can maximize. If they move their position along the scale closer towards the political advocates' while still retaining a militant basis they are more likely to gain the support of the undecided members and supporters while still retaining their core militant support and perhaps stealing some of the voters from the political advocates. Such a movement can significantly marginalize the faction who feel tied down and can negatively impact on the influence which they hold within the movement. Therefore if the factionalism ultimately results in a split it will be, in this hypothetical situation, the militants who are more likely to emerge with the largest levels of support and membership. This supports the previously stated position that the leadership will aim to insure the survival of the organization in a form as close to their ideal as possible. Therefore while the new position taken up by the militants may not be their ideal it at least retains the survival of the movement, and a large proportion of the support and membership, closer to their ideals than if they had retained their original position which may have resulted in a more dramatic split between the two factions. The tied down position of the political advocates in this situation results in minimized levels of support and membership for their grouping in the aftermath of the split and therefore leaves them in a weaker position to attain their objectives. Throughout an organization's existence there may be a number of such linear factionalisms, sometimes more than one may be occurring at a time over different issues. Therefore a successful and long-lasting organization will have to be constantly aware of such dilemmas and deal with them adequately without having a perceived drop in quality of their policies, strategies and goals.

Leaders need to ease in to transition and make sure not to alienate their base. Alienation of the base can make it extremely difficult to make any progress.[67] Such a transition can require a significant amount of patience on behalf of all actors both externally and internally, and the timing of changes in policy must be carefully decided so that the leadership is in maximum control and external events play as minimal a negative effect as possible. Similarly often times they may wish to manipulate the external and internal sentiment at the time of significant incidents which may move people's strategic leanings closer to their ideal political position.

---

[67] Frederick D. Miller, 'The End of SDS and the Emergence of Weathermen: Demise Through Success', in Jo Freeman and Victoria Johnston eds, *Waves of Protest: Social Movements Since the Sixties*. (Oxford: Rowman & Littlefield Publishers INC, 1999), 303–24.

This interpretation of Hirschman's model may be streamlined in conjunction with Irvin's 1999 model. In this she proposes that the opportunities, constraints and resources within which the organization defines its goals and selects its strategies can be affected by three separate factors. These are regime responsiveness, organizational resources and the absence or presence of competing political groups prepared to work with the governments. The interaction between these three variables is said to impact the respective size and influence of three categories of members; *ideologues, radicals* and *politicos.* Similarly the interaction is said to set the strategic context in which the members choose among the variety of violent and non-violent strategies available to them.[68] Taking all of this into consideration the interpretation of Hirschman's model of inter-group competition will say that at an appropriate time an alteration in the strategy adopted by the politicos[69] closer towards that of the ideologues,[70] without significantly compromising their original position will possibly attract a significant proportion of the radicals[71] and even convince a small proportion of the ideologues to join then. This does not specify that merely by moving their strategy slightly 'to the right on the line' that they will automatically gain more supporters for their position. They must justify and legitimize their position and strategy using a combination of the tools available to them. This can be a gradual process of gaining support around the regime from membership and supporters at all levels and waiting for the right time to bring about any proposed changes. They may need to utilize the support and legitimization given to them by various influential individuals and position themselves within the historical context of the movement. Essentially they must convince a significant proportion of the membership and support that the position they are taking and the strategies and tactics they are suggesting are for the good of the organization and their purposive objectives, the specified public goods. They must simultaneously convince a significant proportion that their strategy is not just good for the organization and its objectives but that is also *better* than those being put forward by their internal competitors or any other alternatives which may be on offer at the time. In essence they need to convince that this is the necessary evolution of the terrorist group.

---

[68] Irvin, *Militant Nationalism*, 25.

[69] Those members who support a strategy of 'base-building and political education'. Irvin, *Militant Nationalism*, 29.

[70] Those who are 'drawn to action more than political discussion', Irvin, *Militant Nationalism*, 25.

[71] Those who prefer active struggle but also are more willing than ideologues to 'compromise, though not necessarily abandon, movement principles if those sacrifices appear likely to win real concessions from the incumbent regime'. Irvin, *Militant Nationalism*.

Why should we analyse splits?

It is clear that there are necessary advances to be made in the study of splits in both organizational and terrorism research. In the general organizational literature the discourse needs to move beyond why and how splits take place and focus more on the functionality of the splits across different types of organizations. The theoretical presentation on show in this chapter has strived to advance this by utilizing the splits as the basis for a stage-based process model. The analysis of splits in terrorist groups is still in its naissance and is stunted by its constant inclusion in the 'end of terrorism' literature. It is too blinkered to assess the splits purely in this manner. The occurrence of an organizational split is not analogous to the end of terrorism or the end of the terrorist group. Approaching the topic from this standpoint fails to acknowledge the variety of forms of split which have no relationship with the end of terrorism literature and by considering it with this notion of finality will invariably fail to appreciate the long-term effects which the split may have. Therefore it proves more accurate to describe an organizational split as a mode of terrorist group formation, or the end of an organization as a unified political movement rather than as an end of terrorism.[72]

Within the realms of counter-terrorism it is necessary to understand the problem before one can solve it. It is proposed that the policy-related lessons from this not be seen as the normal negative opportunity of merely splitting off 'pragmatists from radical rejectionists'[73] but as a more positive understanding of how to get a larger proportion of the supporters and membership to advocate a more political solution to their perceived problem. With sufficient consideration and understanding it is believed that successful positive counterterrorist strategies can be developed. This is a theme which will run throughout the entirety of the book. Consequently this book should not only be seen as an analysis of the origins of dissident Irish Republicans but also as a parallel study of the evolution and politicization of modern day Irish Republicanism.

The interpretation of Hirschman's model of party and firm competition presented earlier may prove informative in how we tend to look at organizational splits. Within the terrorism literature when there is a focus on splits there is often the assertion that the splitting of organizations can be utilized, or manipulated, in counter-terrorism initiatives so as to isolate and

---

[72] Oots, 'Organisational Perspectives', 142.
[73] United States Institute for Peace, *How Terrorism Ends Special Report*. (Washington, DC: United States Institute for Peace, 1999).

nullify the radical factions of the organizations.[74] However, it may prove more worthwhile to look at the benefits of such a situation in a somewhat different way. Policy makers and counter-terrorism practitioners can benefit more by regarding such intra-organizational conflict and factionalism not specifically as an opportunity to merely split off 'pragmatists from radical rejectionists'[75] but as a more positive opportunity to get a larger proportion of the supporters and membership to advocate a more political solution to their perceived problem. Within the terrorist movement and their support network at any one time there will only be a percentage who are tied down to a particular viewpoint or strategic policy.

The more successful splits from a counterterrorism perspective may not always be those with a clean divide between the militant and political. The most successful will possibly be those splits which result in the political faction making slight compromises, and therefore moving along the linear scale closer in policy to the militants, and convincing the undecided membership and supporters, and some of the staunch militants, to join and support their grouping. This will result in a larger membership and support structure for those who eventually wish to achieve their objectives through political means. If in the same situation the political faction had believed themselves to be significantly tied down to their position they would have achieved significantly less support both externally and internally. While their position in this situation may have been more in line with that of governmental policy their position is largely inconsequential if they cannot gain sufficient levels of support within their given community and membership. However, in the situation where they have altered their position in order to gain a larger degree of support they will have more influence and therefore will be able to bring a larger grouping on a more gradual process towards politicization and democratization, and consequently isolate the more militant faction weakening their position. In essence what is being proposed here is that splits should not be looked at as a single act where governments and counterterrorist officials see the radical factions of organizations isolated. They should be regarded as an opportunity to bring as many members as possible closer to the acceptance of non-violent strategies. Therefore in these cases organizational splits and factionalism must be analysed to establish how the political wing can best gain the highest levels of membership and support, and therefore lessening the influence of the militants. In such situations they must be perceived as

---

[74] Cronin, *How Terrorism Ends*, 68; United States Institute for Peace, *How Terrorism*, 1; Crenshaw, 'On How Terrorism Ends', in United States Institute for Peace, *How Terrorism Ends: Special Report*. (Washington, DC: United States Institute for Peace, 1999), 2–4.
[75] United States Institute for Peace, *How Terrorism*, 1.

a step in the gradual process towards politicization. Eventually if the political grouping can maintain their high levels of membership, as will be shown with the Provisional IRA and Sinn Fein, and support they may be able to move their position, and that of their followers, back to their ultimate one of a purely political position. In an ideal situation the grouping will not have to compromise political strategies at any point and will be able to bring the majority of the membership and support along with them in the implementation of a purely non-violent political strategy. However, this is not always the case in reality and the political advocates will have to gradually introduce their supporters to non-violent political strategies.

What follows in the remainder of the book is the application of this theoretical understanding to the analysis of splits in Irish Republicanism. However, where necessary and viable the researcher has validated the themes raised through the analysis of both primary documents produced at the time. This is referred to within various footnotes. Similarly previous secondary analysis is referred to for verification purposes. The use of such materials strengthens the validity of the results displayed, and does not detract from the importance of the viewpoints of the participants. Often times the documents referred to were donated to the author by interview participants to support their opinions and analysis of the situation.

3

The tinder piles up

The tinder piled up and it went on fire in '69.[1]

The origins of each of the splits lie in the years and decades previously. A thorough analysis must look a number of years back in order to gain the most comprehensive understanding of not only the cause but the significance of each individual micro-process to fully understand the entire macro-process. Many would suggest that this analysis should not just focus on the actions of the years previous but that there should initially be a clear foundation of understanding of the Republican history from generations past, an opinion put forward by Sean O'Bradaigh in his assessment of the origins of the 1969/70 split.

> I suppose you can find the proximate roots of it, the immediate, within a couple of years and then you can find the approximate roots going back even further. I suppose the approximate roots are going back to the Treaty almost, because each time this comes up we are coming up against the same question, 'do we recognise the Free State?' . . . Will we maintain the Republican position or will we go and take part in [Dail Eireann].[2]

A clear understanding of Republican history enhances ones understanding of each of the splits. However, the majority of interviewees focused on the 'proximate roots' of the divides. The origins of the splits were detailed to lie in the years previous to the ultimate organizational divisions. While those of

---

[1] Interview by the author with Anthony Coughlan.
[2] Interview by the author with Sean O'Bradaigh.

extended organizational experience, especially at a leadership level, at the time of each of the splits were able to go into the most detail about the significant events of the years previous. However, those with less operational experience at the very least acknowledged the significance of specific incidents, policies and strategies from the years prior to their affiliation. The process leading up to and including the split of 1969/70 has been identified as the derivation of Irish Republican involvement in Troubles.

Of all the splits 1969/70 is the one which has most defined modern day Irish Republicanism. It resulted in the birth of the Provisional IRA and Sinn Fein as well as the formal introduction to Republicanism of many of its most influential modern day actors. The significance is observable throughout all elements of Irish Republicanism from 1969 to today. Therefore without a clear understanding of this divide one cannot completely understand modern day Irish Republicanism.

The present chapter presents the process in the lead-up to the 1969/70 split. The process has been divided into five stages. The dominant themes are illustrated within the sub-sections of each stage. These are the themes which the analysis showed to be the most important in each of the separate stages. They should not be interpreted as separate sub-stages but as, at times, overlapping themes relevant during the specific stage of the process. The title of each stage illustrates the stage's dominant characteristic and function. The title of each sub-section illustrates the dominant themes described. Analysis presented in this and each of the chapters was guided by the analysis of the interview data. However, this was expanded to also include relevant primary and secondary sources.

The five stages identified in the process of the 1969/70 split are supportive of the even split model proposed in Chapter 2:

Stage 1: The origins of 1969/70

Stage 2: Factional development

Stage 3: Inevitability of and preparation for split

Stage 4: Organizational exit and breakaway group formation

Stage 5 and Stage 1: Aftermath of split: Competition and re-organization.

The fifth and final stage of the micro-process must also be regarded, in combination with the rest of the split process, as the opening stage of the micro-processes of the 1974 and 1986 splits.

Stage 1: The origins of 1969/70

While the 'approximate' origins of the split lie within the history of Irish Republicanism each of the participants interviewed who had extended experience prior to 1969 identified the culmination of the Border Campaign of the late 1950s and early 1960s as the requisite starting point for any understanding of the 'proximate' origins of the split.[3] Similarly six of the participants without extensive Republican experience discussed the effect of the aftermath of the Campaign. However, for the majority of new recruits to the movement in the lead up to and after 1969/70 the origins of the split through their own experiences took place in the immediate lead up to the formal division of the movement.

Of those participants who outlined the importance of the aftermath of the Border Campaign all agreed to its transitional nature. This is reflected in the analysis of those from both sides of the split.

Within this first stage of the 1969/70 split the dominant themes to be covered are

- Public Support: Weakened
- Membership: Exit, Weakening and Disillusionment
- The Origins of Factionalism

Public support: Weakened

One of the major consequences of the Border Campaign was that there was deterioration in the public support for the Movement and what it could offer the general public of Ireland. This was a campaign which initially gained the support of the people. This support was displayed at the election of four Sinn Fein candidates to the Dail in 1957, each of whom was an abstentionist candidate. However, this support was short lived and in 1962 the Army Council of the IRA officially declared its end. Whatever support the Republican Movement had gained at the beginning of the campaign had dissipated and was probably even lower than it had been prior to the beginning of the operation. This decline was evident in the weakening of both passive and active support.

---

[3] For description of the Border Campaign see, Tim Pat Coogan, *The IRA*. (London: Harper Collins, 2000), 297–329.

> After beginning the campaign it was obvious that we didn't have enough weapons or support, safe houses etc.[4]

This lack of support was a result of a public feeling that the Republican Movement was not representative of the beliefs of the wider Irish population in general, and the nationalist population particularly. There was disconnect between the actions and beliefs of the Republican leadership and the populations they claimed to represent. With this decline in support it proved extremely difficult for the IRA to operate to any significant degree of success. The Irish public were not supportive of any form of armed action to achieve a united Ireland. This proved a critical issue in the failure of the campaign. It is recognized by those within the Movement that in order to sustain any form of paramilitary campaign they needed support within the community. Without this support the armed campaign invariably fails. This would later prove to be a lesson which future generations of Republican leaders would bestow on new recruits.

> It is vital you cannot sustain a military campaign without the support of a substantial section of the population. . . . Why the 56 campaign failed is because the Republican Movement had become isolated from the people, had become divorced from the people, had become elitist, had become obsessed with ending partition and had turned a blind eye to issues like unemployment and poverty and emigration and bad housing.[5]

This reaffirms that if a movement is to gain the public support it requires it is first of all necessary to make their groups objectives relevant among their existing and potential support base.[6] During the Border Campaign the focus of the leadership was not on those issues of importance to the general Irish population. Instead there was perceived to be an almost blinkered focus on the achievement of a united Ireland and the ending of partition. This issue of disconnect with the wider public was one which was sought to be addressed in the aftermath of this failed armed campaign.

With the end of the Border Campaign in 1962 the deterioration of support for the Irish Republican Movement continued. Even for those who remained supportive of the movement there was a heightened disillusionment with its trajectory. This lack of support led to a drop in the finances of the

---

[4] Interview by the author with Mick Ryan.
[5] Interview by the author with 'Paul'.
[6] Kent Layne Oots, 'Organisational Perspectives on the Formation and Disintegration of Terrorist Groups'. *Terrorism*, 12 (1989), 145.

movement and resultantly a drop in their accessibility to new weapons and artillery.[7] Without a significant degree of public support it proves impossible to succeed in achieving objectives, unless they can alter the issues which have distanced them from the population they claim to represent. Each of the interviewees across the splits emphasized the importance of public support in determining the results of an intra-organizational conflict.

Membership: Exit, weakening and disillusionment

This disillusionment with the IRA and Sinn Fein within the public sphere was reflected in the membership with a number of members exiting at both armed and political levels. The disillusionment within the movement during the Border Campaign is illustrated in an extensive IRA statement from April 1964. The IRA outlined the fractious nature of the relationship between the IRA and Sinn Fein during the Border Campaign, and especially when the campaign was called off by the IRA.[8] The Border Campaign was seen by members as a failure. This is a view put across by both sides of the split. This is illustrated in the quotes below, the first from Tomas MacGiolla the 1960s president of Sinn Fein and after the split president of Official Sinn Fein and the second from 'Alex' an influential Belfast IRA member who was among those Belfast Republicans who overthrew the Belfast IRA leadership and refused to support the national leadership of Cathal Goulding in 1969. 'Alex' was an influential northern member in the formation of the Provisional IRA and in the aftermath of the 1986 split chose to support the Continuity IRA and Republican Sinn Fein.

> When the campaign eventually ended, that's the 1950s campaign, which was Operation Harvest. . . . It was a disaster from the very beginning and after a couple of years there were many people who already were disillusioned and didn't want the campaign and wanted it to stop. It went on for another four years.[9]

> The Border Campaign was a fiasco, looking back on it now it was a total fiasco. I don't think they had a clue to be honest with you about what they were up against.[10]

---

[7] This is why it is essential for organizations to continue to recruit new members and support so as to maintain organizational survival, and therefore the continued actions of the group should look to maximize support. Kevin Siqueira, 'Political and Militant Wings within Dissident Movements and Organisations'. *Journal of Conflict Resolution*, 49(2) (2005), 220–2.

[8] IRA Department of Publicity. *IRA Army Council Statement.* (April, 1964), 5.

[9] Interview by the author with Tomas MacGiolla.

[10] Interview by the author with 'Alex'.

As with the public this operational failure resulted in the disillusionment of large proportions of the organizational membership which in turn brought about the exit of members who neither saw the possibility of success nor agreed with the strategies and tactics of the organization at that point in time.

As well as a large number of members exiting the movement there were also a significant number either interned or on the run. With large proportions of the IRA leadership on the run for the concluding years of the campaign the standing and relevance of IRA was further weakened. There were also those who were forced to exit for reasons not directly related to the Republican Movement, largely due to economic issues. As with all sectors of the population this significantly affected the IRA and Sinn Fein during the 1950s and 60s as numerous existing and potential members were forced to emigrate, and in turn the majority of them ceased active involvement with the movement. Therefore the public good which the Republican Movement were aiming to achieve, a united Ireland, was significantly detached from the public goods desired by the majority of the population, economic stability.[11]

The aftermath of the Border Campaign resulted in such a detrimental weakening of the IRA that it can be considered from both a morale and physical capability point of view and that it was at one of its weakest points. Resultantly in the aftermath of the campaign even within those areas which historically would be considered as strong Republican regions the membership levels were extremely sparse. This was evident in the Republican heartlands of Belfast where the IRA membership was close to non-existent.

> When I got out I reported back to the Republican Movement. . . . I think there was only about eight people in the Movement in Belfast, most of them just didn't come back in. . . . So basically it was starting from scratch all over again.[12]

This deterioration in the membership cannot purely be blamed on the failure of the Border Campaign and outward migration. The weakening of the movement was taking place prior to the Border Campaign. As with the deterioration in support many people no longer saw the relevance of joining the IRA or Sinn Fein. As a result there were very few members in the 1950s and early 1960s. The Republican Movement for the most part was a deteriorating group irrelevant to the vast majority of the population of Ireland, and therefore ineffective in operations and in attaining objectives. It

---

[11] This can be regarded as a 'push' factor for both members and supporters. John Horgan. 'Disengaging from Terrorism'. *Jane's Intelligence Review*, 18(12) (2006), 34–7.
[12] Interview by the author with 'Alex'.

is invariably the levels of membership, and their choices of who to side with in an intra-organizational conflict and the resultant split, which decides the successes and failures of either side.[13]

The origins of factionalism

The fragility of Republicanism in the aftermath of this campaign emphasized the need for a re-evaluation in order to maintain organizational survival.[14] This necessity resulted in an overhaul of the national leadership, a move widely supported. The new leadership with Cathal Goulding as the IRA Chief of Staff distanced their policies from the armed struggle and placed a greater emphasis on a left-wing political approach.[15] They realized that in order to achieve the basic aim of organizational survival that they needed to first of all reconnect with both their membership and support base. The emphasis was placed on making the aims and strategies of the organization relevant to the wider Irish population. At this stage of the process the new leadership was largely setting about re-organizing both the IRA and Sinn Fein. This resulted in moving away from the armed struggle and the introduction of new strategies and policies largely centred on politically left-wing ideals.

The left-wing political policies espoused by the Goulding leadership at this time were significantly removed from the policies traditionally promoted by the organization. For many of the traditional old-guard within both the IRA and Sinn Fein these policies would have been considered negatively as 'extreme socialism'. This led to discontent among a number of old-guard traditionalists at this initial stage of the process of split, a discontent which resulted in a number of them exiting. This theme is resonant throughout each of the micro-processes and is supportive of the belief that the immediate goal for each sub-group at the time of split is organizational survival in a form which they respect and recognize.

The immediate objective for all organizations is the survival of the organization. While this requires the recruitment of new members it also requires the maintenance of the existing support. Times of significant change within an organization, such as in the aftermath of the Border Campaign, are

---

[13] Throughout this and the subsequent chapters there is an analysis of individual participants' allegiance choice in the aftermath of and process of the splits. The reasons established in these sub-chapters are generally focusing on reasons linked to the reasons for organizational split. However, allegiance choice is often times made for non-split related reasons.

[14] Richard English, *Armed Struggle: The History of the IRA*. (London: Pan MacMillan, 2003), 83.

[15] For an explanation of the choice of Goulding as Chief of Staff see, Patrick Bishop and Eamon Mallie, *The Provisional IRA*. (London: William Heimann, 1988), 33–4.

the most likely times of membership exit. Therefore it must be the aim of the organizational leadership to convince a significant majority of the membership of the necessity for these changes. At this stage of the process the exit of these members was not as damaging to organizational survival as it is in later stages. The necessity for change in the movement provided the Goulding leadership an opportunity to adjust the policies and strategies to fit better with their aspirations for the left-wing politicization of the movement.

The new left-wing ideology advocated by Cathal Goulding and his affiliates was largely influenced and formulated by some of the new members and advisors introduced to organized Republicanism at the dawn of the new leadership. The most influential of these was the left-wing academic Dr Roy Johnston.[16]

One of the methods Johnston and others utilized to open debate within the movement, as well as externally, was the development of the Wolfe Tone Society in 1963. This group was made up of individuals who were predominantly external to the movement. In their meetings they discussed the future development of Republicanism in Ireland. The ideas generated from the Society in turn influenced much of the positioning of Republican policy of the time. These groupings were predominantly made up of left wing political activists and academics. Some of the most prominent voices were those promoting and supporting the politicization of the IRA and Sinn Fein. The politicization process took place independent of the Wolfe Tone Society. However, it was within these meetings that many of the influential policies were developed in depth and resultantly adopted either in part or completely by the leadership.[17] Prominent to this influence was their distancing from armed Republicanism.

While the promotion of peaceful political strategies was the cornerstone of the leadership's re-organization this was not fully supported by all members. Many of the old-guard traditionalists were wary of the growing left-wing influence within the movement. This rise of left-wing ideals coupled with the demotion of the armed campaign resulted in the origins of internal factionalism.

It was only after I came out [of prison], because from the inside you are cut off, it was only after I came out. When you seen the way these people were going. Their attitude was that physical force was unwanted . . . they

---

[16] For an account of Johnston's view of Irish Republicanism in the 1960s of Roy H. W. Johnston, *Century of Endeavour: A Biographical and Autobiographical View of the Twentieth Century in Ireland.* (Dublin: Tyndall Publications, 2006), 167–289.

[17] This is an example of the application of voice in the attempt to change the direction of the movement.

were following the Communist Party line and objectives. . . . It was not long till you realised that that is what was happening and people who were objecting to it were dismissed.[18]

While a number of members exited the movement as a result of their discontent, and others were dismissed from the organization, there were also those traditionalist members who stayed and internally displayed their dissatisfaction. There were a number of disgruntled members at this stage of the process but they could not yet be considered an organized dissident faction. There were dispersed showings of rebellion, none of which characterized as an organized campaign against the strategic policies of the leadership. For many the origins of their discontent lay in the downgrading in importance of the IRA and the resultant decline in military training and operations. There were small regional pockets of Republican activists who resisted this move and continued with small scale armed training and operations.

For the new leadership and their advisors the IRA was seen as an out of date entity, one which in its historical form could stand in the way of the politicization and rise of Sinn Fein. They wished for IRA members to become political and less militarily minded, and hence required all IRA volunteers to join Sinn Fein. This promotion of political strategies in the place of the armed campaign was resisted by some volunteers who carried on with the utilization of physical force Republicanism in spite of the national leadership's wishes.

The IRA was considered moribund, virtually moribund, at that time. I mean there was obviously some grouping there in the background. . . . He [Goulding] was trying to get Republicans to go political. . . . Famously of course there were incidents, there was some trading dispute down in the west, there was some action some boats were blown up.[19]

This discontent was not extensively on display in the initial periods of this stage of the process. However, towards the end as the left-wing political direction was becoming firmly established the voices of discontent became louder and more constant. This could still not yet be considered as a highly organized dissident sub-group at this stage.

Not all of the discontent can be seen to originate as a result of strategy or policy specific issues. There were also some personality based issues at the heart of this initial factionalism. While this was evident in some instances at a national leadership level it was similarly illustrated locally in the Republican

---

[18] Interview by the author with 'Alex'.
[19] Interview by the author with Anthony Coughlan.

regions of Ireland. As with all human organizations internal grievances need not always be with strategic, tactical or policy based disputes. Some of the factionalism and ultimately the decisions made by individuals during the process of split can be seen to have their basis in personal as well as, or at times in spite of, strategic and policy issues. This is illustrated by the late Dolours Price in her description of the Republican community in Belfast in the 1960s.

> I knew the Sullivans and Billy McMillen and all the people that became Stickies [Officials].[20] I would have known them all before there was any idea of splits, discussions or talk. I would have heard my father talk about . . . he didn't like that crowd, he didn't like Billy McMillen. A lot of personality things went on. He didn't like Billy McMillen on a personal basis and didn't like Malachy McGurran, didn't like Billy Sullivan and Jimmy Sullivan.[21]

This displays that while much of the factionalism may have been policy and strategy driven throughout the process of split that people's affiliations may have originated from their personal attitude to the people on either side of the divide.

This present stage viewed as the origin of the 1969/70 split provides significant support for the hypothesis that the conflict at the centre of a split is, for at least one of the sub-groups, threatening to the organizational identity.

The emerging change of focus by the movement at this stage was for a number of the old-guard traditionalists seen as detrimental to the organizational identity. For many of them they would have been significantly sceptical of an extreme left-wing influence on the movement especially when it was detracting from the armed campaign and the pursuit of a united Ireland. This change of focus was due in part to the growing heterogeneity of the membership with the introduction of a number of left-wing politicizers with no desire to continue the armed campaign. Not only was there a divergence of policy related viewpoints at this stage but there was also a clash of personalities.

At this early stage of the intra-organizational conflict the dissidents were still of the belief that the division could be resolved by internal measures rather

---

[20] This is a derogatory term used to refer to members of the Official Republican Movement. The origin of it can be seen in the different ways that the members of the Officials and Provisionals attached their commemorative Easter lilies. After 1969/70 the Officials attached their lilies to their clothes using an adhesive gum, hence the name 'Sticky', and the Provisionals used a pin. The Provisionals for a time were referred to as the 'Pinheads' or 'Pinnies', but this did not last as long as term 'Sticky'.

[21] Interview by the author with Dolours Price.

than by exiting to form an autonomous organization. They were attempting the utilization of voice in an attempt to bring about change while also defying orders. A number of small units were still actively preparing for an armed campaign, thus defying the intentions of the leadership and illustrating their belief that there was still the possibility of resolving their grievance and partaking in future armed campaigns. However, the most resonant reason for the avoidance of split at this stage was that the dissidents were not adequately organized to exit in a collective manner to form a new grouping or to overthrow the existing leadership.

Stage 2: Factional development

The Republican Movement of the late twentieth century is defined by its policies and actions in Northern Ireland. However, the policies and strategies employed in the immediate aftermath of the Border Campaign focused predominantly on actions in the Republic of Ireland. The purposive goal of the movement was still the unification of Ireland. However, this was not the immediate priority of the new leadership. Their central aim was organizational survival.

In order to begin thinking about unification they first had to re-establish some degree of membership and public support. This led to the re-organization of the movement and the establishment of more left-wing political tactics. Therefore the leadership was revising and expanding the public goods which they were aiming to achieve, and in doing so they were attempting to become more relevant to the Irish public. While this was successful to some degree in gaining support and recruiting, to a small degree, a new breed of left-wing political supporters it also led to discontent within the organization. This discontent was mainly from the traditionalist old-guard. The central theme can be defined as development of the organization into a form close to the leadership's ideal. Parallel to this, however, must be regarded the emerging dissident specific theme of survival of the traditional values, policies and tactics. While this conflict does not cause organizational split at this stage of the process it is during this stage that it is identified as threatening to organizational identity, and therefore the dissidents begin to attempt to maintain the survival of their intended organizational identity.

Throughout the process it is the competition between the aims of the dissidents and the leadership which decides the outcome of the split. In this stage concrete strategic and policy changes were attempted by the leadership through internal constitutional reform. While this succeeded in firmly placing their agenda on the table one of the most significant developments from this was the growth and organization of a dissident sub-group.

Within this politicization was the introduction of multiple actual and proposed changes. The most significant result of this was multi-platform intra-organizational conflict. The vast majority of interviewees outlined the nature of the factionalisms within the movement in the lead up to the 1969/70 split. A number of these participants described a variety of separate conflicts which were developing concurrently. The conflicts at the heart of the factionalism were conflicts due to the armed or political strategy.

With respect to factionalism due to political strategy of the movement at this stage the analysis shows that there were a number of different political elements which were causing factionalism at the time. There was particular reference both in the interview process and in the analysis of primary and secondary sources that the core political conflicts within the movement were due to the proposal of left-wing political strategy or the proposal to drop the traditional abstentionist policy.

Much of the factionalism within the movement can be defined by the strategy or issue over which the conflict is based. However, the location within the movement where the conflict was dominant is similarly important. Two key areas within the movement were identified by participants, these are within the national leadership and in the membership between the religious old-guard and the left-wing politicizers. The most dominant of these two was the developing factionalism within the national leadership which eventually contributed most to the split. Most notable in the factionalism in the national leadership is the fact that five members of this leadership interviewed emphasized its importance.

What follows now is the analysis of why and how these factionalisms developed and their importance in the micro-process of the split. As has been stated above the central theme to this stage is *policy changes: too much too soon.*[22]

Policy changes: Too much too soon?

The foundations of factionalism were laid in the initial stage with the emphasis being placed on the development of a left-wing political movement and the

---

[22] For the dissidents these policy changes can be considered as push factors each contributing to their exit from the organization. The net result of each of them combined makes them a more prominent cumulative push factor than if there was only one change. Horgan 'Disengaging from Terrorism'; The significant proposed changes in tactics and strategies of the leadership brought about intra-organizational conflict, E. Burke Rochford Jr, 'Factionalism, Group Defection, and Schism in the Hare Krishna Movement'. *Journal for the Scientific Study of Religion*, 28(2) 1989, 163.

downgrading in importance of the IRA. However, it was not until the full extent of the proposed changes was nationally apparent that the dissident factions became more vocal and organized. Five interviewees, four Provisionals two at a leadership level and one siding with the Goulding leadership in a leadership advisory capacity, outlined the prominent role played by the outlining of and voting on a set of proposals for change at both General Army Conventions of the IRA and Ard Fheiseanna of Sinn Fein in 1965 and 1966. While there were multiple proposed changes put forward by the leadership the one which caused the most discontent among the dissenters was the issue of abstentionism.[23] The changes proposed that the abstentionist policies to all three parliaments, Dail Eireann, Westminster and Stormont, would be dropped.[24] For many traditionalist members these policies were the cornerstone of what it was to be an Irish Republican. In essence this coupled with the other proposed changes was read by the dissidents as the politicization of the Irish Republican Movement and the downgrading of the armed struggle and therefore threatening in their eyes to the organizational identity. This is emphasized by Ruairi O'Bradaigh, a leading dissident member in the splits of both 1969 and 1986.

> When you added it up the aim was quite clear, it was to convert a revolutionary republican movement into a constitutional party. Although that wasn't said as such that was the effect of it and in keeping with that, as was logical, the IRA was to be run down.[25]

For O'Bradaigh and many other leadership and experienced members the most important, and damaging, of the proposed amendments was the dropping of the abstentionist policies. However, there were multiple other proposed and real changes which were taking place in the movement at both a political and armed level simultaneously. The politicization of the movement, combined with a heightened emphasis on the civil rights movement, provided multiple platforms for internal dissent. The analysis of the interview data suggests that the leadership was trying to change too much too soon and therefore this provided a stronger support for the development of dissenting sub-groups.[26]

---

[23] For a discussion of Sinn Fein as an abstentionist party see, Agnes Maillot, *New Sinn Fein: Irish Republicanism in the Twenty First Century.* (London: Routledge, 2005), 8–20.

[24] Sean MacStiofain, *Memoirs of a Revolutionary.* (London: Gordon Cremonisi, 1975), 92–3.

[25] Interview by the author with Ruairi O'Bradaigh.

[26] This is supportive of the belief that if organizational changes are dramatic and rapid that they could lead to the significant exit of those tied to the original model. Donatella Della Porta 'Leaving Underground Organizations: A Sociological Analysis of the Italisn Case', in Tore Bjorgo and John Horgan eds, *Leaving Terrorism Behind: Individual and Collective Disengagement.* (London: Routledge, 2009), 66–87; see also Sandy Kristin Piderit, 'Rethinking Resistance and Recognising Ambivalence: A Multidimensional View of Attitudes Toward and Organisational Change'. *The Academy of Management Review*, 25(4) (2000), 783.

The opinion that the leadership was trying to do too much too soon was delineated by seven participants, three Officials and four Provisionals. Of these seven participants six were experienced members prior to the split in 1969/70 and one Provisional was a new recruit in 1968. The thematic analysis of the present stage of the process outlines the key areas of proposed strategic change as well as the actions taken by the movement at this time and how they contributed to the strengthening and development of intra-organizational conflict on a number of different fronts. What follows is the analysis of some of the changes being implemented and proposed at this time at the effect they had in causing both factionalism and intra-organizational conflict. The themes are

- Armed to Political
- Politically Left-Wing
- Abstentionism[27]

There is similarly analysis of factionalism specifically within the national leadership. The excess of the changes and factionalisms illustrates the notion that the leadership was trying to change too much too soon.

Armed to political[28]

Central to their politicization of the movement the leadership wished to downgrade the importance of the IRA. The roles of the two wings of the movement, Sinn Fein and the IRA, were reversed and the objective was for the IRA to promote the political policies of Sinn Fein.

> In the IRA the Army had democratised. The Army was used to promote Sinn Fein. We didn't say this is how you have to vote but the policies should determine who should vote in what way.[29]

While there were many would be Provisionals who saw the need for a strong political party their opinion was that this should work in unison with the IRA.

---

[27] It is also acknowledged that there was minor factionalism due to Republican involvement in the civil rights movement and also between the traditional Catholic membership and the left-wing.
[28] The dominance of the debate about and relationship between the armed and political strategies in each of the four splits supports the assertion by both Cynthia L. Irvin, *Militant Nationalism: Between Movement and Party in Ireland and the Basque Country.* (Minneapolis, MN: Minnesota University Press, 1999), 41 and Martha Crenshaw, 'An Organisational Approach to the Analysis of Political Terrorism'. *Orbis*, (1985), 465–89 of the centrality of these strategies and their relationship in intra-organizational conflicts within terrorist organizations.
[29] Interview by the author with Mick Ryan.

Therefore they believed in the need for a movement which was both political *and* armed, not one or the other.

> I thought that the two could go in tandem. . . . This was all being phased out. Goulding said at an army meeting in Connacht that 'the time is long past going around barns with a Thompson.'[30]

This downgrading of the IRA specifically and the armed struggle in general were too severe for some members. The weakening of the IRA and the armed campaign was seen to be weakening the entire movement and its opportunities to achieve its objectives. There were even those who would ultimately remain loyal to the Goulding leadership, and some who would be considered part of that leadership, who believed in the need for a strong IRA.

> In 1965 I resigned as Quartermaster. I felt that the Movement had to get weapons, had to re-arm. Even a small amount would have been helpful.[31]

Some of the major forces behind this politicization have, with hindsight, come to believe that the only significant achievement of the process should be viewed as negative. In no way did they turn the Republican Movement into a strong political force. The primary consequence of this pursuit of politicization must ultimately be regarded as the split of 1969/70. While it must not be viewed as the sole cause of the split it must certainly be regarded among the primary factors. This is emphasized by the left-wing politicizer, Anthony Coughlan, who was brought in by the Goulding leadership in the aftermath of the Border Campaign.

> The politicisation of the Republican Movement in the 60s, what did it lead to? It led to the famous split which was a disaster. In retrospect if I was back in my twenties again I am not so sure I would have followed the same political force.[32]

At this stage of the process a number of opponents to this expressed their discontent to this downgrading of what many regarded as an essential element of the strategy of the Irish Republican Movement. This dissatisfaction was expressed at both leadership and rank and file levels and predominantly but, not exclusively, among members of the IRA.

> Most of the IRA felt that the only way to achieve a 32-county independent Ireland was by military force alone. They saw Sinn Fein as separate. This

---

[30] Interview by the author with Des Long.
[31] Interview by the author with Mick Ryan.
[32] Interview by the author with Anthony Coughlan.

was never thought out fully. It was my view that the IRA was there to complete the job which was 'suspended' in 1921. My view was that the struggle was just in hiatus.[33]

The discontent within the membership and among certain elements of the leadership with respect to the downgrading of the armed struggle is viewed by many as the most decisive element at play in both the reasoning for and the result of the split.

That [the split] was always going to come because it was kind of based on very basic, you are either for armed struggle or you are not, or you are for politics.[34]

While for many this may have been the dominant element it was not the sole intra-organizational conflict in the lead up to 1969/70.

Politically left-wing

The political development was very much moving towards the left. To a large extent they were moving the organization away from the traditional republican ethos and it was becoming dominated by left-wing political ideals and values. With the low levels of membership and support they were shaping what could have been perceived as an entirely new organization. The emphasis of debates both locally and nationally was no longer military based but were focused on the alleviation of perceived social injustices. In its new form the organization was almost unrecognizable from the traditional Republican Movement.

This change to a socialist approach in turn brought with it a modification on the purposive goals of the organization. The movement would have historically considered itself to be a left-leaning political and armed movement. However, this stronger emphasis on socialism brought the aspiration for the organization to achieve a 32 county socialist republic to prominence. This required members and supporters not only to aspire to a united Ireland but to a *socialist* united Ireland. For many of the future Provisionals, especially those old-guard traditionalists, the prominence of socialism in the place, to a large extent, of the pursuit of a united Ireland was significantly and negatively moving the goals of the movement in the wrong direction.

You had the introduction into the Republican Movement of a degree of socialism, which was extreme, which was a diversion really. If that becomes

---

[33] Interview by the author with Mick Ryan.
[34] Interview by the author with Dolours Price.

the main thrust then the question of national liberation becomes a bit of a side show from there on.[35]

This shift towards a left-wing set of goals isolated a significant proportion of the traditionalist membership and support. When this is coupled with the downgrading of the IRA a larger and more significant section of the population were effectively isolated. By changing the goals and strategy of a movement from the pursuit of a 32 county Irish Republic through the use of armed struggle to the pursuit of a 32 county Irish socialist Republic by political means the leadership was, in a short space of time, severely altering the emphasis of the organization. Resultantly their new aspirations could now realistically only be supported and aspired to by a different and somewhat narrower base.

One specific element within the left-wing proposal put forward towards the end of this stage of the process was a proposed coalition with like-minded left-wing parties and movements for the purpose of promoting the left-wing aims of the combined movement.[36] This proposed union acquired the moniker of National Liberation Front [NLF]. In Cathal Goulding's oration in Bodenstown in June 1967 he stated 'to all radical and progressive groups, to all individual revolutionaries, the Republican Movement should be a rallying ground, the point of unity'. This can be seen as a call for what became known as the NLF.[37] When proposed this succeeded in heightening the traditionalist's apprehension of the new left-wing strategy. The issue was seized by the growing dissenting sub-group as a negative example of the direction the movement was taking. They began to spread their message of distrust of the left-wing trajectory which the movement was taking.[38] This was led by prominent dissenters within Republicanism, prominent among them Sean MacStiofain and Ruairi O'Bradaigh.

As the movement was moving more towards the left he [Sean MacStiofain] started to talk to people on his side locally about how this wasn't right for the Movement. MacStiofain was very much anti-Communist. However, there were very few people within the IRA who would have been Communist

---

[35] Interview by the author with Sean O'Bradaigh.

[36] This proposed coalition was central to the intra-organizational conflict as proposed by Irvin, *Militant Nationalism*, 41.

[37] Cathal Goulding 'Bodenstown' 67: Oration by CathalGoulding.' In *United Irishman* (July 1967), 10–11.

[38] This is a classic example of the initial utilization of voice prior to exit to see if they could change the internal workings of the movement and opinions of the leadership and membership. Albert O. Hirschman, *Exit, Voice and Loyalty: Responses to Decline in Firms, Organisations and States.* (New York: Columbia University Press, 1970).

. . . He was against the dropping of abstentionism and the leftward trend of the Movement.[39]

These voices of dissent were negatively portraying the Goulding leadership as being Communists and emphasizing what they perceived to be the negative aspects of the left-wing political ideology being put forward. Some of the strongest voices of discontent came from a number of influence old-guard traditionalist Republicans who had left the movement in the aftermath of the Border Campaign but had since returned due to their disillusionment with the direction of the movement under this new leadership. The influence of this returning old guard in conjunction with the influential dissidents who had remained provided a legitimization for the position of the dissidents.[40]

Abstentionism

As has been mentioned previously to the fore of many people's analysis of the 1969/70 split is the issue of abstentionism, an issue which is later revisited in the lead up to the 1986 split.[41] Historically the Republican Movement viewed the three parliaments as institutions which by their very nature promoted the partition of Ireland.[42] Therefore any Sinn Fein member who was elected to any of the three houses would abstain from taking their seats on strategic and policy grounds. This became an issue debated within the leadership of both Sinn Fein and the IRA as well as in the Wolfe Tone Society. For the new leadership this policy was seen as a burden debilitating the progress of their politicization of the movement.

When in the mid-1960s this was brought to an initial vote, along with a variety of other proposals, the vote was to drop the abstentionist policy completely for all three parliaments. This was read in turn by some members as the recognition of the legitimacy of the three parliaments and the acceptance of the partition of Ireland. For many at that time abstentionism was a central tenet of Irish Republicanism, and for some modern day

---

[39] Interview by the author with Mick Ryan.

[40] This is supportive of the Dyck and Starke model which posits the presence of legitimizing voices in favour of the dissidents as a trigger event for the progress of the process of split. See, Bruno Dyck and Frederick A. Starke, 'The Formation of Breakaway Organisations: Observations and a Process Model', *Administrative Science Quarterly*, 44(4) (1999), 804–11.

[41] For an analysis of debates on republican abstentionist policies see, Brendan Lynn, 'Tactic or Principle? The Evolution of Republican Thinking on Abstentionism in Ireland, 1970–1998', *Irish Political Studies*, 17(2) 2002.

[42] Abstentionism was also a dominant theme in Sinn Fein at the beginning of the twentieth century. See, Peter Pyne, 'The Politics of Parliamentary Abstentionism: Ireland's Four Sinn Fein Parties 1905–1926'. *Commonwealth and Comparative Politics*, 12(2) (1974), 206–27.

dissidents this continues to be the case. It was considered to be beyond a strategy or tactic but was regarded as a principle and even part of their ideology. Therefore the proposed change of these policies was viewed by many of the old-guard as significantly threatening to organizational identity. Since the partition of the state there was the acceptance that the organizational position was the denouncement of the legitimacy of each of the parliaments and now the leadership was proposing an alteration to this strategy by recommending the policy's abolition. Interviews with members of both sides of the split indicate the deep rooted and historical sentiment that went with the abstentionist policy.

> Abstentionism was always a Republican policy. For instance today's situation, how can you say you are a Republican and have to run this state with the British?[43]

> The suspicion of taking seats was deep rooted. [Future] Provisional leaders like the O'Bradaighs [Sean and Ruairi], [Eamon] MacThomais, [John Joe] McGirl and others had spoken publicly at meetings recruiting into Sinn Fein and the IRA under the guise of not taking seats. They said that the Dail would corrupt you. Then these people were asked by the leadership to consider that what was once a mortal sin was suddenly no longer so.[44]

While this may be phrased as a singular policy change in practice this proposal elicited three major changes in policy. These were hugely significant changes individually, but by proposing to drop the policy to all three parliaments the leadership was calling for a monumental turnaround in strategy. For many participants retrospective analysis says that the Goulding leadership may have been better advised to alter the position with respect to one parliament at a time. The leadership believed in taking their seats in each of the three. However, if they could not bring a significant portion of the membership and support with them this change was to be inconsequential.

The overriding theme of this stage with respect to strategic changes, 'too much, too soon', is not only applicable to the full range of strategic and policy changes but is specifically applicable to the issue of the proposed changes in the abstentionist policies. When these are combined with the various other concrete and proposed changes the leadership was always likely to isolate a large number of their supporters, as well as fellow members of the leadership.

---

[43] Interview by the author with Alex.
[44] Interview by the author with Mick Ryan.

This retrospective analysis may suggest the obvious problems to be faced by trying to impose these changes to the abstentionist policies. However, at the time it was believed that in order to sustain the existence of the movement that drastic changes were needed. The leadership inferred that they would be more likely to attract new members and supporters if they were to take their seats and be seen to be actively involved in the political set-up, rather than being the eternal external agitators.[45] However, in order to maintain organizational survival one must not only attract new membership and support but they need also to preserve a significant proportion of the old-guard and bring them along with them. For many of the traditionalist old-guard these sweeping changes to a deep-rooted policy were to prove 'too much, too soon.' The stance taken by both sides of the conflict provided the basis for continuous and developing factionalism from the mid 1960s up until the official division in Sinn Fein in 1970.

With this battery of fluctuation, change and proposed change tensions mounted within the membership and across the leadership resulting in intense intra-organizational conflict and factionalism.

National leadership

One of the clearest examples of this factionalism was within the national leadership of both the IRA and Sinn Fein.[46] This was particularly evident in the IRA Army Council. During the mid to late-1960s this seven person council was divided evenly with three sitting members supportive of politicization and three in favour of the advancement of the armed campaign and one, Tomas MacGiolla, generally described as taking a 'neutral' position until his final decision to side with the Officials.[47] This division was also evident within the leadership of Sinn Fein as well as within other factions of the Republican leadership. It is alleged by Provisionals under their title of 'internal methods' that the Goulding leadership manipulated who would take vital roles within the organization so as to push forward their socialist agenda.

People had largely been identified as to what side they took in this brewing situation and because the people in favour of all these things were in

---

[45] Brian Hanley and Scott Millar, *The Lost Revolution: The Story of the Official IRA and the Worker's Party.* (Dublin: Penguin Ireland, 2009), 40.

[46] This supports the claim that areas of power-relations are one of the prominent venues for intra-organizational conflict. James March and Herbert Simon, *Organizations: Second Edition* (Cambridge, MA: Blackwell Publishers, 1993), 142.

[47] Robert W. White, *Ruairi O'Bradaigh: The Life and Politics of an Irish Revolutionary.* (Bloomington, IN: Indiana University Press, 2006).

charge of the Army, and they had a very good say in Sinn Fein as well, and they controlled the newspaper The United Irishman, then they were in the position to use great influence.[48]

As the mouthpiece of the movement the Republican newspaper, the United Irishman, was a powerful tool to put across the preferred message of the movement to the membership. Therefore at a time of intra-organizational conflict whichever side was in editorial control were better positioned to transmit and justify their viewpoints to the wider membership. In the lead up to the split the left-leaning leadership was in control of the paper. Therefore, they decided what was to be published and, at times more importantly, what was to be omitted from the publication.

This factionalism within the national leadership while evident during this stage of the process grew in strength and significance in the final stages. The presence of these multiple proposed changes and the resultant intra-organizational conflicts was seen as threatening to the organizational identity of the movement by a larger proportion of the movement than it was deemed to be during the previous stage. The multiple changes inevitably isolated a growing number of members and resultantly created a stronger dissident sub-group. These intra-organizational conflicts were not only threatening to the organizational identity on an individual level. The immediate aim of organizational survival was not given the attention it required by the leadership at this time of multiple change as it was significantly isolating a larger proportion of the membership with each proposed change and therefore strengthening the dissidents. While it was deemed threatening to the identity it was still viewed to be reconcilable. Due to the fact that the votes for change were being defeated throughout this stage the internal dissenters believed that the issues could be solved internally. In marked contrast to the opening stage the dissidents were becoming more and more organized at this stage.

Stage 3: Inevitability of and preparation for split

The opening two stages of this process may be regarded as laying the groundwork for the split. However, this third stage should be regarded as the most critical in deciding the outcome of the division. Each of the 30 participants who discussed the 1969/70 split emphasized the importance

---

[48] Interview by the author with Ruairi O'Bradaigh.

of the actions taken, or not taken, by the IRA in the summer of 1969. This is therefore regarded as the most dominant reasoning not only for the split taking place but also as the dominant factor in deciding its outcome. While the opening two stages created situations where sections of the membership and supporters were disillusioned with the direction the movement was taking, these dissidents while expressing their concerns had yet to garner a sufficient degree of internal or external support for their position. Without this support any move away from the parent organization would have proved counterproductive and the resulting splinter group would have been close to irrelevant within the wider society. However, in late 1968 and early 1969 the situation in Northern Ireland began to gain widespread national and international attention. Civil rights marches were attacked by loyalist groups as members of the RUC and B-Specials stood by. At other times officers themselves baton-charged and injured marchers. With growing violence and the resultant riots on both sides of the sectarian divide there were constant calls for the IRA to defend the nationalist communities and provide weapons. However, the leadership resisted as it was not their intention to get involved in armed conflict. They wished to maintain their plans to politicize the movement. The Northern Irish situation came to a fore in August 1969 with incidents such as the Battle of the Bogside[49] and the ensuing sectarian rioting across Northern Ireland.[50] In Belfast hundreds of houses were burned to the ground, leaving thousands of people, mainly Catholics, homeless. By 14 August the British government sent army troops into Northern Ireland. These events of 1969 proved vital in the process leading up to the split, and the escalation of violence in Northern Ireland.[51] The violence and the calls for weapons provided a new impetus to the dissident sub-group. Their dissidence was now purely focused on the need for defence and an armed strategy. This was especially the case with the returning old-guard members.[52] This belief is emphasized by Joe Doherty, a man who would go on to join the Provisional Movement in a post-split West-Belfast.

---

[49] This refers to rioting which followed the Apprentice Boys of Derry march on 12 August.

[50] For discussion of the 'Battle of the Bogside' see O'Dochartaigh, N., *From Civil Rights to Armalites: Derry and the Birth of the Irish Troubles.* (second edn) (Cork: Palgrave, 2004).

[51] Leonard Weinberg and Louise Richardson, 'Conflict Theory and the Trajectory of Terrorist Campaigns in Western Europe', in Andrew Silke ed. *Research on Terrorism: Trends, Achievements and Failures.* (London: Frank Cass, 2004), 156 cite the ensuing communal riots in Belfast and Derry during the summer of 1969 as the precursor to the escalation of terrorist violence in Northern Ireland.

[52] For a specific account of an individual old-guard member's return to the movement see Brendan Anderson, *Joe Cahill: A Life in the IRA.* (Dublin: O'Brien Press, 2007), 152–86.

I think the split in the early seventies was down to a lot of republicans on our side were old-style republicans. And the whole thing that was happening in Belfast and Derry, where people were burnt out of their homes, I think the reactionary element took over.[53]

The growing tensions within the organization cemented the inevitability of split. Throughout this period the mounting tension in Northern Ireland and the perceived inaction of the IRA succeeded in bringing back additional old-guard members to those who had already returned. Many attempted to defend the Republican communities. Parallel to this a growing number of young Northern nationalists became involved in the defence of their communities. While this was not always under the auspices of the IRA a number of the young recruits went on to join and played a crucial role within the Provisional movement in the aftermath of the split. For 21 of the participants in this research this stage of the process represented their first involvement with organized republicanism and signalled the beginning of the split in their eyes.

Within this ten-month time period the voices of dissent grew louder and reached a wider audience. The dissidents became more organized and began to prepare for the eventuality of split. The Goulding leadership on the other hand continued their push for constitutional change, to drop the abstentionist policies and put forward their left wing objectives and policies. This is illustrated in the publication of *Ireland Today* in March 1969 which was a report resulting from the development of a review commission in the Ard Fheis of 1969. Even though it acknowledged membership reticence towards entering Stormont and Westminster it still advised that the abstentionist policies should be dropped.[54] Their desire for organizational change was parallel to a weakening of their position and support, and the strengthening of the alternative being provided by the 'Provisionals'. While no official split was to take place until late 1969 it is noted that it is when referring to this third stage of the process that participants start to prominently refer to two distinct Republican groupings, the 'Officials' and the 'Provisionals'. This is particularly prominent in reference to defence provided in Republican areas by the returning old-guard who became founding members of the Provisional IRA and the failure to provide defence and weapons by future Officials. This deliberate labelling of groups shows how it was within this period that the two distinct groups began to take shape, a move which rendered the split inevitable.

---

[53] Interview by the author with Joe Doherty.
[54] Republican Education Department for the Commission set up by the 1968 ArdFheis, *Ireland Today: and some questions on the way forward (including 1969 Addendum)*, (March 1969).

Within the analysis of this stage the dominant themes focused on are:

- Preparation for Split
- Republican Expectations and Leadership Disconnect

Preparation for split

As the situation in Northern Ireland grew more hostile at the end of 1968 and the beginning of 1969, especially with incidents such as the attacks on marchers at Burntollet Bridge, the growing dissident grouping became more organized and vocal in their dissent. They called on the leadership to refocus their strategies on armed struggle and to move away from left-wing political proposals being put forward. In these months there were preparations made by leading 'Provisionals' for the upcoming split. They sounded out individuals for recruitment and support by criticizing the 'Communist' trajectory that the movement was taking. They strengthened their position in opposition to the politicizing leadership. This was carried out across Ireland at a local level and is reflected on by Mick Ryan, a leading member of the Goulding leadership.

> In early 1969 I called in to Ned Dempsey in Carlow. Ned told me that he had had a visitor from Belfast, Liam Burke and Miles Shevlin, the Dublin solicitor. They were criticising the 'Communist takeover' of the Movement . . . [Sean] MacStiofain would have been in touch with each unit and was finding out from them what was going on locally. As the Movement was moving more towards the left he started to talk to people on his side locally about how this wasn't right for the Movement.[55]

As this took place on the side of the dissidents the national leadership was also putting forward their case for politicization. They promoted their preference for left-wing Republicanism and dropping the abstentionist policies. It was their aim to prevent a split and continue the promotion of their political strategies, even in light of the events in Northern Ireland. However, they were aware from 1968 that a split was inevitable due to the growing organization by this dissident sub-group. It was their task then to lessen the impact of the split.

> I personally from the beginning of my contact had hoped that an actual split could be avoided; people who were unable to adapt to a socially critical

---

[55] Interview by the author with Mick Ryan.

political approach would, we expected, drop out individually. It became evident however that a split was being organised prior to the 1968 Ard Fheis which launched the 'Garland Commission' process; this latter was a conscious attempt to counter it. . . . We did our best to avoid it happening, on the whole; we tried to bring everyone along the political road, but the proto-Provisionals were organising against us all the time.[56]

And there was an escalating situation, and just as a final push was being made by Cathal Goulding and company in '68 at the Ard Fheis. . . . They employed full time organisers, and the full time organisers were sorting us out as to probables and possibles and all the rest of it.[57]

For the dissidents their most national show of dissent came at the re-interment of Peter Barnes and James McCormack[58] in Mullingar in July 1969. At the graveside Jimmy Steele, one of the leading Belfast old-guard, gave a speech which was to send out a signal to all both within and outside of Republicanism that there was a growing dissenting faction who significantly disagreed with the course of action being taken by the leadership. This speech is acknowledged by both sides as a significant moment in the process of the split and ultimately the development of the Provisional IRA. In his speech Steele sidestepped the issues of civil rights and instead promoted and defended the use of force by the IRA. He also showed his contempt for left-wing politics and the notion that members were to be 'more conversant with the teaching of Chairman Mao than those of our dead comrades'. He was dismissed from the IRA due to the criticisms of the IRA in the speech. However, the sentiments he portrayed had effect throughout the movement. It put forward an alternative voice to that of the politicizing leadership.

With the Jimmy Steele speech in Mullingar in July 1969 they were laying the groundwork for what was to come[59]

While this was the public face of the internal dissidence the preparation for the split on behalf of both sides was continuing. On the side of the dissidents members of the national leadership such as Sean MacStiofain and Ruairi O'Bradaigh were being very vocal in their criticisms and their intentions if this left-wing politicization continued.

---

[56] Interview by the author with Roy Johnston.
[57] Interview by the author with Ruairi O'Bradaigh.
[58] Two IRA volunteers who had been hanged in Birmingham in 1940.
[59] Interview by the author with Mick Ryan.

> MacStiofain was letting me know since July 1969 'we are never going to accept a vote on the Dail, Stormont, Westminster and the NLF [National Liberation Front]. We are hoping you will be on our side.'[60]

This continued with the dissidents actively approaching members of both the rank and file membership and leadership to side with them on the issues causing intra-organizational conflict. In the aftermath of the 'pogroms' of August 1969 their organizing moved beyond the pursuit of support for their position and now included the acquisition of IRA arms and artillery for future use.

> After the pogroms the organisation of dissidents started taking place. At one point in August 1969 weapons from a HQ dump were given to MacStiofain by the person in charge of that particular dump. I find it amazing that MacStiofain was left in as Director of Intelligence.[61]

As this took place and the situation in Northern Ireland became more violent the Goulding leadership pushed ahead with their politicization process. They realized that in order to be successful that this required additional effort and promotion on their behalf and they similarly attempted to recruit new members to advance their position.

> Around August 69 . . . Goulding and [Sean] Garland came to me and I was invited to join the IRA . . . I think they were inviting me because they thought I might be helpful to them and they wanted me to maintain the political line on top, tried to maintain the hegemony of the political line, better able to do it than Roy [Johnston] they put it.[62]

With the majority now calling for the IRA to defend the areas under attack and to provide weapons the appeal for the promotion of the political process was out of touch and disconnected with the expectations which the public had for the IRA and Sinn Fein.

Republican expectations and leadership disconnect

The escalating violence in Northern Ireland raised the expectations of many in the nationalist areas, and across the rest of the island, for the IRA to defend

---

[60] Ibid.
[61] Ibid.
[62] Interview by the author with Anthony Coughlan.

the communities and to provide weapons for the newly forming defence committees. In the years previous many of these people regarded the IRA as an obsolete grouping. But in light of the violence this viewpoint changed. Many now desired an IRA presence to supply defence and weapons. However, the intentions of the leadership were disconnected from these expectations as they wished to continue their politicization process and not for the IRA to act as a defender of the communities. Thomas MacGiolla on 13 August 1969 said that the Irish government should act in defence of the republican and nationalist communities. This was distancing the IRA from the responsibility of doing so, but also portrays a disconnect between the leadership and its membership.[63] This was deemed to be one of the most critical factors in deciding the result of the split. For many members the split did not take place because of abstentionism or left-wing politics, but it was the result of the failure of the national leadership to defend the people they claimed to represent during these months, a point argued here by future leading Provisional Danny Morrison. Morrison at the time of the split was a fresh recruit on the ground in Belfast who like many only had a detailed awareness of what was taking place at a local level.

> So the '69 split, yes you were aware of, in simplistic terms I would have said. If you had said to me in January '70 'what is the split over?' I would have turned around and I would have said to you 'The IRA leadership sold us out, they left us defenceless, they sold the guns, they decommissioned'[64]

The expectation of both the Republican membership and the public at this time was for weapons and defence of the regions. However, participants acknowledged that the national leadership's actions and sentiments were significantly disconnected from these expectations. The analysis of the interview data confirms the presumption that there was a significant disconnect between membership expectations and leadership strategy. This was a viewpoint most dominant among the Provisionals, and especially from those who like Morrison joined the movement in or around the time of split. Even if the leadership wished to meet the expectations of their public and membership it was acknowledged that they were unprepared for the circumstances of the summer of 1969.

It is recognized by members of both sides that this failure by the leadership to provide defence and weapons for the nationalist communities of Northern Ireland strengthened the position of their internal detractors. No longer was

---

[63] Tomas MacGiolla, *Republican Statement on Northern Crisis.* (13 August 1969).
[64] Interview by the author with Danny Morrison.

the internal conflict dominated with the pros and cons of abstentionism and left-wing politics, issues which did not affect everyday lives. The issues of defence and the supply of weapons did have this significant impact. In light of this there were now people who years previously had dismissed the relevance of the IRA calling for them to defend them and disapproving when this defence did not arrive.

It is at this stage that the process moves from intra-organizational conflict to a process of split. For the old-guard traditionalist members one of the most dominant historical purposes and identities of the IRA was that of Catholic and Nationalist defenders. However, in this time of violence perpetrated against and by these communities the IRA leadership was hesitant to subscribe to this identity. This is due to the heterogeneous nature of the membership at this stage. Within the movement there were two diverse standpoints being put forward. There were the old-guard traditionalists, many just recently returned, calling for decisive armed action and defence by the IRA. In stark contrast to this was the viewpoint of the politicizers who did not wish for the IRA to partake in an armed campaign any longer. In the lead-up to and during the summer of 1969 it was clear that neither side was willing to compromise on their position and therefore creating the inevitability of split. The discontent about the IRA's reluctance to partake was not just present within the movement but also among the general public.

> And then you had the explosion of all of 1969. You had a very, very strong sense of anger at the IRA's lack of preparation for the defence.[65]

There was a large number of new recruits entering the movement at this time who were not joining due to their views on left-wing politics or the much debated abstentionist policies, or even the target of attaining a united Ireland. They were joining so as to get arms to protect their families and communities.

> The discontent came in afterwards when there was a panic 'where do we get guns?' All people wanted was guns. Even people of a left-wing persuasion would have sold their political beliefs to get their hands on guns to defend the areas, not for philosophical reasons, but in order to have protection for the families in those areas.[66]

While there were a small number of weapons supplied to defend the communities these were mainly provided by the old-guard traditionalists.

---

[65] Interview by the author with 'Paul'.
[66] Interview by the author with Sean O'Hare.

This significantly strengthened the dissidents' standing among young recruits and the public whose expectation was for the IRA to defend the communities. It was not just would be 'Provisionals' who regard the failure to provide weapons and defence at this stage as a mistake by the Goulding leadership. There are those who sided with the leadership, and those who advised them, who believed that if they had met the expectations of the population that the result of the split could have been significantly different, or could even have been avoided. The newly recruited politicizer Anthony Coughlan states that

> . . . it is regrettable perhaps that Goulding and company didn't have a few more guns on the Falls Rd [West Belfast] in August 69 to defend the locals. That might have enabled them to keep on top of the situation politically.[67]

While these sentiments are put forward with the benefit of hindsight at the time of the events the policies put forward, and actions taken, by the Dublin leadership were severely disconnected from those of their membership and public. In the months after the failure of the leadership to provide defence for the communities in August 1969 was used and manipulated by the 'Provisional' leadership to further strengthen support for their position and their movement away from the leadership.

> The pogroms were the catalyst which aided the Provos, and they are manipulating the facts of what happened then and in events after.[68]

The view of a large proportion of the people within the affected areas was that it was the role of the IRA to defend them. However, this opinion was not shared by the national leadership. They no longer saw their role as that of Catholic defenders.They saw this as an opportunity for the British army and the RUC to defend the areas against the loyalists and the B-Specials, a viewpoint which only succeeded in cementing the idea of leadership disconnect in the minds of many.

> Goulding would have seen things politically; it was an opportunity where a clash could occur. With the British troops coming in and Loyalists, or some Orange elements or B-Specials going around parishes. It was an ideal situation for a clash between ultra-loyalism and the British authorities, who were supposed to be in charge of law and order. That is the view that I would have ascribed to at the time.[69]

---

[67] Interview by the author with Anthony Coughlan.
[68] Interview by the author with Mick Ryan.
[69] Interview by the author with Anthony Coughlan.

The sense of leadership abandonment was uppermost in the minds of those in the worst affected areas of Belfast and Derry. This further accentuated a growing notion of north/south divide within the movement as the belief was that the national leadership, based in Dublin, had the time and space to develop and debate political policy and was therefore disconnected from the daily hardship for Republicans in Northern Ireland, a notion that is returned to in each of the splits. They were unaware of what was needed in the communities on a day to day basis.

> I would say that either there would be a lot more ideology taught in Dublin than there ever would have been in Belfast and that is understandable because we were dealing with the constant threat of Loyalist attack and pogroms. We had to live with that notion. So that was uppermost in most people's minds, not the ideology of each according to their needs and from each according to their means, or whatever.[70]

Even if the Goulding leadership had seen their role as that of Catholic defenders it is unlikely that they would have been able to provide any adequate form of defence for the population. This lack of preparedness was criticized both during and after the events, a point recounted by Gerry Adams reflecting on

> And of course some of the people who had been active in other campaigns, but not so active in the sixties, some of the older people who had come back were very critical of this lack of preparedness. Because it was clear to everybody, including me as a young person that things were getting into a very serious situation.[71]

At this critical stage of the process it was clearly not only the intent of a grouping to gain membership and support, but they also had to be able to display a clear ability to protect and partake in armed action. In order to display this ability they needed a more substantial weaponry.

Officials claim that a significant amount of responsibility for the Provisionals' development rests with key members of Fianna Fail, the governmental party of the Republic of Ireland at that time.[72] This viewpoint was promoted by the Officials in the aftermath of the split and was used as a justification for their failure to become the dominant Republican force.[73] The argument put forward

---

[70] Interview by the author with Dolours Price.
[71] Interview by the author with Gerry Adams.
[72] Oots, 'Organisational Perspectives', 145.
[73] See Official Republican Movement, *Fianna Fail and the IRA*. (1971).

was that certain members of Fianna Fail were wary of the electoral challenge which they could meet from a successfully politicized left-wing Sinn Fein. Therefore they sought to split the organization by funding the development of the Provisionals if they would move away from the Dublin leadership and concentrate exclusively on Northern Ireland.

In the 1960s it went from inactivity to the revival of republicanism, from non-involvement to very active involvement in issues like fish ins, land, ground rents, rivers, lakes, mortgages societies, housing etc.[74] We were really beginning to make headway. People weren't saying that this is wrong. Participation in the Dail and more action in councils would have benefited from this growing support. Fianna Fail feared this. The IRA were now involved in the civil rights movement and fighting the Brits. It wasn't just disorganised loyalist mobs in pogroms but they were supported by the state to force the IRA into action and divert the focus to the armed campaign. This brought an effective end to the IRA/Sinn Fein impetus in the south, the concentration had been in the south.[75]

Information was reaching the Republican leadership from early 1969 that individuals were being approached by representatives of Fianna Fail members and they were discussing the possibility of a breakaway group, and how they could help in its development. The people approached were predominantly old-guard Republicans who would have been believed to have been against the left-wing politicization of the Republican movement. For any politically violent organization, especially a newly developing one, they must have sources of finance as well as the availability of weapons and artillery. The accusation from the Officials is that the Provisionals acquired a significant proportion of this from members of the Fianna Fail party, most notably cabinet ministers Charles Haughey and Neil Blaney with the assistance of Irish army intelligence officer Captain James Kelly.[76]

Stage 4: Organizational exit and breakaway group formation

During stage 3 it transpired that a split in Irish Republicanism was to be inevitable. However, it is in stage 4 that the split actually took place. Continuing

---

[74] Economic agitations used by the Irish Republican Movement in the 1960s.
[75] Interview by the author with Mick Ryan.
[76] Justin O'Brien, *The Arms Trial*. (Dublin: Gill and McMillan, 2000).

on from the previous stage the 'Provisionals' attempted to maximize their position due to the circumstances of the time, especially with the perceived failure of the leadership to provide weapons and defence. A number of divisive issues came to the fore in the years leading up to 1969. But it was the divided opinion on IRA responsibilities at this time which accelerated the process.

> I get a sense that in the autumn of 1969/1970 things start to move very, very quickly. I think what is happening is the lid is off and there is an entirely new situation for everyone and the situation has a momentum after August 69 which is in a way very different from what went before.[77]

The split officially took place in both sections of the movement over the issue of abstentionism. However, there were numerous issues at the heart of the conflict but most notably it was the continued failure of the IRA to defend communities which ultimately decided the outcome. While the specific regional sections moved away from the leadership prior to the Army Convention and Ard Fheis, most notably the Belfast IRA, the official split took place in the aftermath of these two national conventions. The split took place in the IRA prior to the one in Sinn Fein. The purpose of the description of this stage is to illustrate how the Goulding leadership attempted to minimize the effect of the split while continuing with their politicization of the Republican Movement. Concurrent to this is an analysis of how the 'Provisionals' attempted to maximize their position and gain as much support as possible.

Within the present stage the themes focused on are:

- The Split
- Competition for Support
- Personality Clashes and Trust

This is followed by an overview of the split process.

The split

At the will of the national leadership during the Army Convention of 1969 a vote was taken on two of the main divisive issues of the time, the development of a National Liberation Front and the abolition of the constitutional abstentionist

---

[77] Interview by the author with Tom Hartley.

policies.[78] Both votes were passed by their required majorities.[79] In the days and weeks after the Convention the dissidents formed the Provisional Army Council and the Provisional IRA.[80] Among the leadership figures within this breakaway grouping were Sean MacStiofain as Chief of Staff alongside fellow leadership figures such Ruairi O'Bradaigh and Daithi O'Conail and a number of the Belfast Republicans who had exited prior to the Convention, people such as Leo Martin.

When the split within the IRA took place in December 1969[81] Sinn Fein remained theoretically intact. However, this all changed when at the Ard Fheis on 11 January 1970 a number of political dissenters staged a walk-out. During the Ard Fheis the Sinn Fein leadership were still attempting to prevent a split from taking place, or at least significantly weaken the support for the Provisionals. This is displayed in the final sentiments of MacGiolla's presidential address. 'I . . . close with an appeal to all members of the movement, once our decision has been made, to close ranks, and face the enemy forces together'.[82] Akin to the IRA Army Convention there was a vote taken on the dropping of the abstentionist policies. When the vote was taken this received a simple majority but not by the necessary two-thirds.[83] Following what was effectively a defeat for the motion a new motion was called from the floor by Seamus Costello, a leading member of the Officials, for the Ard Fheis to recognize the vote that was passed at the Army Convention the month previous. With the calling of this motion there was the walk-out of dissidents. This was due to the fact that as a non-constitutional vote it only required a simple majority to be passed, a vote the dissenters knew they would be defeated on. The dissidents, a number of whom

---

[78] The NLF vote required a simple majority and the abstentionist vote required a two-thirds majority; this continuation of the politicization of the movement is in contradiction with belief that organizations will be more conservative when there is a threat to organizational survival, Mayer N. Zald and Roberta Ash, 'Social Movement Organisations: Growth, Decay and Change', *Social Forces*, 44(3) (1966), 327. While the acceptance of peaceful politics may be looked upon as more conservative than the 'radical' option of armed violence within a long-standing armed group such as the IRA there is a reversal of roles with political participation as more radical for the membership than armed action. This suggests that the leadership was dismissive of the significance of the threat to organizational survival and hence continued with their politicization. This is further proof of the disconnect between them and their membership. In the aftermath of the split there was a reticence to partake in armed conflict against the British or loyalists and again jeopardized the survival of their organization.

[79] MacStiofain, *Memoirs*, 134–5 for a Provisional analysis of these votes; Patterson, 140–1 for an academic analysis.

[80] The birth of the Provisional IRA and Sinn Fein from this split, and their growth in the years after, shows how it is irrational to classify splits within the end of terrorism literature.

[81] Provisional IRA was already generating a significant amount of support around the country.

[82] Tomas MacGiolla, *Sinn Fein Oraidan Uachtarain Tomas McGiollaag Ard-Fheis 1969.* (11 Janurary 1970).

[83] Brian Feeney, *Sinn Fein: A Hundred Turbulent Years.* (Dublin: O'Brien Press, 2002), 250.

had been present at the Army Convention as well, after their walk-out elected a new 'caretaker Sinn Fein Ard Chomhairle' [Executive]. They were ready for the eventuality of defeat and had prior to the Ard Fheis put plans in place for the development of a new political party to align itself with the newly developing Provisional IRA. The events of late 1969/70 support the belief that the sub-group most willing to make compromises is the one most likely to be successful in the aftermath of a split.

The continued push by the national leadership for the politicization of the movement shows a distinct reluctance to compromise. In the lead-up to both the Convention and Ard Fheis they were aware of the preparations for split on behalf of the dissidents. However, they were reluctant to adapt to the changing circumstances and the changing expectations of the membership and public. They were therefore unwilling to compromise. By fixing themselves to their politicizing position and not moving their strategies and policies in anyway closer to the dissidents' position they as a result experienced a more damaging split than may have otherwise taken place.

What follows now is the analysis of two dominant themes which were identified by participants in this fourth stage of the Provisional/Official split. These themes are *competition for support* and *personality clashes and trust*. The focus here is not on why the split took place. Rather this assessment outlines these two issues in relation to how both sides acquired, or attempted to acquire, sufficient support for their position during the split.

Competition for support

With the inevitability of the split the main task for both sides during this stage of the process was to attempt to secure and retain as much support as possible. The Officials wished to minimize the effect of the divide while their Provisional adversaries hoped to accentuate the split. They were competing for the support of both IRA and Sinn Fein members. This task principally took place in the aftermath of the split as the two groupings vied for membership and support. It essentially started in the mid to late 1960s as members of both sides were canvassing across the country. However, at this stage of the process the main competition was to gain the adequate numbers of support among those attending both the Army Convention and the Ard Fheis.

For the Goulding leadership the years leading up to the split had seen them attempting to fend off or postpone a split. It was their belief that by doing so their politicization process would be in a stronger position to succeed. If it were not for the events of 1969 they may have been right, a point considered by the late Thomas MacGiolla, the first president of the newly formed Official Sinn Fein.

> While we had been pushing for this for a while we wanted to slow it down at that stage [1969], we were just trying to avoid a split. I always felt, and Cathal did too that the longer you avoid splits, the better you will be, the stronger you will be. You would be developing where you weren't developed before.[84]

While survival is at the cornerstone of all organizational behaviour the leadership puts this in jeopardy by retaining the membership of the internal dissident grouping for too long. The dissidents were preparing for a division for a number of years previous to the actual split. However, if the leadership had pre-empted this move away in the years prior and forced their exit the emerging breakaway organization would have been significantly weaker in membership and support due to the inability to adequately prepare. It was purely a result of the Northern Irish situation of 1969 and the early 1970s that the emerging Provisionals emerged in such a dominant position within Republicanism close to their formation.

The accusation from the Provisionals is that the national leadership's attempts to acquire more support for their position, and postpone a split, were carried out through what they define as 'internal methods'. They contend that the Officials manipulated the makeup of the delegates at both the Army Convention and the Ard Fheis so as that the votes would be falsely weighted in their favour. This was accomplished by failing to collect a number of known dissidents for the Convention while also bringing an excess of delegates from areas where the support for their position was strong.

> The split came first in the army before Sinn Fein and the Limerick and Clare delegates to the Army Convention were left behind, they were not picked up. On the night of the 22nd and 23rd of December those who didn't agree with the result of this convention met in Athlone and set up the Provisional Army Council.[85]

In addition to this the Belfast IRA and others who had exited the movement pre-split were not eligible to attend.

This tactic succeeded in helping the Goulding leadership achieve their two-thirds majority. This though only solved the short-term issue of passing the

---

[84] Interview by the author with Tomas MacGiolla.
[85] Interview by the author with Des Long.

vote. They had not succeeded in fending off or postponing a split. The real competition for support was to take place in the months and years after the split.

For the Ard Fheis a similar tactic of delegate manipulation was deemed to have been used. The Provisionals contend that new supportive cumanns were developed, as some dissident ones were closed down.

> There are a whole lot of rules, all organisations have rules, but inevitably like in all organisations it slips a bit. You are supposed to have a meeting of the cumann every month, but you might only have ten a year, you mightn't have one in August because someone is always away on holidays. There is always little bits and pieces like this.[86]

This accusation of corruption provided further rationale for their movement away from the politicizing leadership. They embraced the issue and utilized it as they sought to achieve dominance in the resultant recruitment contest. It provided yet another justification in their eyes for their movement away from the parent group.

By placing an overemphasis on organizational survival the leadership had actually weakened the movement. A united movement is only beneficial when the viewpoints are also united rather than having irreconcilable intra-organizational conflicts internally damaging the group. Therefore the notion of organizational survival should not be confused with full membership retention and unity. In extreme situations of intra-organizational conflict it is at times more beneficial for the survival of the movement to allow the dissidents exit prior to them organizing, strengthening and significantly damaging the organization.

Personality clashes and trust

You just can't extricate personalities as a factor in any situation.[87]

To date the analysis of this split has mainly focused on the issues which were dividing Republicanism in the 1960s. However, while much of the reasoning for the divide was organizationally based one must also appreciate that personality also played a significant role. The role played here was twofold. This theme had a significant influence on why the split took place, but it also played a role in deciding the outcome of the split. While much of a person's decision-making process was based on the organizationally divisive issues,

[86] Interview by the author with Sean O'Bradaigh.
[87] Interview by the author with Tom Hartley.

be they to do with the armed or the political strategy, the influence of the allegiances of others also impacted on this choice. At times the decision was made dependent on what side trusted individuals were joining.

> Many people made up their mind on the basis of who was on particular sides, people they trusted and liked more. . . . It was not clear cut hard political people deciding. It was human factors that were deciding why some people went with one side over another, and this is not in hindsight. The political orientation would have counted but to what degree with certain individuals is unclear.[88]

Conversely the allegiance of others who were less trusted, or simply disliked, may have had a negative impact on the choice made. Some of these personality clashes also played a significant role in the split actually taking place in the first place. This is especially relevant with respect to personality clashes at a leadership level.

While these personality clashes were not the main cause of the schism they were certainly a dominant factor throughout. Related to the theme of significance of personality 21 participants outlined the importance of influential individuals in the outcome of and the reasoning for the split. In all, 12 of these participants were Provisionals and nine Officials. Each of them alluded to the influence of individual members of the national leadership with the most dominant individuals mentioned being Cathal Goulding and Roy Johnston. A total of 17 participants outlined the influence of the old guard while a further 13 discussed the influence of specific members of their local leadership.

Overview of the split

In the stages previous the reasons for intra-organizational conflict were detailed. These included abstentionism, politicization, the influence of left-wing political thinking, the decline of the armed strategy and the failure of the IRA to meet Republican expectations in 1969. No one single issue can, or should, be perceived as being the sole reason for the split of 1969/70. Each contributed to the justification for a split on behalf of the Provisionals. A statement issued by the Caretaker Executive of the Provisional IRA on 17 January 1970 outlined what they believed to be the main reasons for the split. These were: the recognition of the parliaments by the Goulding leadership, the creation of a formal alliance with radical left-wing groups, the influence of

---

[88] Interview by the author with Mick Ryan.

'extreme socialism', internal methods,[89] how the northern Catholics had been 'let down' by the IRA[90] and campaigning for the retention of Stormont.[91] The Official Republican Movement issued a number of statements through their newspaper the United Irishman, and other forums noting their perception of the split. In these statements they comprehensively outlined the rationale for their economic, social, political and military decisions in the 1960s.[92] Significantly they placed an amount of the responsibility for the development of the Provisionals with Fianna Fail who they believed had funded and armed the Provisionals as they feared the competition which they would have faced from a political left wing Republican Movement.[93]

What must be acknowledged though is that the combination of the issues and the changes which the IRA and Sinn Fein were going through did accentuate and significantly affected the outcome of the split. If the split had been purely about abstentionism, for example, the exiting Provisionals would have been a significantly weaker organization with a lower level of support. This is due to the fact that only those with an intrinsic reluctance to the dropping of the abstentionist policy would have sided with them.

There is variance in the emphasis on issues and events across participants. However, each interviewee was in agreement that the violence in Northern Ireland of 1969 and the IRA's inability to provide defence and weapons was the most significant factor in deciding the outcome of the split. The schism was predicted to take place anyway due to the disillusionment with the politicization process. However, it was the decisions made by the Dublin leadership especially in August 1969 and the inadequacy of the IRA at this time which succeeded in making the Provisional IRA a more dominant force in the aftermath of the split. This is a belief echoed across allegiances and across generations.

A split does not end with the official division of the organization and the formation of a breakaway group. It is important to analyse the aftermath and the effect of the split. Due to the fact that this research is treating the four splits as micro-processes within the macro-process of Republican evolution this final stage of the 1969/70 split should also be considered as the opening stage of the 1974 and 1986 splits. In order to fully understand both of these micro-processes one must consider the consequences and the continuation of the process which led up to the division of 1969/70.

---

[89] This referred to the suspensions and rigging of important votes.
[90] Crenshaw, 'An Organisational Approach', 483.
[91] Cited in Sinn Fein Education Department (1979).
[92] The United Irishman, The IRA in the 70s. In *The United Irishman.* (January, 1970), 8.
[93] Official Republican Movement, *Fianna Fail and the IRA.* (1971).

Stage 5 and stage 1: Aftermath of split: Competition and re-organization

Following the formal split in the movement the main undertaking for the Officials was re-organization after the significant depletion of their membership and leadership.[94] For their part the Provisionals had to develop a whole new organizational structure from scratch. One of their first tasks was the development of their own newspaper, *An Phoblacht.* This was viewed as a priority as they needed to set out their purpose and their account of the splits to the Republican public.[95] For both groups the organizational newspaper was seen as a vital tool. The Provisionals realized that it was of immediate import in the initial organization of the splinter group. The decision to publish *An Phoblacht* was made at the same time as the development of the leadership structure, and the first issue was published in February 1970.

> There were four members of the Ard Comhairle, and then they elected a number of people as a Caretaker Executive. The expression that was used in the army was a Provisional Executive and a Provisional Army Council, until such time as the position could be regularised. So similarly in Sinn Fein Caretaker Executive and a decision to launch a new newspaper and so on.[96]

The re-organization was an extensive process in itself. It required a significant amount of national and regional organization. As well as the structuring process it also required the training of new recruits and the acquisition of weapons.

> It [re-organisation] was an ongoing thing. Even after the Provisional campaign started, it is an ongoing thing weapons and training. The main thing in Belfast was to make sure that areas were properly sufficient at defending themselves. It was a long struggle, it seemed an age but when you look back on it now it boils down to months.[97]

---

[94] For an Official analysis of the 1969/70 split see, The United Irishman, *The IRA in the 70s.* (January, 1970), 8.
[95] Within the first issue of *An Phoblacht* the Caretaker Executive of Provisional Sinn Fein outline to their membership and supporters what they saw as the five main reasons for the split from the Officials. Sinn Fein Caretaker Executive, Attempt to Takeover the Republican Movement. In *AnPhoblacht.* (February, 1970), 4–5.
[96] Interview by the author with Ruairi O'Bradaigh.
[97] Interview by the author with 'Alex'.

While the split took place towards the end of 1969 and the beginning of 1970 the dynamic nature of the process meant that in certain sections of the membership the true effects of the split were not felt until sometime after. There was a number of members and supporters who were oblivious to the fact that a split had even taken place, or if they were conscious to the fact there were some unaware of the defining differences between the two groups. For this reason there were a number of new members who initially joined one group before leaving to join the other sometime after the split.

Many of the Republican regions were bitterly divided between Officials and Provisionals in the aftermath. However, there were other areas which still cooperated together. The bitterness that was displayed immediately in areas such as West Belfast was not necessarily the case in every Republican community. This is a point emphasized by Joe O'Neill, a Donegal based member of the Provisional movement at the time of the split.

> Even in 1970 we had a joint commemoration, Easter commemoration in Drumbo, at that time because we said we would not let anybody interfere with us and we would go ahead with the Donegal Tir Conaill commemoration committee and not have any Dublin interference in it or anything like that so we had a joint commemoration at that time in 1970 in Drumbo.[98]

The organization and re-organization of the groups were the priorities in the immediate aftermath of the split. However, the dominant theme throughout this stage was that of *competition*.

Competition

The immediate consequence of any split is that of inter-organizational competition. The two groups competed on a number of fronts, but most notably for membership and support. In the aftermath of split the Officials and Provisionals were not just competing for the membership of people from the original Republican Movement but also for numerous new recruits. They therefore had to actively recruit and justify the position of the group in contrast to that of their opposition. In the Provisional IRA's Easter Message 1970 they outlined their intentions. 'Irish freedom will not be won by involvement with an internal movement of extreme socialism'.[99] In the direct

---

[98] Interview by the author with Joe O'Neill.
[99] Provisional Army Council, 'No Opportunity Will Be Lost: Army Council's Easter Message.' In *AnPhoblacht*. (April 1970), 1.

aftermath of the split the two organizations were relatively numerically even in membership and support terms. Both sides were trying to prove that they were stronger than their opposition and that they were the legitimate voice of Republicanism. As a result of this, acting in conjunction with the acrimonious nature of the split, this competition resulted in the outbreak of violent feuds between former comrades. These violent feuds engulfed Republicanism in the years after the split which supports the theoretical belief that in the presence of significant inter-organizational conflict the purposive goals of the organization will be substituted with the aspiration of harming the rival organization.

Competition for membership and support

For any organization to sustain survival they must be able to constantly recruit new members as well as maintain the membership which they already have. When there is another organization vying to attract membership and support from the same population this task becomes more challenging, especially when the population is too small to successfully accommodate the survival of two similar groups. Therefore the aftermath of a split leads to intense competition for membership and support between the two organizations in what is a finite population. In the aftermath of the 1969/70 split it would be remiss to assume that what was necessary to attract support and membership across Republicanism was the same in each region. The split of 1969/70, and the subsequent splits, saw divisions form in the support structures in place in the US as well as Ireland.[100] As I previously detailed in an analysis of why people become dissident Irish Republicans the location of a specific population had significant impact on what their expectations were for the organization.[101] In the aftermath of 1969/70 in Belfast the issues of community defence and the acquisition of weapons were at the forefront for people when considering which of the two groups to support or join. This caused significant problems for the local Official IRA as the national leadership was reluctant to supply weapons for an armed strategy against the security services and/or the loyalist paramilitaries, yet the Provisional campaign in the area was building and a significant number of Republicans were joining the new breakaway group. This again revisits the theme of

---

[100] See Niall O'Dochartaigh, N., '"Sure, it's Hard to Keep up with the Splits here": Irish-American Responses to the Outbreak of Conflict in Northern Ireland 1968–1974'. *Irish Political Studies*, 100 (1995), 138–60.
[101] John Morrison, 'Why Do People Become Dissident Irish Republicans?', in P. M. Currie and Max Taylor eds. *Dissident Irish Republicanism*. (New York: Continuum, 2011), 17–42.

leadership disconnect. The national leadership wanted to avoid an armed campaign. However, the Belfast membership was demanding it.

> The Provisional campaign intensified and the pressure was on the Official leadership in Belfast to implement a more robust policy of defence and retaliation against the British. It was obvious that [Billy] McMillen [Belfast leader of the OIRA] was walking a tightrope with what needed to be done in Belfast and what the Dublin leadership were requiring . . . it was obvious that the Dublin leadership were embarking on a course of strategies and tactics which were far removed from the situation in Belfast. They didn't seem to realise that the Provisionals were creating a situation which would make a lot of their strategies and policies impossible to implement.[102]

Initially the split was characterized by the evenness of the divide. However, in the long run the competition for membership and support was numerically won by the Provisionals. This was acknowledged by Official Sinn Fein in a statement in July 1972 in which MacGiolla stated that 'the Provisional Alliance appears to be in the antecedent' they 'have won publicity because their demands are simple, easily presented and easily understood'.[103] This is mainly due to the aggressive nature of their tactics in contrast to the more controlled response of the Officials to the violence on the streets of Northern Ireland. Their violent reactions to loyalist and British attacks significantly raised their profile and support. While the Officials did not completely adhere to a purely political strategy their armed response was more considered and restrained than that of the Provisionals. However, when it came to their armed reaction to the Provisionals there was a significant difference.

New enemy: Violent feuds

At times of intense competition for membership and support between violent political groupings this often results in violent feuds.[104] This is especially true in intensely bitter feuds such as 1969/70, and similarly when the divide is relatively even. From the outset of the competition between the Officials and Provisionals was expressed in the form of violent feuding. It proved to be the prominent theme in the aftermath of the split. This feuding was especially

---

[102] Interview by the author with 'Paul'.

[103] Tomas MacGiolla, *Where we Stand: The Republican Position*. (Dublin: Official Republican Movement, July 1972), 5–6.

[104] For an account of the feuds from the perspective of the Officials see, Six County Executive of the Republican Clubs, *Pogroms!* (Six County Executive of the Republican Clubs, 1974).

visible in areas such as west Belfast where the two groupings were living in close proximity and the split had been particularly personal. There was significantly more expected of the armed Republicans here with respect to defence and weapons. The community was visibly divided.

> It was very, very difficult and realising then that the situation had been brought about whereby the community of the Falls Rd would never be the same again, the community on the Falls Rd. would be torn apart, it would never be the community which we had known, a sense of disillusionment if you can't unite the people of the Falls Rd. how are you going to establish a thirty two county Republic, a thirty two county socialist Republic, there was a sense of disillusionment there.[105]

However, while Belfast was the most visible location of violent feuds between the groups it would be wrong to state that feuds were isolated to Belfast or to Northern Ireland as a whole.

The split of 1969/70 created tensions within the wider Republican community that were not largely repeated in the aftermath of the other splits. While there was feuding after each of the other splits, especially after 1974, it was never again as all-consuming for the entire Republican population as it was in 1970. The two groups shared a common enemy, the British, and a common goal, the unification of Ireland. In spite of this much of their concentration at this time was given to dismantling each other's organizational structures. The national Official leadership intended not to get involved in the any form of armed campaign but the attacks on them by Provisionals provoked a response.

> We made the decision that we wouldn't get involved in the situation in the north, but we began to get involved then in the north. Also the Provos later in 71 or 72 got involved in shooting us, our members, and our members were responding.[106]

In essence they each had a new enemy. This was a very different form of enemy though. It was one who knew the tactics and strategies which would be employed in certain circumstances as they had until very recently been comrades.

> Similar feelings must have been felt in the Civil War. These people knew our methodology, and now they were our worst enemy.[107]

---

[105] Interview by the author with 'Paul'.
[106] Interview by the author with Tomas MacGiolla.
[107] Interview by the author with Mick Ryan.

This was demoralizing for much of the membership and support, especially those who were not actively involved in the actual split. For many Officials it seemed like there were weapons made readily available when they wished to fight against the Provisionals, but yet not when they wished to attack the British or loyalist forces.

> We began to ascertain that there was a trend here whereby you could get access to weapons if it was trouble with the Provisionals, you never get access to them if you were wanting to defend an area against the British Army or otherwise incursion. There was a question mark over that and why this was happening.[108]

As with the split itself the reasoning for the feuds could be ascribed to the policy and strategic differences between the two groups. However, more often these feuds were personality driven, with some former comrades using this as a method of settling old scores. The bitterness of this split is still evident in certain communities to this day, over 40 years after the split took place.

> Certainly there are people to this day who have a whole bitterness towards the Stickies [Officials], and Stickies who hold bitterness towards the Provos [Provisionals]. That is still there, its myopic, but it is still there.[109]

In response to the escalating violence by both republican and loyalist paramilitary groups in the early 1970s in August 1971 the British parliament passed legislation which introduced internment without trial for suspected paramilitaries in Northern Ireland. This resulted in a large number of suspected members of both the Provisional and Official IRA being interned in prison for an indefinite period of time. This led not only to members of both groups being incarcerated but to a number of innocent civilians, unjustly accused of paramilitary membership and activity, being interned for extended periods of time. This caused additional anger among the nationalist and republican communities of Northern Ireland, anger which resulted in a larger number of new members entering the groups than may have without this aggressive measure.

The Republican feuds on the streets and in the prisons continued. However, so did the Republican offensive against the British and loyalists. There were similarly loyalist attacks against Republicans and at times highly questionable

---

[108] Interview by the author with 'Paul'.
[109] Interview by the author with Richard O'Rawe.

tactics employed by the British forces. The end of the 1960s and the turn of the 1970s saw Northern Ireland engulfed in a protracted conflict, 'The Troubles', which would last for close to 30 years. This conflict at times spread to Great Britain and the Republic of Ireland. Throughout the 'Troubles' the actions of each of the conflicting groups resulted in the injuries, death and distress of innocent civilians. The conflict was to see three more significant splits in Irish Republicanism. While none of these three were as dramatic and defining as their predecessor of 1969/70 each was significant in their own right.

4

The Officials split again

As the process for the 1969/70 split came to a close two new processes of splits began. This chapter covers the relatively short process which resulted in the division in the Official Republican Movement resulting in the formation of the Irish Republican Socialist Movement (IRSM) which consisted of an armed wing, the Irish National Liberation Army (INLA) and a political wing, the Irish Republican Socialist Party (IRSP).

In 1974 the Official Republican Movement court martialled and expelled Seamus Costello, in the aftermath of which he developed the IRSM in conjunction with a number of other erstwhile Officials. Therefore there is an obvious difference between this and the other splits. The 1974 split was a result of the expulsion of a leadership figure. The other splits resulted from the voluntary departure of key leadership figures. However, similar to the others the 1974 divide was the result of an organizational stage-based process. By the time of the divide the Officials were a significantly smaller grouping than their Provisional rivals. Even with their relatively small size of the group the 1974 split should still be regarded as significant in the macro-process of Irish Republican evolution.

Of the participants interviewed only 12 individuals were involved in this split. There were six who stayed with the Officials and another six who joined the IRSM. Of these two of the Officials and one IRSM were members of their organization's national leadership. One additional IRSM member was to become a member of the national leadership but at a time significantly detached from the split. It is acknowledged that various subsequent splits happened within the IRSM in the years after their initial split from the Officials. However, due to the sensitive and volatile nature of the issues none of the members involved were willing to talk about these splits in any detail. Therefore there can only be a cursory acknowledgement of their existence.

As with the previous chapter the present analysis details the 1974 split as a stage-based micro-process. Distinct from the 1969/70 split the analysis of the 1974 split has identified four stages as opposed to the five stages of the previous split. This is due to the forced nature of the organizational exit and breakaway group formation brought on by the pre-emptive actions of the Official leadership against Seamus Costello and his followers. The themes presented in this and other chapters should not be regarded as separate themes but as themes dominant during that specific stage of the process. The title of each stage illustrates the stage's dominant characteristic and function.

The stages of the 1974 split are:

Stage 1: Aftermath of split: Competition and re-organization[1]

Stage 2: Factional development

Stage 3: Forced exit and breakaway group formation

Stage 4: Aftermath of split: Multiple feuds.

This does not fit either the models of split or split avoidance. It may more accurately be described as a model of forced split. Within this framework the Official leadership effectively bypassed the third stage of the hypothesized model from Chapter 2 and forced a split by expelling members. This expulsion declined the dissidents the opportunity to adequately prepare for either split or change.

Stage 2: Factional development

The previous split analysed is notable for the variety of intra-organizational conflicts in the lead up to the divide. In contrast the 1974 split had one central intra-organizational conflict. The factionalism within the movement in the lead up to this split was focused on armed strategy. While the split in 1969/70 was partially a result of the Official's lack of engagement in paramilitary activity the birth of the Troubles saw a perceived necessity on behalf of the leadership to participate in 'acceptable' forms of paramilitarism. In the aftermath of Bloody Sunday[2] the Army Council of the Official IRA ordered that any British soldier,

---

[1] This stage has been detailed within the end of the previous chapter.
[2] 30 January 1972, British paratroopers shoot dead 13 people participating in a civil rights march in Derry.

on or off duty, was to be shot.[3] Following these orders on 25 May the Derry Officials 'arrested' and executed Ranger William Best as he was walking through the Creggan. This proved to be one of the most unpopular attacks ever sanctioned by the Officials and resulted in numerous protests against the movement. This came in the aftermath of three other publicly disparaged Official attacks in which innocent civilians proved the main casualties. These attacks were the Aldershot barracks bombing where the casualties were all civilian and included the death of a Catholic priest, the murder of Minister for Home Affairs John Taylor and Sidney Agnew a Protestant resident of Mountpottinger East Belfast who was due to give evidence against three Officials charged with hijacking a bus.

By 29 May the Official GHQ in Dublin declared a ceasefire[4] and issued an order to all members that they were to only attack in situations of defence or retaliation, and this had to take place within 48 hours of the initial event and the resultant attack had to be approved of and justified by Dublin HQ. This policy proved to further factionalize the movement as members found the process frustrating and restricting.

This second stage of the process starts with this change in armed strategy in 1972 and focuses on the developing factionalism between members wishing to expand the armed strategy and their internal rivals aspiring for the movement to restrain all forms of armed conflict. This is regarded as an extension of *disillusionment* and *disconnect* which originated in the first stage in the aftermath of the 1969/70 split. Each of the IRSM members interviewed outlined the central role of the change in the armed strategy.

Membership disillusionment and leadership disconnect

The composition of the Official Republican Movement in the early 1970s was diverse. The national leadership was still predominantly based in Dublin. They were extolling a purely political strategy with the complete removal of

---

[3] Martha Crenshaw, 'Theories of Terrorism: Instrumental and Organisational Approaches', in David C. Rapoport ed., *Inside Terrorist Organisations*. (London: Frank Cass, 2001) (originally published in 1987, 22 and Martha Crenshaw, 'An Organisational Approach to the Analysis of Political Terrorism'. *Orbis*, (1985), 483 outlines that the Officials' heightened use of violence against both the Provisionals and British at this stage of the conflict, and in the direct aftermath of the split, can be understood as former moderates consenting to collective radicalization in order to prevent the departure of a sub-group.

[4] J. Bowyer Bell, *IRA Tactics and Targets: An Analysis of Tactical Aspects of the Armed Struggle 1969–1989*. (Dublin: Poolbeg, 1990), 21.

the armed component. In line with their left-leaning non-sectarian political philosophy they wished to reach out to the unionist and loyalist communities in order to work together in the fight for the working classes. While this may have been viewed from Dublin as the right course of action it was met with disdain by many members and supporters across Northern Ireland. It was difficult for them to accept such an overture to the loyalist communities when Republican areas were facing numerous sectarian attacks perpetrated by members of these communities. The northern Officials attempted to voice this discontent and concern about the strategy to the national leadership. These concerns were even being voiced by some of those who would stay with the Officials in the aftermath of the split, people such as Liam [Billy] McMillen.

> The other paramilitaries were involved in very, very grizzly sectarian murders. I remember Liam McMillen at the September 1972 Ard Fheis reading a quotation from one of the pamphlets, a Loyalist pamphlet, to try and emphasise to the southern membership of Official Sinn Fein the depth of the sectarian bigotry among Unionists, essentially the Unionist population in the North, how deep it was. We thought that overtures to Loyalist paramilitaries at this point in time were being interpreted by Loyalist paramilitaries as a sign of weakness and it was actually giving them a greater confidence to commit more sectarian murders; that was our belief. This created a greater increase in tension within the Official Republican Movement.[5]

This factionalism was not solely based in Northern Ireland. There were militant Officials across Ireland, both north and south of the border, who were sceptical of the policy, as displayed in the quote below from Patrick Kennelly, a Limerick Republican who was a member of the INLA leadership at the time of the split.

> I would have been happy to go along with that if they kept fighting the Brits but they came along with a policy that said 'we are trying to get contact with the Loyalists, get the Loyalist involvement', which was a load of rubbish. They weren't going to make any move, Loyalism weren't going to make any move towards any Republican organisation, irrespective of socialism, I don't know if the Loyalists had any socialism in them, I don't think they would have had any socialism.[6]

---

[5] Interview by the author with 'Paul'.
[6] Interview by the author with Patrick Kennelly.

With respect to the immediate target of organizational survival this again fits with one of the dominant themes of the 1969/70 process, 'too much too soon'. The violence in Northern Ireland was at an all-time high and the Official membership was being targeted by the British, Provisionals and the loyalist paramilitaries. For the northern membership which was taking the force of these attacks, they wanted their leadership to take decisive action to aid in this struggle and provide them with the ability to fight back.

The predominance of violence in Northern Ireland at this time had provided a context where a significant proportion of the Official membership advocated a stronger armed campaign on behalf of the organization. The 'defence and retaliation' strategy was seen as providing too many constraints and was viewed by many to be debilitating in the fight against the Provisional and loyalist paramilitaries, as well as the British occupation.

> At the time we had to be active in defence and retaliation. There was little done in retaliation as there were so many factors to take in to consideration; the time element, we had to be sure who carried out the attack which we were retaliating against so we couldn't be seen to be starting the aggression. There was a good deal of disgruntlement and frustration with the in built conditions, the conditions of defence and retaliation. We had to contact GHQ before any operation and know the organisation responsible. The retaliation had to be carried out within 48 hours of the attack so it wasn't looked as us starting a fresh campaign. Therefore it was very difficult to implement.[7]

While they were being personally constrained by their leadership in taking part in any significant offensives the Official membership was seeing the Provisionals acquiring an abundance of weapons. For many this was to prove disheartening.

> . . . as things got worse in the north the Provos were at the forefront of defending the Catholics at the time when there was a lot of pressure with pogroms and setting fire to homes. As that progressed and got worse people within the Official Sinn Fein Movement were, the Official IRA, were beginning to get disillusioned because they saw that the Official IRA were standing back and weren't sort of taking the lead, the Provos were taking the lead. A lot of fellas that were in the Official Sinn Fein Movement, the Official IRA, they wanted to bring physical force back to the forefront of policies.[8]

---

[7] Interview by the author with Mick Ryan.
[8] Interview by the author with Mick Murtagh.

As Director of Operations at this time Seamus Costello found the strategy of defence and retaliation debilitating and from an early stage voiced his discontent. While supportive of the need for the party to have a strong political basis he believed that in light of the Northern Irish context that the priority at that time should have been having a strong IRA.[9] He believed that the strategy promoted by the national leadership was naïve and had misguided priorities.

> Costello would have been for greater engagement by the Official IRA. As Director of Operations a key element for him was the failure to implement 'defence and retaliation' due to the restrictions placed. Costello was very upfront with his complaints. . . . From then on Costello realised the frustration of local Directors of Operations in the North about not being able to take action. The leadership didn't want to take action against the UDR as this would turn into a sectarian war. Costello's reaction was 'so what if it turns into a sectarian war?' This proved to Costello that the Republican Movement in the north was driven to a situation of appeasement of the Protestant working class. . . . There should have been stronger emphasis on IRA military action against the British. Costello saw the role for the political but thought that the IRA should have been carried out as a primary role, not a secondary role.[10]

The dominant theme at this stage of the split was that of disillusionment among the rank and file membership at the failure of the national leadership to implement a 'strong' armed strategy. This was coupled with a significant leadership disconnect to their northern membership. This disconnect between membership expectations and leadership actions resulted in heightened division within the group between those calling for a purely political campaign and those wishing for stronger armed action.

In light of the constant violence within the republican and nationalist areas of Northern Ireland at this stage of the process, and the specific violence directed against the Official IRA members and supporter by the Provisionals, a significant number of the Northern Irish membership in particular felt that the survival of the organization was under threat. The threat to survival of the organization at this stage was twofold. The physical threat to the survival of the organization was in the death of members due to the on-going feuds, arrests and violence, and there was similarly a numerical threat to

---

[9] Ironically it was originally Costello who toured the country to 'sell' the ceasefire to members in 1972. Jack Holland and Henry McDonald, *INLA: Deadly Divisions*. (Dublin: Torc, 1994), 19.
[10] Interview by the author with Mick Ryan.

organizational survival due to on-going competition for membership with the Provisional IRA.[11]

In the aftermath of the 1969/70 split and in light of the on-going violence described a number of longstanding Officials, as well as those new members, revised their perceived organizational identity. This was particularly true in the areas most affected by violence. A significant number of the members in the worst effected regions believed that the OIRA should have a stronger armed presence both in a defensive and agitational manner. However, the majority of the national leadership still professed the necessity of a restrained use of the armed strategy, with many denouncing any use of violence at all. Therefore they believed that due to the strict promotion of the defence and retaliation strategy and the deficiency of weapons to partake in offensives that the purpose and identity of the organization was being diminished. At this stage there was an attempt to rectify this perceived threat through the application of 'voice'. This was particularly carried out by the local leadership as well as disapproving national leadership figures such as Seamus Costello.

It was unmistakable that at this stage of the process the national leadership was unwilling to compromise on what they believed to be the necessary role and strategy employed by the organization. The continued application of the defence and retaliation strategy, which the advocates of a strengthened armed campaign believed to be purposively restrictive, and the active engagement with the loyalist and unionist communities illustrated even in the aftermath of the application of critical voice on behalf of the disillusioned that the national leadership was unwilling to compromise. This continued strict adherence to their stated principles and strategies outlined to the emerging dissidents that the growing conflict was possibly irreconcilable.

As a consequence of the active and continuing politicizing campaign by the Official leadership the organization at this stage was a significantly heterogeneous grouping. A significant proportion of the organizational leadership was very much in favour of the politicization of the movement. However, in the context of the violence this was significantly disconnected from the expectations of a significant proportion of the membership. This heterogeneity of viewpoints about both the short-term and long-term strategic prioritizing of the group provided a fertile setting for a possible split.

---

[11] As is illustrated in John Morrison, 'Why Do People Become Dissident Irish Republicans?', in P. M. Currie and Max Taylor eds, *Dissident Irish Republicanism.* (New York: Continuum, 2011), a number of young members who joined the Officials during this stage of the Troubles left to join the Provisionals due to their disillusionment with the organization.

Preparation for split

This split more than any of the others was driven by one dominant individual. As is displayed throughout the process it was Costello who was the predominant voice in the call for a more militaristic Official IRA. Each of the participants who participated in the 1974 split, as well as three external observers, indicated the centrality of the leadership of Seamus Costello to the split.

At the Army Convention of 1972 he put forward the motion for the continuation of the armed campaign, a motion which was passed. In the year subsequent it was clear that Costello was making moves to form a new more militant armed group, a move which was countered by the rest of the national leadership. The discontent already illustrated transformed into decisive action. A section of the membership, led by Costello, started to form a more organized dissident grouping with the possibility of moving away from the OIRA. Costello was actively putting forward arguments for the reinforcement of the armed strategy. Even though he could not rely on the support of the majority of the movement he did have the backing of a significant minority. It was with this minority that he began to prepare a dissident organization. Costello's voicing of discontent was not restricted to the national leadership. His misgivings about the organization's armed strategy were also promoted to the discontented rank and file. In specific areas where there was significant discontent especially among the local leadership Costello's strategy was welcomed as an alternative to the restrictive 'defence and retaliation'.

> Costello acted as subversive in the Army and Sinn Fein, and was not just restricted to the Army Council and Sinn Fein. He was going along the route of pandering to dissatisfaction at local level.[12]

The strategy latched on to the sentiment of those who had joined the organization to take part in an armed struggle. The argument put forward to them by Costello and his supporters at a local leadership level was that while there was the necessity for a strong political strategy that in order to have any chance of achieving the organization's ultimate objective that there must similarly be a strong armed campaign. This was a strategy which appealed to many at the forefront of the conflict.

> Our attitude was we didn't want to be like that [purely political]. If we're going to have weapons we wanted to use them, and that's what we joined

---

[12] Interview by the author with Mick Ryan.

the movement for. . . . So what we were saying was 'yes there needed to be a certain political direction, but the gun is an extension of politics'. Throughout history the gun is an extension of politics, it just depends what way you use it. But they didn't want the gun in the politics, the Officials didn't want . . . the gun in the politics at all. So people were all getting disillusioned. Most people, the old ones who were still there were starting to go 'what's the point?' . . . Then came the mention of going back [to an armed campaign] and eyes lit up.[13]

With these growing levels of support for his alternative strategy Costello's stance transformed from changing the movement's armed strategy to preparing for a takeover of the leadership, or alternatively splitting to form a new Republican organization. Acting on this sentiment necessitated significant preparation. The possibility of a split was clear from 1972. However, Costello wished to gain greater levels of support or if at all possible the support of the majority of the movement.

The reason it didn't happen was because Costello wanted to take the whole Movement. He could have gone in Autumn of 72, that is when a split could have taken place.[14]

In his preparations for a split, or alternatively a coup, Costello through his role as Director of Operations had gained the loyalty of units across the island. A number of these would carry out his orders ahead of those of Cathal Goulding.

The Derry people wouldn't take any orders from Cathal, they would only take orders from Seamus Costello. He went up to find out and Costello had all the Derry unit in his hands and had policies to do this and do that and the other, and was all military action in other words. The Provos were at it at this time and we weren't, we were doing nothing, and Costello said that we should be doing something.[15]

As he gained the backing of a significant minority his preparation moved on to include the securing of sufficient levels of weapons for the potential new grouping. For the participants interviewed this was a key issue. Eight interviewees, three Officials and five IRSM, outlined the importance of

---

13 Interview by the author with 'Denis'.
14 Interview by the author with 'Paul'.
15 Interview by the author with Tomas MacGiolla.

this pre-split preparation through the attempted acquisition of armaments. However, the Official leadership, and those loyal to Goulding, were privy to these preparations and countered this by disarming and discontinuing the rearming of units suspected of dissidence. This move was made so as to weaken any possible coup or future external opposition. The disarming of units was taking place when it became apparent to the leadership of the possibility of another split.

> At that stage the unit that we were in, the Fianna [Republican youth wing] and the Army in Divis Flats [Belfast] were known as a head cases because they were always wanting guns, they were always firing out operations, 'can we get this? Can we do that? Can we have more weapons? I want more weapons. Give us more. Let us do. Come on we do' . . . So we were finding then that weapons weren't coming into the areas, just whatever weapons you had, you had. And then you would be asked for maybe someone would want a Shorty and it was going out of the area, but it wasn't coming back.[16]

> They were strapped for arms. The Official IRA ensured that they would disarm most of us at the time. A lot of fellas in Limerick and Clare and Cork and Waterford guns were taken off them months before the split.[17]

The Officials had learned their lesson from the experience with the pre-split Provisionals and were now taking decisive action to prevent or at least minimize the effects of the split. As will be displayed in the subsequent sections this pre-split intervention by the Official leadership proved significant in affecting the subsequent strength of the dissidents. By not allowing them to adequately prepare for the formation of a new group, as the Provisionals had been allowed in the lead-up to 1969, the dissidents were therefore a much weaker organization in the aftermath of split. This is not solely in reference to numerical strength and the possession of weapons. The dissidents had also failed to prepare a significant organizational structure for the now impending new movement. In the aftermath of the split, in the resultant violent feuds Seamus Costello was killed and without a clear succession plan the organization once again entered into further conflict and feuds, this time purely due to a leadership struggle.

---

[16] Interview by the author with 'Denis'.
[17] Interview by the author with 'Frank'.

This stage of the process suggests the significance of the desire for power as a dominant factor in the lead up to the 1974 split.[18] This is an issue which was not previously hypothesized. However, it may prove significant in the analysis of splits and coups led by influential or charismatic individuals rather than groups. The influence of Seamus Costello as the predominant leader of the dissidents was one of the overarching themes within this stage. It is proposed here that his growing dissidence was not solely motivated by the wish for a more combative armed campaign. Although it is clear that he believed in the necessity for an armed campaign it is not clear whether his motivation for dissidence was linked to a belief that the leadership strategy was threatening to the organizational identity. It is posited that his dissidence in particular was also linked to his wish for control of the organization.[19] At this stage of the split Costello was putting forward claims for control. However, in order to gain sufficient control of the organization he needed significant levels of support both numerically in members and physically with respect to weapons and artillery. Therefore it was necessary to frame his push for leadership with the discontent within certain sections of the organization. This desire for power is particularly illustrated in the quote from Tomas MacGiolla detailing Costello's Derry specific usurping of leadership control. Costello's desire for power was similarly emphasized by the former Provisional, turned informer, Sean O'Callaghan. In this quote O'Callaghan compares Costello's personality type to those of some high profile modern day dissidents as well his fellow INLA activists Gerard Steenson and Dominic McGlinchey.

> Costello was always going to run the organisation his way . . . same kind of personality traits, macho male if you like. You look at Gerard Steenson, even [Gary] Donnelly to some extent. You look at Colin [Duffy] in some ways. Of course there are other factors than just that. It often seems to me that while the situation was continuing, while the struggle was going on, that the kind of guys who were big names and heavily attracted or began splits, or then became the leaders. They seemed to me to be particular kinds of characters, that they really weren't suited to being the smallish leaders. [Dominic] McGlinchey never took to orders, neither did Costello, neither did Gerard Steenson.

---

[18] This supports the claim that areas of power-relations are one of the prominent venues for intra-organizational conflict. James March and Herbert Simon, *Organizations: Second Edition* (Cambridge, MA: Blackwell Publishers, 1993), 142; It is similarly supportive of the claim that in armed movements that leadership rivalries can invariably lead to intra-organizational conflict.
[19] This form of split may be more analogous to a national revolution than an organizational split. See Charles Tilly and Sidney Tarrow, *Contentious Politics*. (Boulder Colorado: Paradigm Publishers, 2007), 155–61.

Stage 3: Forced exit and breakaway group formation

This awareness of Costello's organization of dissident factions led the rest of the national leadership to take steps to remove him from a position of power and ultimately expel him. The first major move against him by the leadership came in the wake of the 1973 Official Sinn Fein Ard Fheis where he was accused, alongside a number of his supporters, of vote rigging by the national leadership. Although his dissidence was focused upon the armed campaign and the military leadership he had also attempted to utilize his influence within the political wing to gain ground.

> His conspiracy would develop into 'Goulding, Garland and Ryan are going soft.' He was conspiratorial and undermining our credibility. It became more than opposition and change at Army Council. He also wanted to change things secretly at local councils and had lists of voters at Ard Fheiseanna.[20]

Official IRA units around the country were briefed on multiple accusations against 'Vol. Clancy'[21] by leading members of the movement. Ultimately on 21 February 1974 an Official IRA Court of Inquiry dismissed Costello from the movement. Upon being dismissed Costello requested a court martial. When this was convened he was accused of undermining the IRA through his conduct, misappropriating army funds and faction building. The 'judges' of this court martial found him guilty on all charges and he was dismissed 'with ignominy'.[22] When it came to his membership in Sinn Fein he was originally suspended for a six month period but was subsequently dismissed from the political party, along with a number of his supporters, as he did not adhere to the guidelines of his suspension. He competed in a county council election as an 'Independent Sinn Fein' candidate even though he had been informed that this was against the guidelines of his suspension. His ultimate dismissal from the political party came after a vote to reinstate him was defeated at the 1974 Ard Fheis.

In the aftermath of the court martial the Official leadership de-briefed the national membership on the reasoning for the judgement. Within the ranks of the northern membership in particular this was at times met with anger due

---

[20] Interview by the author with Mick Ryan.
[21] This was a codename used for Costello.
[22] Brian Hanley and Scott Millar, *The Lost Revolution: The Story of the Official IRA and the Worker's Party.* (Dublin: Penguin Ireland, 2009), 271–2.

to what Costello loyalists believed to be an unfair ruling. Many believed that his positioning with respect to a strengthened armed campaign was justified in light of the situation across Northern Ireland. However, not all of these people angered and vocal in their concerns exited in the formation of a new Republican grouping. A number of these critiques stayed out of loyalty to the movement, and at the dismay of having to develop yet another movement from scratch so soon after the split with the Provisionals.

> Costello had been court martialed in June/July 74. I remember we were all called to a meeting in Cyprus St, it was the Officials then headquarters in Belfast, and Goulding was brought up. The entire membership were summoned to the meeting and they read out the whole details of Costello's court martial and why he had been dismissed. . . . It was a witch hunt. They wanted to get rid of Costello. Costello was also basing his position on moves which had been made by a lot of people in Belfast and in Derry saying to him to take a firmer line. Some of those people when it came to the crunch then backtracked and stayed with the Officials.[23]

The position of those calling for an armed campaign in the place of the politically led movement of the time was understood and empathized with by many of those who stayed on in the movement. For those northern Republicans especially who remained with the Officials in 1974 the calls for a re-focusing of the armed campaign were not wholly uncalled for.

> People at the coalface here, you will notice that any splits that happened here were to do with weapons or military tactics or things. They didn't have the luxury of sitting back and falling out over philosophical issues.[24]

With the imposed exit of Costello and a number of his internal supporters the decision for them then was to either remain external to organized Republicanism as independent dissidents or to develop a new organization. As they collectively believed in the need for a strong republican socialist armed campaign they selected to set up the Irish Republican Socialist Movement. They were joined in the new movement by a number of disillusioned members who had not been dismissed from the organization. There was also a portion of the disillusioned that chose to join the Provisionals.

With Seamus Costello regarded as the figurehead for a stronger armed campaign his dismissal from the movement was regarded by many of those

---

[23] Interview by the author with 'Paul'.
[24] Interview by the author with Sean O'Hare.

exiting to join the IRSM as a sign that the intra-organizational conflict about the strengthening of the armed struggle had reached an irreconcilable stage. With the development of the IRSM they now had a new alternative more in line with their beliefs and expectations for an Irish Republican organization.

Breakaway group formation

Even though the split was predominantly a division from within the OIRA the organization which was initially publicly developed was a political party, the Irish Republican Socialist Party (IRSP). The new party included former members of the Official Republican Movement alongside a number of prominent civil rights figures such as Bernadette McAliskey (nee Devlin). One of the main features which differentiated the IRSP from Official Sinn Fein was the new party's dismissal of the potential for beneficial engagement with the loyalist paramilitary groups on socialist issues.[25] However, for a large proportion of the membership the most notable differentiating factor was the presence of an armed campaign. Unbeknownst to purely political members of the IRSP Costello, along with a number of former Official IRA members, set up a new left-wing paramilitary organization the People's Liberation Army (PLA). This organization was the precursor to the Irish National Liberation Army (INLA), a name it changed to in 1975.

The rationale for the initial clandestine nature of the armed wing was twofold. First, the armed leadership was aware that the existence of an armed wing would compel the political recruits to leave the organization, an exit which took place during the walk out from the 1975 Ard Fheis. These political figures gave the new movement an air of legitimacy which was needed in order to have Costello's desired political impact. This provides further support for the power based proposal contained within a previous stage of this process. Costello's wish for power was not confined to power within Irish Republicanism. This desire spread externally to his desire for personal political success at times ahead of the purposive goals of a united Ireland. This is an observation which was made by four members of the Official movement, two in a leadership position. With his new movement he wished to gain significant political success and therefore recruited these politically legitimizing figures. However, he was aware that in order to achieve this political success that he would need to retain both their legitimizing presence as well as the core Republican grouping who expected the organization to provide a strengthened armed campaign. This may be

---

[25] Pat Walsh, *Irish Republicanism and Socialism: The Politics of the Republican Movement 1905 to 1994.* (Belfast: Athol Books, 1994), 147.

a further explanation for hiding the presence of the armed wing from the purely political membership.

Due to the pre-emptive moves by the Official leadership to expel Costello and commandeer weapons the armed grouping was not fully ready for a sustained armed campaign. The pre-emption of his move away by the Official leadership had impaired the preparations for a new movement. They had yet to acquire adequate arms or personnel, even though they had been recruiting and organizing months prior to the split.

> So what happened was when we were still there we hadn't officially put a resignation in because what we needed to do was to stay underground until we got ourselves strong, until we got ourselves organised in units and OCs and adjutants and brigades, because it wasn't just a case of walking away. The Officials wouldn't let you just walk away one on one. You needed to do it on block when it wouldn't have been just as simple, that's the theory.[26]

Due to the need for organizational stability and maintenance the armed movement did not wish to declare their existence until they had developed a sufficiently ready and equipped paramilitary organization. They were wary that due to the animosity on the ground that they would be faced with the prospect of entering into a violent feud with their former comrades.

> Seamus didn't want it to become public knowledge until they had acquired finances, weaponry, had drilled and trained and were in a position to launch attacks on a proper scale.[27]

However, it was this very mistake which they needed to avoid that defines the path of the organization for the rest of the twentieth century.

> What happened with the INLA/IRSP was Costello had made a blunder of making it public to effect that he had a new power a new political power in the Irish Republican Socialist Party. People in Belfast had forewarned him that that was dangerous, unless they were in the position to militarily defend themselves. The Belfast people knew their city better than Costello and they knew that the Official IRA and Liam McMillen would not tolerate another organisation, and would come down heavily.[28]

---

[26] Interview by the author with 'Denis'.
[27] Interview by the author with Fra Halligan.
[28] Interview by the author with 'Paul'.

Stage 4: Aftermath of split: Multiple feuds

As with all splits the aftermath of 1974 was notable for the competition of membership and support. The leadership of both sides was aware of the necessity of a strong membership and support in order to have any chance of achieving the organization's immediate aim of survival, let alone their purposive goal.

> They [organisational policies] may be the best in the world but that is irrelevant if you haven't got people putting their support behind you, you are going nowhere.[29]

The result of this pursuit of membership and support was the explicit regional division of previously Official dominated areas. For example in the aftermath of the 1969/70 split the Lower Falls Road and Divis Street area stayed loyal to the Goulding leadership. As a result of 1974 this was further sub-divided with Divis Street moving to the INLA and Leeson Street and other nearby Official areas staying loyal. This regional divide coupled with the post-split hostility resulted in some of the most violent feuds in the history of Irish Republicanism.

> Everybody came out, Divis Flats was a no-go area for the Sticks, it actually became known as Planet of the Irps.[30, 31]

Alongside the influence of Seamus Costello these feuds were the most dominant theme throughout the analysis of the 1974 split. Each participant involved in the split, as well as four external observers, commented in detail about the feuds. As with all splits both groups wished to put forward the impression that they were the true republican socialist group, and also that they were the stronger of the two groups.

> In paramilitarism there is a lot of macho attitude, 'we are the real ones and we should do this and we should do that.' Then I think you had a situation were each side thought the other side was going to do something and you better not show any weakness. That kind of thing builds up and then tensions build up and tensions build up and then something happens.[32]

---

[29] Interview by the author with Martin McGonagle.
[30] Irps was a slang term used to refer to the Irish Republican Socialist Movement.
[31] Interview by the author with 'Denis'.
[32] Interview by the author with Sean O'Hare.

With the new organization trying to put forward an air of political legitimacy these violent feuds were to prove a significantly regressive step. Not only did both organizations lose a number of significant figures through interment and death, but the IRSP in particular was degraded by the exit en masse of a considerable proportion of their newly recruited political membership. This inevitably stunted any political growth.

> In hindsight it [feuds] didn't allow the politics to flourish the way it should have been . . . I think that that done more damage than Costello's stance. With political people once the guns came out and the Officials attacked them, which was a very deliberate thing, people said 'right I don't want part of that. It is bad enough having the British out after us but you know . . .' that scared a lot of political people as well.[33]

Both groups lost significant leadership figures through the violence, the most significant for the Officials was the murder of Billy McMillen in 1975. However, the defining death of the entire feud was that of Costello himself in 1977. As a result of his death the INLA became embroiled in additional feuds as there was no obvious successor to Costello within the movement.

> Another year or two of him living would have just maybe, he would have had more people politically aware, or organisationally aware, and would have left the Movement on a stronger base. That's not his fault unfortunately, but him leaving at that particular time in a transitional period where we were just out of the feud, people were banged up in jail. We were just starting to get back on our feet, and then bang. The man who had started it everybody looked up to, he was the one we were going to follow, bang away. It was like cutting the head off, so you needed somebody else to take his place who was as charismatic, who was as strong, who had his leadership qualities and who was as politically aware as him. Unfortunately there wasn't that one there at that particular time, there was just that many issues.[34]

It was this issue of internal feuding which would define the IRSM right up to the 1990s. During the feud with the Officials a number of new members were recruited purely for the purpose of partaking in the feuds. These new members had little to no aspirations for a socialist Irish Republic. Their sole purpose in the movement was to take part in combat against the Officials.

---

[33] Interview by the author with Martin McGonagle.
[34] Interview by the author with 'Denis'.

When a number of these new recruits became involved in a leadership battle in the aftermath of Costello's death it led to the development of a number of new smaller Republican organizations, which to a large extent were violent criminal gangs with little to no political aspirations. The net result of all of these feuds was the loss of public support, a necessity for organizational survival, for all groups involved.

> Unfortunately what happens with any feud is the public don't support feuds at all. In the time that you are involved in the feud you're ignoring the public entirely and this applies to all groups because the public come out and protest about feuds. But the attitude of a feud is if you step down you get destroyed and walked on and you have to do to them what they have done to you, and a bit more maybe.[35]

The INLA feuds in the aftermath of the death of Costello succeeded in decimating the organization, and none of the resultant groups ever made as significant an impact on the Troubles as the Provisionals.

> The first split with the IPLO and Gerard Steenson in Belfast, he wiped out quite a good few of the INLA figures at the time, but eventually they shot him. They cornered him in some part of Belfast and shot him. That seemed to put an end to that feud. There have been several feuds after that.[36]

As stated previously in the presence of significant inter-organizational conflict the purposive goals of the organization will be substituted with the aspiration of harming the rival organization. This is particularly illustrated in the recruitment by the INLA of a violent criminal membership with no link to Irish Republicanism for the sole reason of taking part in the feuds. No longer was the organizational priority the achievement of a unified socialist Irish Republic. The perceived necessity now was to harm their rival organization, the Official IRA, and secure organizational power and survival in this competitive environment. Even though the purposive goal of the two groups was the same the concentration was now on destroying the rival Republican organization. Therefore it similarly lends support to a further hypothesis that the immediate goal for each sub-group at the time of split is organizational survival in a form which they respect and recognize. At this point of group inception and immediate aftermath of a close split, similar to the aftermath

---

[35] Interview by the author with Sean O'Hare.
[36] Interview by the author with Patrick Kennelly.

of 1969/79, this immediate goal of organizational survival is accentuated. Due to the closeness in strength of the two rival organizations they are both competing for organizational survival.

The resultant feuds in the aftermath of the death of Seamus Costello further suggests the presence of a power driven motivation for organizational split. However, due to the insignificant level of data gathered on this it requires further investigation. Regarding the Official Republican Movement they rebranded themselves as 'Sinn Fein The Workers Party' with a purely political focus, later dropping all titular signs of their Republican past by becoming 'The Worker's Party'. This party had a small amount of electoral success particularly in the Republic of Ireland before splitting again with the foundation of Democratic Left in 1992.[37] The reason for this split was twofold, those exiting wished for the party to recognize free market economics and they were against the continued existence of the Official IRA, even though it was existent in name alone.

Split summary

In his official analysis of this split Tomas MacGiolla outlines that the intentions of the Official Republican Movement were not to settle just for a 32 County Free State but their aim was to change the way the political system in the whole of Ireland was to work. They wished to 'organise the people to build a revolution and not just build an army to start a campaign'. In this document, which was originally a speech given to the Boston Irish Forum, he outlines his analysis of the 1969/70 split as well as detailing how Republicanism should move forward. The points he raised are resonant of what took place over two decades after with the success of the peace process. In this he outlined the necessity to achieve peace for the people's benefit and in order to achieve this, among other points, he outlined the necessity for amnesty for political prisoners, the reform of the police and the abolishen of 'repressive legislation'. He also detailed that 'only when people can move about and talk without fear can progressive idea once more flourish'.[38] It is the ability for this peaceful dialogue which proved to be the cornerstone of the peace process of the 1990s and early 2000s.

---

[37] There was one other minor split in 1991 when a small number of members left to form the autonomous 'Official Republican Movement' as they believed that the party had moved away from its Republican heritage too much.

[38] For an Official analysis of Irish Republicanism from the early 1960s to 1975 see, Tomas MacGiolla, *The Making of the Irish Revolution: A Short Analysis*. Repsol Pamphlet No.17, 1975, 5.

It has been illustrated here how the 1974 split in the Official Republican Movement was distinctly different from the other three splits analysed in the present research. The dissident faction within the movement was predominantly led by one figurehead leadership figure rather than a group of likeminded dissidents. While this figurehead, Seamus Costello, had significant levels of support from sections of the membership due to his stance on the armed strategy the split can be seen not only as a result of armed strategy based dissidence but also due to Costello's aspirations of power. The split is also distinct as the impending split or coup was pre-empted by the Official leadership and they took decisive action through the safeguarding of weapons from known dissidents and the expulsion of Seamus Costello from the movement. The even nature of the divide in the aftermath of the split as with 1969/70 resulted in a significant level of violent feuds and therefore a shift in the immediate goals of the new movements. The focus was now on weakening their Republican opponents as opposed to fighting against the British presence in Northern Ireland or loyalist attacks on nationalist and Republican communities.

5

The beginning of the end

The mid '70s and early '80s in Northern Ireland are rightly remembered as being among the most violent years of the Troubles. Perhaps paradoxically the analysis in this book shows that this period should also be considered as the beginning of the Republican Movement's gradual advancement into peaceful politics. The culmination of this was the split of '86 and 'mainstream' Provisional Republicanism's dropping of the abstentionist policy to Dail Eireann. While this split was the start of the politicization of the Provisionals it also saw the birth of one of the most dangerous of the modern day dissident groups, the Continuity IRA and their political wing Republican Sinn Fein. After a General Army Convention in '86, which saw the vote to drop the abstentionist policy to the Dail passed, those opposed to the change, mainly from the outgoing Army Executive, met to develop this new armed movement. This was shortly followed by a walk-out from the subsequent Sinn Fein Ard Fheis when the same motion was passed by the requisite two-thirds majority. These walkouts were led by Ruairi O'Bradaigh, Daithi O'Conaill and others, many of whom were the 'old-guard' southern Republicans who a decade and a half earlier had left the IRA and Sinn Fein to establish the Provisionals. For them history was repeating itself.

However, while the split saw the emergence of this dangerous grouping it is also analysed as part of a successful politicization process on behalf of the Provisional leadership of the '80s. Much of the focus of the analysis is therefore on how the newly emerging Gerry Adams and Martin McGuinness leadership successfully maintained their core membership while gradually politicizing the organization towards the end of this process. It is acknowledged that the '86 split is a different form of split from '69/70 and '74. The '69/70 was a split resulting from the dissident faction exiting to form an autonomous organization and '74 resulted from the expulsion of the dissident faction before they were ready to make their move. However, '86 was the result of the original dissenting voices gaining power from the old leadership, and in turn this old leadership exiting to form their new group.

The opening stage of this process has already been outlined in the aftermath of the '69/70 split. In the years after that split the Provisional Movement embarked on an extended terrorist campaign across Ireland and Great Britain resulting in the deaths and injuries of service men and women, innocent civilians and fellow paramilitaries. Their campaign was ostensibly focused on aggressively countering British presence in Northern Ireland. However, they also entered into violent feuds with the Official IRA and loyalist paramilitaries and were regularly seen to be attacking civilian targets across Ireland and Britain.

As with the previous two the present chapter presents the analysis of the '86 split as a stage-based micro process. Similar to '69/70 the analysis illustrates that it was a five-stage process. The significant difference between the two splits lies in the third stage. While the function of the third stage in '69/70 was the inevitability of and the preparation for the split in the process in the lead-up to '86 there was a transition of power from the old-guard leadership of the likes of O'Bradaigh and O'Conaill to the new-guard leadership of the so called 'young Turks', included among them the modern day leadership of Gerry Adams, Martin McGuinness, Pat Doherty, Gerry Kelly and others. A distinct difference also lies in the final stage. While the aftermath of both '69/70 and '74 was notable for violent feuds this was not the same for '86. The absence of feuds is explained by the dominance of the Provisional Movement in the aftermath of this split and the weakness of the Continuity IRA and Republican Sinn Fein.

The stages of the process of the 1986 split fit within the model of an uneven split. Even with the successful application of voice resulting in a change of leadership and strategy at stage 3 this still resulted in an organizational split.

Stage 1: The origins of split

Stage 2: Factional development

Stage 3: Successful application of voice *and* inevitability of and preparation for split

Stage 4: Organizational change *and* organizational exit and breakaway group formation

Stage 5: Aftermath of split: Inter-organizational competition and re-organization

It is therefore argued that this was a minor split in comparison to 1969/70 and the split of the small grouping which formed the Continuity IRA, and Republican Sinn Fein was a minority organization which deemed the political changes as significantly threatening to the organizational identity, even with the compromises. However, as recent history has shown us even though the split itself was minor the resultant activity on both sides of the divide has proven to be highly significant.

Stage 2: Factional development

The initial stage of this process was analysed as the aftermath of '69/70. It was shown to be significant for the feuds which took place between Provisionals and Officials. However, with respect to the process of this split the most notable consequences were the introduction of internment and the influx of a young, mainly northern, membership into the Provisionals. Many of this young membership, as well as those who joined in the late '60s, played a significant role in shaping the course of modern day Irish Republicanism. The names of Gerry Adams, Martin McGuinness, Pat Doherty, Danny Morrison, Gerry Kelly and others still resonate as being the most influential voices in the shaping of modern day Republicanism. It was under their leadership that the Provisional IRA took part in a sustained terrorist campaign during the Troubles. However, it is also under this leadership that the majority of the Irish Republican Movement accepted the necessity for peaceful politics in the place of armed force. This majority move to peaceful politics began here in the process of the 1986 split, a move that partly originated in the debates between many of the interned and imprisoned Republicans. The present stage analyses the developing intra-organizational conflicts within the movement in the mid to late 1970s and assesses how these were significantly different to those present in the process of '69/70. There is also a continuous examination of the growing influence of this new, mainly northern, leadership and the direction in which they wished to take the movement.

All of the active participants acknowledged that the process of change in the 1986 split began in the mid-1970s. While the RSF/CIRA participants generally did not agree on one specific event to signify the instigation of this change the majority of Provisional participants were in agreement. Twelve Provisionals specified that the Provisional ceasefire of '74/75 was the beginning of the change. One member of the RSF/CIRA leadership also identified this as the starting point for the split. The cessation referred to was initiated in December 1974 after a meeting between leading Republicans and Protestant clergymen[1] from Northern Ireland, in Feakle, Co. Clare. The purpose of the talks was to discuss the parameters whereby a cessation of paramilitary violence could take place, with the IRA leadership adamant that this could only happen with a British commitment to their withdrawal from Northern Ireland. During the talks the clergymen presented a British government approved policy document to the IRA members. While the secret talks were prematurely broken up by the Gardai (Irish police) in the aftermath discussions continued between the Provisionals and intermediaries about the possibility of a December ceasefire. The Provisionals announced a ten-day cessation on 20 December 1974. This was extended to last until 17 January, while the Provisionals negotiated with NIO officials. However, the Republicans brought it to an end as their demands had not been met. The end of the ceasefire was marked by continued bombings and attacks in both England and Northern Ireland. The following month on 9 February the Provisionals announced an indefinite ceasefire and again entered into negotiations with the British. Key to their demands was the construction of a plan for British withdrawal from Northern Ireland. These talks and ceasefire eventually came to a close with no development on the Provisionals' demands.[2] The ceasefire officially ended in November 1975. However, during the period of cessation there was growing unrest within the Provisional movement about the handling of the talks by the leadership. A number of members broke the ceasefire, often times claiming their actions under names other than the Provisional IRA. This discontent was evident not only within the communities but also among the Republican prisoners and internees. For many observers the IRA had been 'duped' into the talks by a British government intent on weakening the organization.

The talks were led on the Republican side by Ruairi O'Bradaigh and Daithi O'Conaill who are characterized by many as principal members of the old southern leadership of the time. Throughout my interviews and beyond, these negotiations have been much maligned by the Provisionals as having a detrimental effect on the movement. However, O'Bradaigh defends his and the leadership's position of entering into and continuing with the negotiations.

The invitation was from the British government to 'discuss structures of British disengagement from Ireland.' Now how could one refuse that? Except that they were being deceitful, but how could one refuse that?[3]

---

[1] Members of this group were in contact with the Northern Ireland Office (NIO).
[2] Paul Bew and Gordon Gillespie, *Northern Ireland: Chronology of the Troubles 1968–1993*. (Dublin: Gill and MacMillan, 1993), 95–105; J. Bowyer Bell, *The Secret Army: The IRA (Revised Third Edition)*. (Dublin: Poolbeg, 1989), 414–23.
[3] Interview by the author with Ruairi O'Bradaigh.

His position is that the Republican negotiators were led to believe that there was a possibility of achieving British withdrawal from Northern Ireland. However, there was a failure to agree on the proposed timeline, and that the British would not publicly announce their intention for withdrawal.

The ceasefire and the protracted negotiations have been criticized both during that time and in the years after. In both instances criticisms have principally, but not exclusively, come from the newly emerging northern leadership of the time. The accusation is that the lengthy nature of the combined cessation and talks, which resulted in no real benefits for Republicanism, led to a sense of disillusionment among the membership and support. There was a growing belief that the Provisional leadership of the time had effectively run its course. They no longer knew how to move the Republican movement forward and it was therefore, in their view, time for a new leadership to take over, a point emphasized by Pat Doherty.

> I think it [1975 ceasefire] had a big effect. If you like the then, and I stress then, young leadership would have seen that period as a time where the old days, it was totally out-manoeuvred by the British in terms of how they were dealing with them, what was on offer and the reality of it. After that had run its phase it was time to move on.[4]

The viewpoint expressed by the 'Young Turks' is that the leadership of the time were politically naïve and consequently unable to pragmatically deal with the British. It has retrospectively been promoted that they had brought the movement as far as they possibly could, and therefore it was time for a change, both in personnel and policy.

> In terms of the ceasefire, this is without being overly critical, I think the leadership was military as opposed to political. That doesn't mean you can't be military and political or that you can't have military thoughts when you are political, but really I think it was politically naïve. I mean the Brits were saying things like they were going to leave, but they weren't. They were saying that there was an economic argument that it was inevitable to leave. But all of that was frankly a bit of bullshit to try and prolong the ceasefire and make it harder for them to go back to armed struggle, to all of those things.[5]

Throughout the negotiations there were critical voices coming out especially from the prisons about the way the national leadership was handling the

---

[4] Interview by the author with Pat Doherty.
[5] Interview by the author with Gerry Kelly.

situation and questioning the benefits which the talks and ceasefire had for the Republican cause. The criticisms were chiefly coming from leading northern republicans, people such as Gerry Adams and Ivor Bell. These people had a significant influence on the prison population, as well as on republicans external to the prison.

> People who were in jail, like Adams and Ivor Bell and other people who were querying what was going on and their influence would have been felt amongst the prison population, some of whom were coming out of jail and also in late August 1975 Adams started to write for Republican News . . . So there was a big lot disillusioned about what was going on in '75. And also it had been felt that the IRA had lost its way.[6]

The longer the negotiations went on without any significant benefits for the republican cause the more demoralizing it became for the membership. Retrospectively it may seem that the newly emerging leadership used this demoralization as an opportunity to begin their gradual takeover of the movement both politically and militarily.

> To be quite critical I think that there wasn't a particularly strong view of British objectives at the time, and the ceasefire then created tensions. I suppose then at that point you have a new . . . the other side of the ceasefire in late 1975/76 you begin to see a new leadership emerge, a leadership that has brought the movement right along to where we are today.[7]

While it is proposed that the political success of the early to mid-'80s and beyond stems from the debates and discussions of the mid-'70s, this is not to say that the successful politicization was being comprehensively planned out at this stage with great forethought. As will be shown later in the chapter much of this success was also down to circumstance, but circumstance which could not be taken advantage of without this foundation of debate. The members of this new leadership, which gradually came into position in the late '70s and early '80s, now look upon this as an essential transition which was carried out for the good of republicanism. While not arguing with the point that it was these negotiations which laid the foundations necessary for the new leadership a number of rank and file interviewees, the majority of whom became independent dissidents in the '80s or '90s and one who joined the 32 County Sovereignty Movement (the political wing of the Real

---

[6] Interview by the author with Danny Morrison.
[7] Interview by the author with Tom Hartley.

IRA) in 1998, were critical of the moves to acquire power. They specify that individuals within this newly emerging leadership were using the situation for their own personal and selfish benefits. It was not necessarily the case that they were opposed to the actions of the O'Bradaigh leadership at the time. However, they saw this as an opportunity to utilize the disillusionment within republicanism not only to acquire positions of power but to also isolate certain leadership members.

> I think it was probably called for the best reasons, but I think it was used by certain individuals within the Provisional Movement to enhance their status.[8]

This is a similar argument to the one put forward in the last chapter with respect to Seamus Costello's moves to take power within the Officials in the lead up to 1974. However, in the present situation it was more a collective leadership rather than an individual seeking to takeover.

Those republicans who exited in '86, to form Republican Sinn Fein and the Continuity IRA, believe that the criticism of the '75 leadership was mainly utilized in the years subsequent to the events as opposed to at the time. They argue that some of these emerging leaders were already in positions of power at the time of the ceasefire and negotiations, yet failed to speak out against them at the time. However, in the years later they utilized the situation to critically assess the old leadership. They wished to frame this as a failed leadership, one which had significantly damaged the republican cause. There was not necessarily the purely negative sentiment among the rank and file at the time. Many saw the benefits of the extended ceasefire as it allowed for those on the run to return home and for the IRA to re-organize where necessary. One of the most prominent modern day independent dissidents, Anthony McIntyre, argues this point in specific reference to Martin McGuinness.

> There seemed to be developments only in terms of entering into truces, we didn't see these truces in the way Adams and McGuinness would later, you also have to bear in mind McGuinness was seen by us as a key leader and he wasn't making his opposition to the truce known then in the way that he would later.[9]

The poor handling of the '75 ceasefire and negotiations became a prominent aspect in the subsequent years of the negative portrayal of the 'old southern'

---

[8] Interview by the author with 'Una'.
[9] Interview by the author with Anthony McIntyre.

leadership by their new northern counterparts. It was utilized to illustrate how they were out of touch and were unable to move republicanism forward. However, it most notably provided the catalyst for a more focused discussion to take place about the utility of a more dominant political strategy to work alongside the armed campaign.

Voice: Questioning of strategy[10]

The '86 split is exemplified by the successful start to the politicization process within the Provisionals with the dropping of the abstentionist policy to the Dail. This politicization was only made possible by the extended process of internal debate at both leadership and rank and file levels. One of the most prominent forums for this strategic debate was within the Republican prisoner populations. Throughout the 1970s a large proportion of Provisional republicans were either imprisoned or interned. The prison populations ranged from national and local leadership figures down to ordinary rank and file members, and innocent internees. Within the prisons the inmates organized as they would on the outside in an organizational command structure. At this time, especially from the mid-'70s on leadership figures within the prisons such as Gerry Adams were openly questioning the direction the movement was taking, and the long-term strategies of the national leadership. The external context of a weakening Republican Movement meant that the Republican community was more receptive to critical questioning of the long-term strategy. Prisoners were being asked to think not just militarily but also politically. They were advised to educate themselves on other revolutionary struggles, as well as the Irish one, and see how this could be applied to the situation in Northern Ireland. There was encouragement to look beyond a purely armed campaign and to develop their political thinking. Critical to this, and in stark contrast to the Goulding leadership of the 1960s, was that the prison leadership was not calling for a complete move away from the armed struggle but that a continued armed campaign would be complemented by a strengthened political strategy. This important differentiation allowed this discussion to be more inclusive and did not isolate as many as the political discussions of the 1960s.

I remember Gerry Adams in the jail. We were all sitting there and he says 'you know the armed struggle is only a means to the end, not the end.

---

[10] A more concise discussion of the influence of the prisoners on the politicization of the Irish Republican Movement is contained within Morrison, J. F., 'A Time to Think, A Time to Talk: Irish Republican Prisoners in the Northern Irish Peace Process', in Silke, A. ed., *Prisons, Terrorism and Extremism Critical Issues in Management, Radicalisation and Reform*. (London: Routledge, 2013).

Youse are politicians.' And people said 'we're not really, we're army'. 'No you have to develop your consciousness in here . . . Politics is important and the armed struggle is only a means to an end, and not the end.' So everything I think we see now with Sinn Fein today, I think Adams and them people actually foreseen that. They probably knew that the armed struggle was outmoded, but you couldn't do it because you would have been overthrown, the army would have turned against them.[11]

These discussions led to the gradual acceptance of the utility of the introduction of a political element to the republican struggle. The prisons provided the time and the space for the republicans to actively discuss, argue and think about how this could add to or detract from the armed struggle. It provided the perfect platform for those in favour of a more political struggle to introduce to and convince others of the necessity of this political element while simultaneously questioning the present tactics of the movement. This was all against the background of heightened, and horrific, paramilitary activity.

So I think out of the perhaps initial very violent background, and then people through internment and imprisonment, actually having the time. Because when you were in prison you were removed from that day to day almost kind of survival, or conflict. They began to reflect these arguments, began to examine whether the current kind of structures of republicanism was fit for purpose.[12]

An inevitable consequence of these discussions about the importance of a political element was the debate surrounding electoral politics. As in the lead up to '69/70 there was an innate scepticism about republican participation in electoral politics. However, within the confines of the prison environment the pros and cons were discussed. There were those within the prisons who were strong advocates of electoral involvement and they utilized their time inside to discuss and open others up to the possibility. The debate was one which continued both within the prisons and externally within the republican community through the 1970s, 80s and 90s. The gradual and continuous process of the discussions went on to shape the strategic path taken by the movement.

These discussions over the long-term strategy of the movement had an obvious influence on those who were present and taking part in the process.

---

[11] Interview by the author with Joe Doherty.
[12] Interview by the author with Mitchell McLaughlin.

However, they also had an external influence on the wider republican community. Throughout the history of Irish Republicanism the prison population is revered. This is a point which will be further emphasized when detailing the actions of the modern day dissidents later in the book. During the '70s and '80s in particular their opinions and actions were listened to and appreciated. While many externally would not have been privy to the breadth of the internal discussions taking place there was the strategic utilization by the prisoners of the republican publications to outline their critical analysis of the republican struggle. The most prominent example of this is the series of articles believed to be penned by Gerry Adams, but published under the pen name 'Brownie'. These appeared in the northern Republican newspaper *Republican News* between August 1975 and February 1977. While detailing his experiences of prison life the articles provided a vehicle for 'Brownie' to be critical of national leadership while also putting forward the recommendation of placing a stronger emphasis on the political element of the struggle. These articles proved significantly influential within the republican population as they introduced the wider community to the debates and discussions which were taking place within the prisons at the time. 'Brownie' was one of the methods utilized to gradually introduce the debate around issues such as abstentionism into the wider republican population.[13] While the Goulding leadership introduced the abstentionism debate surrounding the three parliaments this introduction was much more subtle and generally only focused on Dail Eireann, the parliament of the Republic of Ireland, or the '26 counties' as the Republicans called it.

Those who stayed with the Provisionals after the split look to these political debates within the prisons as a positive and necessary step in the process of modern day Irish Republicanism. However, those who exited to form the Continuity IRA and Republican Sinn Fein regard this in a negative manner. They deem it as the start of the downfall of the 'true' Irish republicanism. The influence of these key debates, both within and outside of the prisons, is seen by them as moving the focus away from the armed campaign and towards a corrupt and illegitimate political process. An obvious divide was forming between the northern and the southern leadership. Within the prison the northern influence is blamed by those within the Continuity and Republican Sinn Fein for the ultimate acceptance of Dail Eireann. The blame is laid at their door for not fully understanding the significance of dropping the abstentionist policy to the Dail. This was an 'illegitimate' prospect one that

---

[13] See for example Brownie, 'Active Abstentionism', in *The Republican News* (18 October 1975), 6.

could not be supported in the eyes of those who eventually moved away from the Provisionals in '86.

> I have a suspicion that that [the discussion to drop abstentionism to the Dail] originated probably in Long Kesh camp in the 1970s and again it is people looking for a shortcut to an all-Ireland Republic and I have a suspicion that it was. . . . Well inevitably it was in Long Kesh, it was mostly Northern people. I do feel that unfortunately within the north there is this kind of foolish attitude towards the twenty-six county state.[14]

The obvious influence of these prison debates came with the impact the prisoners had upon release. Many of the leaders of the discussions within the prisons acquired prominent positions within the national and local leadership of the IRA and Sinn Fein. There were great expectations that leaders such as Gerry Adams, while introducing the political element to the campaign, would also lead the Provisionals in a sustained and successful armed resistance against the British presence in Northern Ireland.

> I think in Adams people had a great expectation of him. I think in many ways Adams was trying to influence the debate out there with the Brownie columns and influence Seamus Twomey, who was Chief of Staff of the IRA. It started with the 1975 ceasefire.[15]

Within their leadership roles they extended the discussions which had taken place and introduced the issues to the wider population. They did this through internal local discussions but also through public speeches and addresses.

> I remember at Bodenstown, maybe about 1978 or thereabouts, or in some keynote interview or speech, it might not have been Bodenstown, saying that there could be no military victory for any side that the problem in the north was a political problem and it needed a political solution. That caused all sorts of controversy in a certain generation of republican leaders, and for me it was just so obvious.[16]

While many of the proposals put forward by them were deemed contentious by some of the older traditional membership they also ensured that they

---

[14] Interview by the author with Sean O'Bradaigh.
[15] Interview by the author with Anthony McIntyre.
[16] Interview by the author with Gerry Adams.

gained significant levels of support from this section of the membership as well. This is a factor which proved crucial in eventually passing the proposals both in this micro-process as well as within '97. In order to be successful it was necessary for this newly emerging leadership to gain an air of legitimacy by achieving the support of influential members from all sections of organized republicanism.

Even though this process did eventually result in a split within the movement it was a minimal division of the organization. The actions and preparation taken by the Adams/McGuinness leadership throughout the process significantly contributed to minimizing the effect of the split. The gradual introduction of critical voice was one of the most significant factors at play. The similarities between the intentions the Goulding leadership and the achievements of the Adams/McGuinness leadership are unmistakable. Goulding wished to fully politicize the movement and bring it away from the armed campaign, but failed. However, it was the Adams/McGuinness leadership who gradually achieved this with the Provisionals, while also overseeing some of the worst atrocities by Irish Republican paramilitaries. This on-going politicization started here with the application of voice and compromise. The critical difference between the two situations is that the Goulding leadership attempted to change too much too soon. In contrast the Provisional leadership of the late '70s and early '80s gradually introduced the idea of a strengthened political arm to the movement while stating and displaying their intentions to maintain the armed struggle. This showed a connection between the dissenting voices and the membership and wider republican population. It was a respect for context. As the years and decades after show the leadership only introduced significant changes when they believed that they had the support of the majority of members. It is through this continued appreciation for context and membership sentiment that this was achieved.

IRA restructuring and northern prominence

While the debates about the introduction of a stronger political element were beginning in the mid-1970s the main focus of the northern leadership at this stage was the restructuring of the entire organization, specifically the IRA. They advocated the IRA becoming a cellular organization[17] more capable of adopting the 'long war' strategy which was proposed. This strategy of a long war was articulated by Jimmy Drumm in Bodenstown in June 1977,[18] one

---

[17] The IRA was restructured in the late 1970s.
[18] Jimmy Drumm, 'Annual Commemoration of Wolfe Tone, Bodenstown: Oration Given by Jimmy Drumm', in *Republican News* (18 June 1977).

of many examples of the utilization of the legitimizing voice of the internally respected old-guard to put forward the newly emerging strategic argument. This is a tactic reminiscent of the original Provisionals using Jimmy Steele in the late 1960s to put forward their criticisms of the Goulding leadership. The proposal was that this armed strategy was to go hand in hand with a new form of political pressure.[19] However, at this stage the assertion was that the armed strategy was still to take precedence. While the young northerners were gaining prominence within the movement they were still aware that they needed the support from some of the older members in order to bring about the changes they wished and to retain this air of Republican legitimacy.

Part of the restructuring of the IRA in the late 1970s saw the division of the army into the northern and southern commands. With the vast majority of the armed campaign taking place within Northern Ireland the Northern Command, in conjunction with the Army Council and GHQ, took charge of the active service operations and the Southern Command acted primarily in a quartermaster role in the supply of safe-houses and training. This accentuated a growing divide within the movement between the northern and southern republicans. For some northerners there was resentment in taking orders from those who were geographically separate from the daily struggle.

> In human terms quite naturally, people would resent what they considered to be people who were a hundred miles from the warfront giving orders, and you also had this conception of what was cynically called 'long rifles', people who were very far away from it. There was that element of it.[20]

This establishment of the divided Northern and Southern Commands was seen by some of the southern IRA members as a means by which the emerging northern leadership could take further control of the day to day running of the armed campaign. While this was not the viewpoint of all southern republicans there was a small minority who viewed it as such, and in turn believed that their role was being diminished and their viewpoint isolated.

> They got the Northern Command up and running and by '79 they had complete command of the whole lot and more or less pushed out the southern section of the movement.[21]

---

[19] Martyn Frampton, *The Long March: The Political Strategy of Sinn Fein, 1981–2007.* (London: Palgrave MacMillan, 2009), 10–11.
[20] Interview by the author with Danny Morrison.
[21] Interview by the author with Joe O'Neill.

The ultimate factionalism of the movement was once again established over the issue of abstentionism to Dail Eireann. However, for many volunteers the divide was more accurately defined as one which was north/south in nature. In the comparative analysis of this and the '69 split some of the most prominent differences are within the area of intra-organizational conflict. The prelude to 1969 was defined by the multiple intra-organizational conflicts which were taking place at the one time. This succeeded in strengthening the campaign of those opposed to the proposed changes of the Goulding leadership. In contrast the years prior to 1986 are defined by the narrow focus of the conflict. This is as a result of the gradual introduction of changes and proposed changes. The strategy in turn proved successful in isolating a small minority of dissenters and earning the support of the vast majority of members and supporters. The conflicts in '86 were predominantly located within the national leadership as opposed to '69/70 which were more evident across the entire organization. The '86 conflicts did not spread across the movement until the split was inevitable, and even then it did not have a significant effect on the membership. In essence 1969/70 was the consequence of a collection of intra-organizational conflicts which engulfed the entire membership. In contrast 1986 can be seen as a power struggle within the leadership which was accompanied by tensions surrounding the gradual politicization.

Throughout the interview process interviewees on both sides of the divide from both leadership and rank and file levels described the developing intra-organizational conflict at this stage as being a north/south divide, with a small minority describing it as a division between the old guard traditionalists and the new guard. The prevailing description of any factionalism which was in place at this stage was described as intra-organizational conflict which was centred on struggles taking place within the national leadership. Thirteen participants outlined that the main conflict was taking place within the national leadership of the organization, the majority of whom were members of the leadership themselves.

While the analysis initially pointed to the presence of intra-organizational conflict between the old guard and the new guard, as well as between the northern and southern membership of the movement, upon closer analysis of the data this does not give a fair reflection of what was actually taking place. The emerging divide was not between the northern and southern membership, or between the old members and new members. The minor divide was concentrated within the leadership structures and was between the mainly the old-guard southern leadership and the northern leadership. The new northern leadership actually had the support of much of the northern old-guard, as well as the southern new membership. Therefore the grouping forming in resistance to change was principally concentrated within the southern national leadership. However, at this stage of the process the strategic change was merely being discussed and it was not until the subsequent stage that concrete changes were actively proposed and initiated.

Stage 3: Successful application of voice: Transition of power, one step at a time

From the early 1970s paramilitary prisoners in Northern Ireland were granted 'Special Category' status. This meant that they did not have to wear prison uniforms or take part in prison work with non-political prisoners.[22] However, in March 1976 this status was withdrawn. This resulted in protest by the Republican prisoners in the years which followed. Initially a number went on what has become known as 'the blanket protest.' This form of protest involved prisoners refusing to wear prison uniforms and therefore only wearing their blanket wrapped around them. As this protest was not bringing about the changes wished for by the prisoners they adopted a new strategy in 1978 where they combined the blanket protest with a dirty protest. This new strategy involved prisoners smearing the walls of their cells with their own excrement.[23] While this was attracting more public and media attention it still was not bringing about the changes in prisoners' status. In light of this October 1980 saw the adoption of a protest strategy used the world over, and historically frequently used by Irish Republicans; the hunger strike. The 1980 hunger strike saw seven Republican prisoners in Long Kesh simultaneously start their strike. This strike was led by Brendan 'Darky' Hughes, the OC of the Provisionals in Long Kesh.[24] The seven prisoners continued their strike until 18 December when it was believed that one of the strikers was within hours of death. Hughes was informed that negotiations had been fruitful and that their demands had been met. The strike was therefore stopped without any fatalities. However, it soon transpired that the demands were not met to the full satisfaction of the prisoners. Therefore in March 1981 a new hunger strike was started, this time led by Bobby Sands. One of the major differences between the two hunger strikes was that the 1981 strikers started at staggered intervals for maximum impact. Again the strike was not having the intended impact of the

---

[22] Tim Pat Coogan, *The IRA*. (London: Harper Collins, 2000), 180–7.
[23] Patrick Bishop and Eamon Mallie, *The Provisional IRA*. (London: William Heinmann, 1987), 278–89.
[24] During the hunger strike Bobby Sands took over as OC.

prisoners' demands being met by the British government. Therefore when a by-election was called for the Fermanagh-South Tyrone Westminster seat the Republican Movement decided that Bobby Sands would stand as the Sinn Fein abstentionist candidate, an election which he subsequently won. This shift in strategy saw a swell in public support and sympathy for the prisoners externally from the traditional Republican communities, and in turn support for the Republican Movement as well. The Republican thinking was that the late Margaret Thatcher, the British prime minister at the time, would not let an MP die on hunger strike.[25] However in May 1981 Bobby Sands became the first of ten hunger strikers to die while on strike. His election was followed by the election of two of his fellow hunger strikers as abstentionist TDs in the Dail Eireann general election of June 1981. It was not until 3 October 1981, with 10 hunger-strikers dead, that the protest was called off.

The results of the analysis for this stage show how in this period the new politicizing leadership was able to significantly move forward their agenda and gradually implement some of their desired changes while simultaneously achieving more control and power within the movement at both an armed and political level. This is a point raised by Richard O'Rawe, the IRA public relations officer at the times of the hunger strikes.

> The death of the hunger strikers had a massive political effect on the movement. What it did do was it politicised an awful lot, and it radicalised an awful lot of people throughout Ireland. The national H-Block committee, the H-Block committees firstly became Sinn Fein cumainn overnight. It had a very radicalising effect on ordinary people and Bobby Sands' the hunger strikers' deaths was a departure point for this leadership, for the Adams leadership. It is fairly well acknowledged, and I acknowledge it in my book, that Adams basically set out on the road to engage with the Brits in the months or certainly in the year or so after the hunger strike, but certainly the hunger strike was the point of departure. The hunger strike was the point where Adams could see that there was potential for a mass movement, that there was the potential to eventually overcome the SDLP and become the dominant nationalist party in the north. The hunger strike was the catalyst for the drift into constitutionalism.[26]

In his vocal criticism of the Sinn Fein leadership's managing of the hunger strikes O'Rawe outlines that the Adams leadership extended the situation so

---

[25] This is how the strikes were being framed by the Republicans that the Thatcher government was letting these men die.
[26] Interview by the author with Richard O'Rawe.

as to gain more political traction from the publicity. O'Rawe states the prior to the death of Joe McDonnell, the fifth hunger-striker to die, that the British Foreign Office had conceded to three of the prisoner's five demands, and effectively conceded to a fourth. However, even with this the strikes and the deaths continued.[27]

Strengthening in alternative support: Benefits of circumstance

Prior to the hunger strikes and the election of Bobby Sands the late 1970s is noted as a period of significant disillusionment for the Provisional membership. The 'campaign' was not seen to be making any advance in their objectives of British withdrawal and the unification of Ireland. The IRA membership was coming to this realization and as a result a significant proportion was leaving the movement.

> I think people got to the point that they were getting out, they just weren't going back. I got out of prison I met loads of people saying 'Joe, pressure from the parents, pressure from the wife, I got married, I've got a job, I have to think of my kids and family, I don't think it's worth it anymore, I don't think the revolution is going anywhere.'[28]

Coupled with this was a lack of public support for the extended Provisional armed campaign. The nationalist communities of Ireland were supportive of political rather than armed campaigns. This weakening of public support had played a significant role in the disillusionment of the membership. With the hunger strike campaign and particularly the election of Bobby Sands there was a perceived growing support for Republicanism through the elections of Sinn Fein abstentionist candidates in both the Republic and Northern Ireland.[29] However, the subsequent gradual weakening of support, particularly in the Republic, in the years after the hunger strikes signified that this support was context specific rather than an actual strengthening in support for Provisional Republicanism.

---

[27] See, Richard O'Rawe, *Blanketmen*. (Dublin: New Island, 2005) and Richard O'Rawe, *Afterlives: The Hunger Strike and the Secret Offer that Changed Irish History*. (The Liliput Press: Dublin, 2010).

[28] Interview by the author with Joe Doherty.

[29] For accounts of the hunger strikes see O'Rawe, *Blanketmen*; David Beresford, *Ten Med Dead: Story of the 1981 Hunger Strike*. (London: Grafton, 1987).

So whilst in the June '81 general election in the south of Ireland the H-Blocks and the hunger strikes had an impact to the extent that Kieran Doherty, who was later to die in August '81 was elected TD for Cavan/Monaghan and Paddy Agnew who was 'on the blanket', and who was from Louth, was elected to Leinster House as TD for Louth. In February '82, when another election was called, that vote had completely disappeared, just completely disappeared. So it had come out emotionally in an emergency as a one off.[30] I believed, several of us believed, that there was a major lesson to be learned from this.[31]

This show of electoral success during the hunger strikes displayed to them, and more importantly it displayed to the rest of the movement, the benefits that a strong political element to the Republican campaign could bring.[32] It provided tangible evidence of the benefits of political involvement.[33]

It was a huge event, and it made it easier for us to convince the movement, or the bulk of the movement that we could be involved here in politics and it wouldn't interfere with the progress of the armed struggle. In fact arguably propaganda wise it enhanced it, dove-tailed with it.[34]

However, as with the Goulding leadership they intimated that the abstentionist policy was impeding any further political success during non-emotionally arousing times. The emotionally exaggerated Republican electoral success of '81 therefore provided the necessary impetus for the young leadership to gain more power within Republicanism and significantly strengthened their position in wishing to politicize the movement. The theme of strengthened public support at this stage of the process proved to be one of the most dominant factors in the success of the Adams leadership in gradually implementing their politicizing strategy. A total of 20 participants, across both sides of the

---

[30] This shows the need for modification of strategies as support for political organizations fluctuates with time and the organization needs to adapt to this in order to maintain any significant level of support. Thomas E. Shriver and Chris Messer, 'Ideological Cleavages and Schism in the Czech Environmental Movement.' *Human Ecology Review*, 16(2) (2009), 161–71.

[31] Interview by the author with Danny Morrison.

[32] The mobilization of support for the political changes helped to neutralize the internal dissent from the competing sub-group. Donnatella Della Porta and Mario Diani, *Social Movements: An Introduction.* (Second Edition), (Oxford: Blackwell Publishing, 2008), 329–30.

[33] The most significant results from Republican involvement in electoral politics was that it opened dialogue between the Republicans and other political actors, but it similarly exposed the IRA and Sinn Fein to the negative public response to their ongoing terrorist campaign. Peter R. Neuman, 'The Bullet and the Ballot Box: The Case of the IRA'. *Journal of Strategic Studies*, 28(6) (2005), 941–75.

[34] Interview by the author with Danny Morrison.

divide, emphasized the importance of this theme in the overall process of the politicization of the Provisional Republican Movement not only within this micro-process but within the entire macro-process. However, this growing support for the minimal politicization of the movement did not just grow from the electoral successes achieved by Sinn Fein. There was a concerted effort through a variety of methods which resulted in the ultimate acceptance of the strengthening of the political element.

Control of voice

As has been already intimated in this process the Republican newspapers, in a time prior to internet forums and blog posts, provided a vital vehicle for the leadership to get their desired message across. Therefore as with the '69/70 process when there are developing factions within the movement the editorial control of the paper, and with it the control of potential national voice, proved a significant tool which was actively utilized. Until January 1979 there were two Provisional newspapers, ironically partitioning the Irish Republican message. There was *Republican News* which was southern based and under the editorial control of the traditionalist elements of the southern leadership and *An Phoblacht* northern based and under the control of the emerging young northern leadership. In January 1979 when Deasun Breatnach stepped down as editor of *Republican News* Danny Morrison, editor of *An Phoblacht* and close ally of Adams, came down to Dublin with his staff from Belfast and merged the two papers to form *An Phoblacht/ Republican News*. This move proved significant as the young northerners now had control of the propaganda of the movement and could push their views without fear of alternative points of view within the movement being easily put forward. This also signifies an important step in the gradual process of the northern leadership acquiring control of the movement.

> I became aware that this was part of the politics of change within the movement, the old guard being pushed out, and Danny [Morrison] and [Gerry] Adams and co. moving into Dublin coming from Belfast, becoming national figures. That was all part of the changing of the guard, for want of a better word.[35]

This merger proved to be a significant stepping stone in the strengthening of the newly emerging leadership's position. It provided them an open platform

---

[35] Interview by the author with Richard O'Rawe.

for expressing their views, policies and strategies and simultaneously weakened the voice of those old-guard traditionalists. The membership and supporters of the movement were reliant on the newspaper to provide them with much of their organizational information and policy arguments. Therefore the merger of the papers was a move which gradually diminished the traditionalists' support base.

In the years leading up to the 1986 debates and abstentionist vote the newspaper was utilized as a tool at the forefront of the debate. However, with it in the editorial control of those advocating the dropping of the abstentionist policy the debate, and other policy changes, within the paper was very one-sided with the arguments for politicization at the forefront of opinion pieces published. So therefore in the years leading up to the 1986 vote there was active and patient campaigning for this change in political strategy within not only the IRA and Sinn Fein but also through the medium of *An Phoblacht/Republican News,* as indicated by the leading proponent of this, Danny Morrison.

> My point being is that therefore prior to 1986 debates were also carried out in An Phoblacht, in preparation for the ground, we were chipping away and the argument for continued abstentionism in the Twenty-Six Counties. So you had a debate going on inside the IRA, you had an An Phoblacht debate, you had a Sinn Fein debate over a period of years prior to 86.[36]

While there was a growing appreciation for the need for a stronger political strategy among the membership there were significant elements within the organization that were yet to be convinced that the dropping of the abstentionist policy was the way for this to be best achieved. Therefore in order for this to succeed it was important that the leadership did not force this change upon them but gradually and continuously put forward their arguments for this change while simultaneously stifling the potential for stronger counter-arguments to be put forward by their internal rivals.

Strategy change: One step at a time: Armed to armed and political

The key to the success of the politicizing Provisionals in the 1980s was the gradual process of the changes introduced. The 'young northerners' only officially brought forward their proposed changes when they were certain that they had sufficient levels of support across the movement. This gradual

---

[36] Interview by the author with Danny Morrison.

introduction of change allowed the leadership to ease their base into the transition and therefore succeeded in only alienating a small number of members.[37] At times when they did not have this support they postponed the changes until a time they did, a tactic they utilized across the peace process. This is in stark contrast to the Goulding leadership of the 1960s who tried to change too much too soon. They had pushed forward with votes of abstentionism, NLF and other issues when there were significant levels of opposition across the movement. This respect for timing and support, and the manipulation of circumstance, proved the most significant asset in the on-going support for the leadership across the entire peace process, a process in which they successfully brought the Provisional movement gradually away from terrorism and towards the acceptance of peaceful politics.

One of the tactics utilized throughout this process, in the lead up to '86 and in the years after, was the distancing of the leadership from contentious proposals and debates until it was clear that majority support was in place. In the local and national debates about potential changes to both the armed and political strategies it was rarely the key leadership figures who introduced the potential for change to the debates. They often utilized republican actors external to the leadership structure to 'test the waters' prior to their official backing of the proposal. It was only when the feelings towards the proposals were significantly positive that the leadership officially endorsed it. Richard O'Rawe states that:

> Adams doesn't declare himself until he is absolutely certain that the ground is correct. He wasn't talking about dropping abstentionism, certainly not at a local level, he may have been talking about it at an Ard Comhairle level that we need to revise our strategies. I am aware that at Ard Comhairle level there was friction as early as in the early eighties. In fact there was friction earlier, even before the hunger strikes.[38]

This tactic enabled the key figures to distance themselves from any unsuccessful attempt to implement a controversial change in strategy, and therefore it was more difficult for their internal detractors to accuse or blame them. It also allowed them to take the credit when such changes were successful. However, it was largely down to the groundwork in the months and often years beforehand that allowed for this success. The continuous implementation of

---

[37] Frederick D. Miller, 'The End of SDS and the Emergence of Weathermen: Demise Through Success', in Jo Freeman and Victoria Johnson (eds) *Waves of Protest: Social Movement Since the Sixties.* (Oxford: Rowman & Littlefield Publishers INC, 1983), 303–24.
[38] Interview by the author with Richard O'Rawe.

this distancing tactic is one of the key reasons for the success of the drastic changes implemented by the leadership. It is similarly part of the reason for their prolonged dominance in the Republican leadership.

This patience in the implementation of change allowed the leadership to portray an image of being significantly connected with the expectations of their membership and the communities they claimed to represent. This sets them apart from the disconnect present at the end of the Goulding leadership. It was their relevancy to their base at specific times which maintained their organizational dominance and strength ahead of any internal detractors.

> It's incontrovertible that that kind of seminal formative revolutionary debate, the fact that we had to engage with republicans right throughout, just to prevent the split from being more catastrophic than it was required that you headed off and you started debating this and discussing this. To win the debate required an engagement and negotiation and it was an important lesson that was taken into the peace negotiations, you negotiate with your base every step of the way.[39]

This is a process which was taking place both within the IRA and Sinn Fein. While this took a considerable amount of time the end result is that the leadership was in a stronger position due to the mandate given to them by their base.

This process is looked upon positively by the Provisionals. However, for those who formed or supported Republican Sinn Fein and/or the Continuity IRA they see it otherwise. They regard the tactic less as a form of consultation with the base and more a process of demanding the acceptance of the leadership stance until there is an overall consensus. They contend that the Adams/McGuinness leadership forced a consensus on topics by suppressing active debate within the organization and placing known supporters of their position within leadership positions across the country. This is a similar accusation to that which was directed at the Goulding leadership.

> Every OC in every county was a Belfast man. So they were controlling the Army and then they went for Sinn Fein. The only group that they didn't control was the Executive of the Irish Republican Army.[40]

This claim of suppressed debate was put forward by each of the RSF/CIRA participants as well as two former Provisional members, who are both

---

[39] Interview by the author with Mitchell McLaughlin.
[40] Interview by the author with Des Long.

independent/freelance dissidents. Even if this is the case the analysis of the data indicates that the leadership successfully portrayed the guise of active and constructive engagement with the base.

The key stumbling block for the Goulding leadership, in gaining full support for their strategic changes, was the downgrading in importance of the armed campaign from their long-term strategy especially from the summer of 1969 onwards. This coupled with the further wholesale changes to the organization provided a strong platform for the detractors to base their dissent on and therefore attract stronger support, and in the aftermath of the split greater levels of membership. Conversely the success of the 1986 leadership in achieving majority support for their leadership and their proposed strategic changes was in their maintenance of the paramilitary strategy to continue alongside the stronger political element. This maintenance of the traditional armed campaign placated a significant proportion of would be detractors, a key point emphasized by Pat Doherty, a key member of the new leadership forming within the IRA.

> With the dual strategy you could maybe see that the fact that the armed struggle was going on was giving people a sense that there wasn't a sell-out happening.[41]

The fact that there was a slow gradual implementation and proposal of change, rather than immediate wholesale change, allowed the membership and support to acclimatize to the benefits of the implemented change before any further change is proposed. In the situation where the previous alteration had a perceived positive impact on the movement and had aided in the progress of the organization in the pursuit of their purposive goals membership is more likely to be receptive to the idea of further changes. This movement from a purely armed strategy to a combined armed and political strategy[42] was deemed to be one of the most important factors in the post-split strength of the Provisionals by the majority of interviewees.

The retention of the armed campaign is deemed to be the major factor which kept the PIRA largely intact, an assertion which is supported by those five leadership figures of the armed wing of the movement. While a split was not avoided in '86, the application of 'compromise' and voice successfully lessened the effects of the divide. It was this appreciation and respect for the sentiments of their base which allowed the newly forming leadership

---

[41] Interview by the author with Pat Doherty.
[42] This is often referred to as the 'Armalite and Ballot Box' strategy, see, Peter Taylor, *Provos: The IRA and Sinn Fein*. (London: Bloomsbury Publishing, 1998), 281–2.

to prosper. They were aware that the radical changes they wished to implement were only possible at a time when there were sufficient levels of support throughout the movement. Therefore they were keeping themselves constantly aware of the sentiment and levels of support. By implementing changes in this gradual manner of one step at a time they displayed their willingness to compromise. While they may possibly have wished to implement more sweeping changes there was awareness that this would strengthen the position of their internal detractors. As was displayed in '69/70 the implementation of too many isolating policy and strategy related changes at the one time can prove detrimental to the aspirations of the leadership. Therefore a strategy of one step at a time weakens the detractors' position and therefore weakens any potential competition in the aftermath of a split and resultantly provides the organization with the opportunity to focus on purposive goals rather than having to change focus to competition for membership and support. The strategy of maintaining the armed campaign as well strengthening the political wing of the movement resulted in the isolation of a small number of dissenters. The pledge to continue the armed struggle ensured the support of a wider grouping. Any move to call an end to the armed strategy would have resulted in a stronger RSF and particularly and stronger CIRA.

For many Republicans during the Troubles one of the most defining features of the Provisional Movement was its ability to mount a significant armed campaign against the British 'occupation' of Northern Ireland. Especially for many of those northern Provisionals partaking in almost daily violence across the six counties of Northern Ireland any threat to this element of the movement's make-up, without an illustrated intent for the British to withdraw, would have been defined as threatening to the identity and purpose of the movement. Therefore it was essential for the maintenance of strong support for the gradual changes being made at this stage that the armed campaign be retained as a fundamental element of the strategy. If it was not retained the exiting group would have been more likely to have had a much stronger armed grouping than the Continuity IRA which developed in the aftermath of the split.

Leadership change

As with the strategy changes implemented and proposed the transition of power was similarly a gradual step by step process. Throughout the 1970s the young northerners and their supporters gained and retained leadership positions within both the IRA and Sinn Fein, and in doing so took the place of many of those less supportive of the direction they wished to take the movement. The result was a leadership, local and national, more supportive of the gradual transformation of the organization. Those internal detractors who exited to join or support the Continuity IRA and/or Republican Sinn Fein, as well as a number of freelance dissidents and Provisionals, maintain that this was carried out very purposively and at times aggressively. The Adams/McGuinness leadership deemed that they required to get rid of certain individuals within the movement so as to achieve the necessary control of both the IRA and Sinn Fein so as to progress the movement in the manner they wished.

> He got out and the first thing he done when he got out was to remove Billy McKee as Brigade OC, and then get himself elected onto the Army Council. I think he was also Adjutant General of the IRA around then. But that's what he did, and he started by getting the majority of people who were on the Council, who were in his pocket, and once he had that he had control of the Movement.[43]

The accusation by a number of participants was that the removal of a number of those in disagreement with the newly forming leadership was done by violent means. This was either carried out directly through executions or indirectly by sending IRA members on missions which the leadership knew they would not return from. This forceful removal was not a tactic used against all dissenters. It was principally used to eliminate those individuals who were deemed to pose a threat to the progress of the new leadership.

> They would have conspired to get rid of people who posed a threat to Adams, people who were charismatic, people who had leadership qualities, who would have posed a threat to Adams' position.[44]

Within the Republican Movement the greatest threat posed to the progress of the northern leadership came from the old-guard traditionalist leadership, especially well-respected leaders like Ruairi O'Bradaigh and Daithi O'Conaill. Within Sinn Fein they held the positions of President and Vice President respectively and were also heavily influential within the IRA leadership. These individuals were the main figures within the leadership maintaining the traditionalist Republican position. Their respected and lengthy history within the movement in the view of many members legitimized their position. Due to the respect within which they were held by all members

---

[43] Interview by the author with Richard O'Rawe.
[44] Interview by the author with 'Una'.

an obvious removal would have been significantly damaging to their internal opposition. Therefore they attempted to force their resignations. They did so by calling for the removal of the Eire Nua policy. Eire Nua (New Ireland) was a policy developed with the structuring of the Provisionals in the early 1970s and was approved as policy in 1971. It promotes the federalization of a united Ireland, divided into four federations, one for each province, and is a policy still advocated by the Continuity IRA and Republican Sinn Fein to this day, as well as their subsequent splinter group. In the '80s the Adams leadership, even though they ostensibly supported it throughout the '70s, believed this to be, and sold it as, a 'sop' to the loyalists and unionists.[45] This was a policy portrayed by O'Bradaigh, O'Conaill and other members of the old-guard traditionalists as a fundamental part of the purposive goals of the movement. It was their view that the desired public good that the Republican Movement should aim for was the federalist united Ireland outlined in the document. O'Bradaigh in particular was one of the most vocal advocates of the policy.

> The major disagreement with the Eire Nua programme was that the Adams crowd knew that if you could outmanoeuvre O'Bradaigh on it you could outmanoeuvre him both strategically and organisationally, and you could undermine him within Sinn Fein.[46]

The first attempt to remove the policy from the constitution took place in the 1981 Ard Fheis where they received a majority. However, this did not meet the constitutional requirement of a two-thirds majority, a target which they did reach in 1982. This constitutional withdrawal of the policy highlighted the growing tensions within the leadership of the movement and in 1983 O'Bradaigh, O'Conaill and Cathleen Knowles all stepped down from the Ard Comhairle[47] of Sinn Fein. In O'Bradaigh's resignation speech as president of Sinn Fein he highlighted his belief about the dangers of constitutional politics and the need for the Republican Movement to stick to its 'basic principles'.[48] They saw this as a drop in the quality of Republican policy. These resignations saw the further rise of the new leadership with Adams taking over as president of Sinn Fein. For the likes of O'Bradaigh and O'Conaill the removal of Eire Nua was seen to be threatening to the identity of the movement, and they consequently stepped down from their positions of power within the

---

[45] Brian Feeney, *Sinn Fein: A Hundred Turbulent Years.* (Dublin: O'Brien Press, 2002), 320–1.

[46] Interview by the author with Cathleen Knowles-McGurk.

[47] Directly translated as 'high council'; this is the political party's executive.

[48] O'Bradaigh, R., *Statement by Outgoing President Ruairi O'Bradaigh to the Ard Fheis of Sinn Fein* (13 November 1986).

movement. However, it was not threatening enough to yet justify their exit from the entire organization.

For many the rejection of Eire Nua was less a rejection of the policy and more a method to displace Ruairi O'Bradaigh and others from their position of leadership, a point made previously by Cathleen Knowles-McGurk and re-emphasized here by Ruairi O'Bradaigh himself.

The people who thought as I did just felt they weren't wanted.[49]

This period of time from the late 1970s to the mid-1980s can be defined as a steady rise to power of this young northern leadership. A clear part of this progress to gain significant control was that they changed a number of significant policies while removing from power, the advocates of these policies which they considered to be holding them back.

I just felt that Ruairi was just not up to the job of what the struggle needed . . . no one could stand in the way of progress.[50]

While there is much talk about the political influence of Ruairi O'Bradaigh for observers on both sides of the divide the removal of Daithi O'Conaill was the key to the success of the new leadership. O'Conaill was seen as a highly influential paramilitary and political strategist, one who could shape and influence the decisions made by fellow members. Therefore his isolation was seen as key, even prior to the hunger strikes of 1981.

Even at that time they were looking to sideline O'Conaill, the people within the Movement were looking to sideline O'Conaill. . . . You see O'Conaill had great charisma and he had one of the best, both politically and military brain that ever was.[51]

It was seen as imperative that O'Conaill's influence was to be removed from both the political and the paramilitary leadership. It is alleged that in 1980 he was replaced as the leader of the Southern Command of the IRA by Pat Doherty, a man whose influence within the IRA and the broader Republican Movement was growing significantly. With his removal came his subsequent isolation. In the eyes of some of the young leadership his removal was a more complex and critical issue than that of O'Bradaigh's. While it was clear that

---

[49] Interview by the author with Ruairi O'Bradaigh.
[50] Interview by the author with Danny Morrison.
[51] Interview by the author with Joe O'Neill.

O'Bradaigh was perpetually tied to abstentionism and the Eire Nua policy there were questions asked about O'Conaill's commitment to these strategies and policies. The growing belief was that he was more tied to power than policy, a position emphasized by the former leading IRA member, turned informer, Sean O'Callaghan, and one vehemently denied by Republican Sinn Fein and the Continuity IRA.

> This was about 1980. O'Conail was furious. With O'Bradaigh it was different because O'Bradaigh was still on the Army Council at this stage, whereas O'Conail was really frozen out, he was really frozen out. Yes they saw him as more of a threat than O'Bradaigh. He wasn't even opposed to abstentionism, he got himself in a knot. O'Conail wasn't opposed to lifting abstentionism. He just had nowhere else to ally himself. He was totally outmanoeuvred. He was just too. . . . Whereas O'Bradaigh you knew O'Bradaigh believed in this, absolutely, whether it be flat earth country or not. . . . O'Conail didn't. Neither did Richard Behal or these people. But where were they going to be. These were the people [they were allied with].[52]

The influence and power which O'Conail had within the movement is reflected by some in the weakness and ineptitude of the Continuity IRA after his death in 1991.

> Yeah,[if O'Conail had survived the Continuity would have been stronger.] He would have been formidable in that circumstance. He was particularly astute relatively speaking. He was very astute politically. He was a very astute strategist, and he would have gotten out from under the abstentionist thing. He would have gone with a broad front. He would never have been as rigid or anything.[53]

The aftermath of these significant changes in leadership is defined by the process to remove the abstentionist policy to the Dail. However, as was detailed the leadership did not link themselves to this sensitive issue until they believed that they had enough support to successfully change their policy.

> When Gerry Adams took over in 1983 he said that he was quite happy with the policy of abstentionism. I think it was 1985 before the leadership decided that they would go public on it and the following year they were very very public on it. They did it in a devious way. They don't try to persuade, they tried to instruct and demand.[54]

---

[52] Interview by the author with Sean O'Callaghan.
[53] Interview by the author with Sean O'Callaghan.
[54] Interview by the author with Anthony McIntyre.

This stage in the lead up to the 1986 split is analysed as a contrast to the equivalent stage of the 1969/70 process. While the Goulding leadership attempted to change too much too soon and therefore significantly strengthened the dissidents membership and support the Adams/McGuinness leadership changed policy one step at a time and as a result weakened support for the traditionalists. Most notable within this differentiation is the maintenance of the armed campaign in the 1980s as opposed to its significant destabilization in the 1960s.

However, the success of the 1986 leadership and the failure of the 1969/70 must not be purely attributed to their own internal organizational actions. For the Goulding leadership the violence in Northern Ireland played a more significant role in the post-split strength of the Provisionals than any abstentionist or left wing policy. And in the early 1980s it was the hunger strike campaign and specifically the election of Bobby Sands and others which provided the impetus for a strengthened political strategy. Without this demonstration of the potential for political involvement it is unlikely that the Republican membership would have been as easily convinced of the worth of strengthened political strategy.

Stage 4: Organizational exit and breakaway group formation

As has been detailed throughout this chapter the politicization process up to 1986 was a gradual one marked by individual strategy changes designed to cause minimal dissension at the time of actual change. The changes had all been preceded by internal discussions and were only voted upon or implemented when the leadership believed that they had the support of the majority of the movement. This was the same with the case of dropping the abstentionist policy to Dail Eireann in 1986. The Adams/McGuinness leadership, and their internal supporters, entered into discussions across the movement in order to gauge levels of support for the change to what was a sensitive issue. Part of this process was to emphasize the electoral successes of the party in the past as well as drawing their membership's attention to the utility of active involvement in politics.[55] These discussions continued up to the day of the Convention as well as at the Ard Fheis.

---

[55] See, Gerry Adams, *Sinn Fein Ard Fheis 1985: Presidential Address.* (London: Wolfe Tone Society Publications, 1985), 3.

As with all potentially divisive strategy changes it was extremely important for the leadership to prepare the ground in the years prior to ensure their desired result. This was especially true with the change of the abstentionist policy as it had been the centre of splits in the past. It was a divisive issue, especially for those members in the Republic of Ireland as they were to be the ones most affected by the change, and at the time they were more representative of old-guard traditional republicanism than their northern colleagues, many of whom had initially engaged with Sinn Fein and the IRA in the late 1960s and early 1970s.

> I think in broad terms and this is very broad it wasn't seen as such a fundamental issue in the north, it would have been certainly in some places in the south. It would have certainly been to some older members a real fundamental and defining issue of what the party was about.[56]

As with the Goulding leadership before them the northern politicizers led by Adams and Morrison regarded the abstentionist policy as a burden suppressing their political progress. The electoral support for Sinn Fein significantly dropped in the Republic during elections detached from emotionally arousing moments. While the hunger strikes had seen a dramatic rise in the electoral success of the party the vote returned to its pre-hunger strike base-level in the years after. This decline had not been echoed in Northern Ireland.

The decline in support can be broadly explained by an artificial indication for success given at the time of the hunger-strikes. However, one must also acknowledge the growing sense of hope in the possibility of a peaceful political solution to the growing Northern crisis. In response to the on-going political deadlock the Social Democratic and Labour Party (SDLP) alongside the main nationalist parties of the Republic of Ireland convened *The New Ireland Forum*. The forum met between 1983 and 1984 with the remit of discussing political solutions to the on-going Troubles. In May 1984 the forum, which had excluded any Sinn Fein involvement, presented three alternative political structures to the one in place at the time; a unitary state, a federal or confederal state and joint British and Irish authority over Northern Ireland. The reaction of British Prime Minister Margaret Thatcher was that all options were 'out', in a speech that is frequently referred to as 'out, out, out'. However, even with this apparent reticence to change, and bumpy negotiation process dating back years, Thatcher did negotiate and sign the 1985 Anglo-Irish Agreement with Taoiseach Garret Fitzgerald. This agreement gave hope for a political solution to the Troubles. It gave the Dublin government an advisory

---

[56] Interview by the author with Pat Doherty.

role in Northern Ireland's government through the Anglo-Irish Conference of Ministers. It allowed for them to have representation in areas such as the economy, security, discrimination and rights, and gave the Dublin government an opportunity to make representations on behalf of the minority nationalist communities in Northern Ireland. The key point of the Agreement, however, was that the future of Northern Ireland would be run on a bilateral basis, not by a single community majority.

With this climate of hope in a political process the leadership of Sinn Fein and the IRA believed that they needed to enact political change in their movement. For them and their community at the time it was perceived that active involvement in the Belfast or London institutions was unthinkable. However, the dropping of abstentionism to Dail Eireann was a different matter. The key difference was in public acceptance of the political institutions. As the northern nationalist and republican populations failed to recognize Stormont and especially Westminster as legitimate governing bodies they were more willing to accept the continuation of the abstentionist policies to these institutions than the southern electorate who for the most part regarded Dail Eireann as their rightful legislator. Therefore for many southern nationalists a vote for abstentionist Sinn Fein was seen as a wasted ballot. This was a viewpoint recognized by the young leadership and they resultantly saw it necessary to remove this inhibiting policy. Therefore the continued advocating of southern abstentionism was deemed as a significant obstacle in their attempts make republicanism relevant to a wider southern base.

> So in 1983, after that election in '83/84, it was quite obvious that unless we were prepared to go in to Leinster House that vote was going to remain at rock bottom and could rise occasionally.[57]

It was here where the core difference between the two extremes on either side of the debate lay. The politicizers viewed 26 county abstentionism as a tactic which had failed and was debilitating Republican progress. On the other side of the divide lay the old-guard traditionalists who viewed abstentionism as a cornerstone of Irish Republicanism, closer to part of Republican ideology than a tactic.

> Abstentionism was a policy that had been elevated to a principle[58]

Even though it was northern republicans who were pushing for the dropping of the abstentionist policy to Dail Eireann, and old-guard southern Republicans

---

[57] Interview by the author with Danny Morrison.
[58] Interview by the author with Sean McManus.

leading the calls for policy maintenance, both sides required to widen their support base. As with all intra-organizational conflicts there were firm advocates on either side of the divide. However, there were similarly those undecided members who required convincing before deciding their position. The arguments applied by both sides to justify their position to the Republican base were, as would be expected, polar opposites. The justification put forward by those advocating a policy change suggested that abstentionism in the south was hampering Republican progress. It was argued that without a change in policy that Republicanism would remain irrelevant to the majority of residents within the Republic of Ireland. However, this argument was constantly supported with a reaffirmation of the commitment to armed struggle. This therefore narrowed the prospective support base for the dissenting voices. The main task for the new leadership was to convince those undecided members that political involvement did not equate to a weakening of Republican standards and tradition. This was made simpler by the electoral successes of the years previous.

> I suppose the fact that Bobby Sands was able to be elected and of course the other elections, Kieran Doherty and Paddy Agnew and all of those gave the sense that there was people out there who would respond to Sinn Fein if they were more proactive in engaging in politics and that electoral politics was something that they had to engage in.[59]

On the other side of the divide, in stark contrast, the old-guard traditionalists relied upon historical referencing and moral principle-based arguments to justify their aversion to the arguments for policy change. Their arguments were principally based on the belief that abstentionism was not a tactic which could be utilized or dispatched when the leadership saw fit. Abstentionism, to them, was a historical principle at the centre of what it was to be 'true' Republicans. This was a principle which could not be removed by any leadership at any point during the struggle, and should not even be debated. The only parliament they would recognize was a 32 county parliament elected by the entire population of Ireland. Electoral acceptance of any of the three parliaments would, in their opinion, leave the movement morally bankrupt and would equate to a move away from 'true' Republicanism.

> Then in 1986 whenever the Provos decided to recognise Leinster House at the Ard Fheis of 1986, we left, walked out of the Ard Fheis, because it was never in the constitution of the Republican Movement that you recognised partitionist assemblies. . . . So those who walked out of the Mansion House

---

[59] Interview by the author with Pat Doherty.

in 1986, walked out with the Republican Movement intact, its principles its beliefs and its constitution. Those who remained in the Mansion House dissented from the principles and beliefs of the Republican movement by recognising a partitionist assembly[60] . . . . Those who remained dissented from the Republican Movement and had no right to call themselves Republican after that, because each step they've taken has been further and further and further away from the movement and its goals.[61]

As they held abstentionism as a fundamental part of Republican identity those who left to form both the Continuity IRA and Republican Sinn Fein did so as they believed that an acceptance of seats in Dail Eireann was threatening to organizational identity. As has been stated above the advocates for a change in policy were successful in receiving the necessary two-thirds majority at both the Army Convention and the Ard Fheis. The Provisional leadership under the guidance of Adams and McGuinness when compared to the politicizing Goulding leadership had positioned their policy more strategically to enable the undecided membership to side with them as opposed to the O'Bradaigh leadership, who were firmly tied to their positioning on the issue of abstentionism. The key in this regard was the ability of the new leadership to continuously vocalize their intentions to continue the armed struggle in unison with a now stronger political strategy. The positioning of the two internal sub-groups emphasized the perception of a progressive Adams leadership as opposed to the O'Bradaigh and O'Conaill leadership who displayed no ability to move the organization forward, a leadership unable to adapt with changing circumstances. Related to this was the issue that the changes implemented by the new leadership were not seen to be significantly threatening to organizational identity by the majority of the movement. This is due to the minimal nature of change coupled with the continued reaffirmation of the continuation of the armed struggle.[62]

Preparation for split

It is essential to detail the policy-related differences between the two sub-groups in the analysis of the result of all splits. However, it is equally

---

[60] This shows dissidents are classifying their loyalty not to any organization but to the historical aims of Irish Republicanism in general. They are loyal to a movement, not any one organization. Donnatella Della Porta and Mario Diani, *Social Movements: An Introduction*, 151. Mayer N. Zald and Roberta Ash, 'Social Movement Organisations: Growth, Decay and Change'. *Social Forces*, 44(3) (1966), 328.

[61] Interview by the author with Geraldine Taylor.

[62] An emphasis of the continuation of the armed campaign was present throughout the early to mid-1980s. See, Martin McGuinness, *Bodenstown '86*. (London: Wolfe Tone Society Publications, 22 June 1986), 2.

necessary to understand the non-policy related issues which significantly impacted upon the result. The previous splits emphasize the necessity for pre-split preparation whether it be in organizing a breakaway group at both armed and political levels or alternatively preparation on behalf of the leadership to weaken the potential for a strong breakaway group. In '69/70 the pre-split preparation on behalf of the would be Provisionals enabled the new movement to start their armed and political campaigns immediately at the point of inception, while the pre-split preparation on behalf of the Official leadership in advance of 1974 considerably weakened both the INLA and IRSP. While the IRSM had also prepared for the division the pre-emptive actions of the Officials curtailed this preparation and in turn the IRSM was never the dominant Republican movement it could potentially have been. With respect to the '86 divide the pre-split preparation was truly one-sided. The preparations for change were dominated by the Adams leadership at both paramilitary and political levels. In contrast those wishing to avoid organizational change were noticeably unprepared for a split. This is portrayed in the analysis of the interview data from those on both sides of the divide. Central to this pre-change preparation, and therefore central to the post-split Provisional dominance, was the emphasis placed on gaining internal support for all policy-related changes prior to putting them to a vote. This sets the Adams/McGuinness leadership aside from their predecessors in the Goulding leadership of the 1960s. For Goulding's changes the organization wide support was not there to the same extent as with Adams and McGuinness. This appreciation of the benefits of this preparation was from both sides of the divide.

> Adams and them were better organised [than us]. Adams is a very smart politician and tactician. Nobody can deny that. . . . On the other side, on the army side with regard the Continuity, they hadn't even a water pistol because they had secured all the dumps in between times before this thing took place. They had secured all the dumps and all the guns were in their control.[63]

This pre-split preparation was carried out in order to minimize the possible effects of a divide on the movement. A stronger post-split organization maximizes the potential for the movement to achieve organizational goals, and to maintain organizational survival.

---

[63] Interview by the author with Joe O'Neill.

The most important thing in the course of the struggle and one of the priorities I think for us at all times was to keep as many people with us as we could to prevent as far as possible any fragmentation or slippage from the edges. We were never going to keep everybody. In the course of the struggle you're always going to lose some folks.[64]

An essential part of this preparation was securing the support of influential individuals within the movement for each sub-group's policy positioning, and isolating those who threatened their success. For many members individual allegiance was decided not by arguments for or against abstentionism, but by the positioning of individual members whom they trusted and respected. It was a priority of the Adams leadership to secure the support for change from a broad range of legitimizing figures within the movement. The O'Bradaigh/ O'Conaill sub-group had the ability, through their lengthy and influential membership and leadership of the movement, to provide a claim to the historical continuity of the struggle. They provided a link to the pre-1960s IRA in opposition to the relatively inexperienced involvement of Adams and his supporters. Therefore one of the essential, and most beneficial, steps taken by the leadership was taken in securing the support of other influential old-guard republicans which lessened the continuity claims of O'Bradaigh, O'Conaill and others. The importance of the influential old-guard was referred to by the majority of participants, with each of the RSF/CIRA referring to the importance of this for them. This supports the position taken in this research that there was an over-reliance from this sub-group on the historical past of the movement and in turn a dearth of progressive planning for how the movement was to move forward.

In this respect John-Joe McGirl, Joe Cahill and others spoke out in support of the change in the abstentionist policy to Dail Eireann. Their vocal support came at different and influential times, and culminated in speeches at both the Army Conventions and Ard Fheis, where the split actually took place. The support of these influential individuals from both the Republic and Northern Ireland significantly strengthened the case for change. This was complimented by the wide variety of support for the change from all sections of Republicanism at both armed and political levels, as well as from Republican prisoners. This does not suggest that RSF/CIRA did not gain the support of influential Republicans. However, this took place too late to gain significant traction. After the General Army Convention of 1986, which saw the vote to drop the abstentionist policy to the Dail passed, those opposed to the change, mainly from the outgoing Army Executive, met to develop a new armed movement, a movement which

---

[64] Interview by the author with Richard McAuley.

would become the Continuity IRA. The first public statement by the Continuity IRA Council was not issued until February 1996. In this they declared that their origins had come from 'the gerrymandered General Army Convention of 1986 which deserted the All-Ireland republic and accepted the partitionist and collaborationist 26-County State'.[65]

Upon leaving they contacted General Tom Maguire, the sole survivor of the Second Dail. In the aftermath of the 1969 split he had declared his support for the newly formed Provisional IRA. He wrote 'I hereby further declare that the Provisional Executive and the Provisional Army Council are the lawful Executive and Army Council receptively of the IRA and that the governmental authority delegated in the Proclamation of 1938 now resides in the Provisional Army Council and its lawful successors'. In 1986 he transferred his support to the Continuity IRA and Republican Sinn Fein.[66] The support of Maguire and other influential traditionalist Republicans was utilized by those calling for the maintenance of the status quo as a historical legitimization for their position. The Continuity also gained support of people such as George Harrison and Tom Falvey who ran the American gun-running for the IRA. In an open letter to the Irish Republican Movement they stated that 'we categorically reject any move for elected representation to enter into the Leinster House government, an institution imposed in Ireland in 1922 by British guns and bayonets, to serve the interests of British imperialism'.[67] However, this support was negated to a large extent by the cumulative support from across the movement and across the generations acquired by the Adams leadership.

> I think people like John Joe McGirl and Seamus Twomey and Joe Cahill and having their support was actually crucial. In a historical sense it would have been nice to have Tom Maguire on our side. I know they went to see him and spoke to him, not really to seek his endorsement but just really to appraise him of what was happening. He didn't agree with it. I suppose every generation has to decide for itself how it is going to advance the struggle, and not be hampered by decisions of previous generations, but be mindful of their experiences as well.[68]

When the exiting Executive contacted Maguire[69] he declared the legitimacy of the Continuity Executive as the true IRA, while discounting the claims to

---

[65] B. O'Ruairc '"Runai", "Revolutionary" IRA Emerges.' In *Saoirse* (February, 1996), 9.
[66] Thomas Maguire, *Entering Leinster House: A Veteran Speaks* (22 October 1986).
[67] George Harrison and Tom Falvey, *Open letter to the Irish Republican Movement* (October 1986).
[68] Interview by the author with Pat Doherty.
[69] Ruairi O'Bradaigh, *Dilseacht: The Story of Comdt. General Tom Maguire and the Second (All Ireland) Dail.* (Dublin: Elo Press, 1997).

THE BEGINNING OF THE END

legitimacy of the on-going Provisional IRA. While the existence of an armed wing was heavily suspected it was not until 1994 at a graveside salute to Tom Maguire that the Continuity IRA were brought to the public's awareness. The argument is posited that the declaration of the existence of the Continuity IRA at this stage of the peace process when the Provisionals had declared their first ceasefire, is due to Republican Sinn Fein and the Continuity IRA representing a certain group of Irish Republicans who will support and organize paramilitary activity for as long as there is any sort of British presence in Ireland. In their eyes the announcement of the 1994 Provisional ceasefire made the need for this 'true' form of Republicanism all the more pressing.[70] However, it must also be noted as is supported by the interview evidence that in the direct aftermath of the split in the PIRA that it took a significant amount of time for an efficient dissident armed structure to form, and therefore they may not have had the ability to participate in paramilitary activity until then.

It is not just the insurance of influential individuals' support which was essential for the young leadership but the isolation of detractors. This continued right up until the day of the Army Convention and the Ard Fheis. The previously referred to backhanded respect shown to Daithi O'Conaill was apparent right up until the time of the actual split in Sinn Fein in '86. In a much recounted tale those who walked out of the Mansion House to form Republican Sinn Fein were called to a meeting with the Adams leadership prior to the vote on dropping abstentionism to Dail Eireann. The Adams leadership was willing to meet one last time with the leaders of the future dissidents prior to their walk out. They ostensibly wished to call a truce to the heightened factionalism and prevent a split in the party at the very last minute. However, one person they would not countenance meeting was O'Conaill. While it is portrayed as an attempt at peace talks by those within Sinn Fein, those future members of Republican Sinn Fein and the Continuity IRA recount it as a threatening situation. The isolation was no longer to prevent a split, but it was now to prevent any post-split moves by the inevitably newly forming organization.

At the Ard Fheis they said that they wanted to see myself Ruairi O'Bradaigh and Joe O'Neill, and we could bring one other, but we couldn't bring O'Conail that was the stipulation. So Joe brought Pat Ward and . . . it was very acrimonious. Now O'Bradaigh would never use language, but in the end anyway Pat Ward said, and it wasn't me I have a walking stick

---

[70] Robert W. White and Michael R. Fraser, 'Peronsal and Collective Identities and Long Term Social Movement Activism: Republican Sinn Fein', in Sheldon Stryker, Timothy J. Owens and Robert W. White eds, *Self, Identity and Social Movements.* (Minneapolic, MN: University of Minnesota Press, 2000), 324.

now, but I didn't have it then. Pat Ward hit the table with the walking stick and he said, 'if I was in my health I would wear this stick off you.' 'Ah no Pat we know you, you're alright, you're a hundred percent.' So going out of the meeting [Thomas] Slab Murphy said to Ruairi 'now Ruairi don't be starting anything.' And [Mickey] McKevitt [future Real IRA leader] started to say something to me, the only once I ever spoke to him in my life . . . I never spoke to him before and that was all I said to him. So there was no showing of bullets but Slab Murphy and him were there to be the heavies and we just showed that we weren't afraid of them.[71]

However, it was not just from within the O'Conaill/O'Bradaigh faction that the new leadership had to contend with. Upon his release from prison in the former Chief of Staff of the IRA, Ivor Bell mounted his own unsuccessful opposition against the Adams leadership. Similar to O'Bradaigh and O'Conail the Belfast based Bell was against the increased attention being paid to the political campaign. This hardliner is said to have believed that almost the sole focus of the movement should be on the armed campaign. He was not interested in any political concentration, and that the concentration and spending of the organization should focus on attacks within Northern Ireland. However, even more so than the O'Bradaigh/O'Conail faction Bell had put in little to no groundwork to prepare for his move against the leadership, and was in turn court-martialled and dismissed from the Movement in 1985. The case of Bell, and his few supporters, suggests that the dissenting voices were actually stronger than solely those represented by the Continuity IRA and Republican Sinn Fein. However, due to their lack of preparation, or alternatively their stubbornness against aligning together, the dissidents failed to capitalize. It is speculated that a Continuity IRA including Bell and his allies, or alternatively a Bell led Provisionals including O'Bradaigh and O'Conail in the leadership, would have been able to mount a more serious threat to the Republican dominance of the Adams/McGuinness leadership. If the two sets of dissidents were able to place their differences aside they may have been a dominant force. For Sean O'Callaghan it was the failure of the Bell coup which was key to the success of the Adams/McGuinness leadership.

If Bell had taken over, if Bell had succeeded. Even though Bell might have despised Ruairi O'Bradaigh, and O'Conail . . . He certainly wouldn't have been abstentionist. But for quite a period they might have suited 'Jaysus thank God we did it before the movement was ruined.' But Bell would have been looking at it like 'I will leave those . . . to get on with their thing. I'm

---

[71] Interview by the author with Des Long.

not interested. I'm interested in fighting the war in the north.' He wouldn't have been interested. O'Bradaigh spouting away about not taking part in elections, it wouldn't have bothered Bell. He would have concentrated on the military stuff, so O'Bradaigh would have concentrated on . . . Gerry was gone as president of Sinn Fein. Who was the replacement? O'Bradaigh? '84 O'Bradaigh? Step back into the role again? Bell was the crucial moment. Bell was the big, big moment.[72]

Stage 5 and stage 1: Aftermath of split[73]

The aftermath of the previous two splits is notable for the intense competition for membership and support between the two resultant groupings, leading to violent feuds between the two sets of former comrades. However, this competition was not evident in the same intensity after the 1986 split. Due to the dominance of the Provisional IRA and Sinn Fein, and the resultantly weak Continuity IRA and Republican Sinn Fein, the violent feuds of previous splits failed to escalate. For the Provisionals the Continuity was not seen as a significant threat to their position within Republicanism and consequently the Continuity was in no way strong enough to mount any significant offensive against a grouping which had, in the years since their split from the Officials, acquired the title of 'mainstream' republicanism. For the Provisionals the results of the votes at both the Army Convention and the Ard Fheis allowed them to continue with the politicization of the movement while maintaining a significant terrorist campaign. However, for the breakaway group the years after were dominated by their immediate objective for organizational survival. This included the necessity of acquiring weapons, the recruitment of membership and support and the maintenance of the numbers who originally exited with them.

While both the Provisionals of '69 and the INLA of '74 accumulated a reasonable stockpile of weapons and artillery in the lead-up to and in the aftermath of their splits this was not the case for the Continuity IRA of '86. As has been stated above members of both Republican Sinn Fein and the Continuity IRA admit that they had failed to prepare for the eventuality of split. Resources were close to non-existent for the new organization. Therefore in order to organize any form of armed organization this necessitated the founding members attempting to acquire arms and finances from internal as well as external supporters and members. The Continuity IRA accuse

---

[72] Interview by the author with Sean O'Callaghan.
[73] The aftermath of the 1986 split constitutes the opening stage of the next split in 1997.

leading Provisionals of threatening them against setting up a new armed grouping and similarly Republican Sinn Fein indict that in the naissance of the new political party that members and potential members were warned by Provisionals not to join or support the new movement. As has been already stated these threats never reached the scale of violent feuds. Joe O'Neill emphasizes this in his description of the founding of both Republican Sinn Fein and the Continuity IRA.

> Next thing we set up [Republican Sinn Fein] and we got ourselves an office and we hadn't a penny. On the other side, on the army side with regard the Continuity, they hadn't even a water pistol because they [the Provisionals] had secured all the dumps in between times before this thing took place. They had secured all the dumps and all the guns were in their control . . . . The next thing anyway myself and [Ruairi] O'Bradaigh was called to a meeting in Sligo and we were threatened by [Martin] McGuinness and Pat Doherty and they had two henchmen outside the door, and told that we would be shot if another army was set up[74]

While the 1986 splits did not result in violent feuds similar to '74 and '69/70 one of the comparative outcomes was the refocusing of the Continuity IRA and Republican Sinn Fein with respect to who their main enemy was. It is the belief of the Provisionals that the Continuity and Republican Sinn Fein's immediate exploits were not concentrated on bringing an end to British presence in Northern Ireland. Alternatively their focus was on condemning the actions and intentions of the Provisionals; an accusation that similarly stands with respect to their modern day activity.

> We became the focus [of RSF] over and beyond the role of the British and the Irish governments, we became the focus of the energy of Republican Sinn Fein. They spent their time examining what we were doing and criticising it, rather than providing an alternative that would address the question of independence and self-determination.[75]

This is an accusation made against the Continuity and especially RSF by Provisionals as well as the other Republican groupings and freelance dissidents. However, it is not one confessed to by the membership of the organization in question. Such an admittance would constitute for many the failure of the organization's actions and goals. While not admitted to by members and supporters it is borne out through the interviews. During the interviews

---

[74] Interview by the author with Joe O'Neill.
[75] Interview by the author with Mitchell McLaughlin.

each of the participants across all the organizations was questioned about the modern days activities of their respective groups. During this section of the interviews each RSF and Continuity IRA member placed more emphasis on criticizing the Provisional Republican Movement and its leadership rather than emphasizing the actions of their own organization. It was also noted that four members and supporters were actively critical of the actions of both the armed and political wings of their own grouping. This signifies the failure of both Republican Sinn Fein and the Continuity IRA to make any significant impact on broader Irish Republicanism.

It [the ineffectiveness of the Continuity IRA] is embarrassing, it is not good enough, nothing anywhere near good enough.[76]

Through their critical analysis of the Provisional Republican Movement, and the persistent historical referencing, they were constantly framing themselves as the 'true' Republicans. This belief is further emphasized within the chosen title of the armed wing, *Continuity* IRA. It is their belief that as they have not altered the Republican stance or political strategy that they are the only organization who should be considered as 'true' Irish Republicans maintaining the stance of historical figures throughout Republican history. These criticisms while mainly focused on the Provisional Movement spread across all of the Republican organizations both dissident and mainstream. This is especially true among the old-guard leadership figures such as the now deceased Ruairi O'Bradaigh and his brother Sean. However, even if they wish to portray themselves as 'true' Irish Republicans this is not a message which has resonated among the wider Republican community. Since their inception in 1986 both the Continuity IRA and Republican Sinn Fein have failed in attracting any significant levels of support, a point which is acknowledged and accepted as a failure of the movement by their own members as well as those external. No matter what the intentions or strategies of an organization nothing can be achieved without an adequate level of support, both passive and active. However, even without this support they have been responsible for some of the worst atrocities of a post-Troubles Northern Ireland, as will be detailed in later chapters.

Split summary

The 1986 split was the micro-process which effectively began the politicization of the Provisional Republican Movement. However, it is necessary to

---

[76] Interview by the author with James Scullion.

emphasize that the origins of this divide lie within the process of the 1969/70 split. This longevity of process supports the assumption that the roots of splits will be in previously long-standing cleavages. While the actors from the politicizing side of '69/70 divide had left to form the Officials many of those old-guard traditionalists opposing them stayed and played the same role in the 1986 split. The Republican cleavage of the abstentionists and non-abstentionists continues throughout the movement from its inception up to the present day. Therefore for a cleavage to be long-standing the actors do not necessarily have to be the same, but the reasoning for cleavage needs to remain constant.

Without the rejection of the abstentionist policy to Dail Eireann the gradual movement towards the full acceptance of peaceful politics would not have been possible. The contrasts between the attempted politicization by the Goulding leadership and the 1986 success of the Adams/McGuinness leadership have been portrayed throughout the analysis. The Adams/McGuinness leadership changed policy one step at a time as opposed to the Goulding leadership who tried to change too much too soon.[77] The contrasting effects of the two tactics are borne out in the resultant strengths of the parent and breakaway groups in both instances. The method employed by the 1986 Provisionals successfully maintained the vast majority of the membership and were therefore able to continue with their politicization process in the years after. This is in stark contrast to the dramatic split of 1969/70 which resulted in violent feuds and a significantly depleted Official IRA. It is posited that the Adams/McGuinness leadership of the years preceding 1986 had learned from the mistakes and experiences of the Goulding leadership of the 1960s.[78] The modern leadership did not attempt multiple political and armed strategy changes in unison. Their strategy was to maintain a strong armed campaign throughout their gradual politicization of the movement. This therefore assuaged a number of potential dissidents who saw the armed campaign as central to the purpose of the movement. This incremental change was only viewed as threatening to organizational identity by a small portion of the membership. This therefore weakened the dissident grouping numerically, and the pre-split preparation weakened their potential resources. The concept that the 1986 leadership had learned from the mistakes is acknowledged by numerous interviewees on both sides of the divide. For those Republican Sinn Fein and Continuity IRA

---

[77] If organizational changes are dramatic and rapid, they could lead to the significant exit of those tied to the original model. Donatella Della Porta, 'Leaving Underground Organisations: A Sociological Analysis of the Italian Case', in Tore Bjorgo and John Horgan eds, *Leaving Terrorism Behind: Individual and Collective Disengagement.* (London: Routledge, 2009), 76.

[78] For a justification of the changes in the Irish Republican movement in the 1980s from the point of view of the Provisional Movement see *The Politics of Revolution*, 1–2.

members this perception is portrayed in a negative manner. They regarded it as a cynical and calculated political move to deceive members and supporters of their true intentions for the organization. Their belief is that it was always the intention of the Adams/McGuinness leadership to fully politicize to movement and therefore the maintenance of the armed strategy at this stage was purely to maintain a strong internal support base in their gradual politicising process. A similar assessment is given to their alteration of the abstentionist policy solely to Dail Eireann.

> Number one the Provos had learned from the mistakes the Stickies had made and they didn't put forward the three parliaments they put forward the one, number two they insisted that they were keeping the war going, and that was regarded by many people . . . as the engine of the whole thing.[79]

For those Provisionals who accepted that lessons had been learned from '69/70 while they did acknowledge the importance of gradualism their emphasis was on the value of engaging with the Republican base. One of the most significant themes within the process of '69/70 was in the disconnect between the intentions of the leadership and the expectations of the base. This is deemed to be one of the most significant factors contributing to the result of the '69/70 split. Similarly it was the '86 leadership's ability to connect with and engage the expectations of their membership which significantly contributed to their success. This engagement with the base at times required significant convincing and negotiating on the part of the leadership. It was necessary for them to first convince their membership of the necessity for, and the benefits of, proposed change. It is only when they had convinced the majority that they actively attempted to implement the proposals.

Without the gradualism of change and the engagement with the base it is likely that the result of the split would have been a much more even divide numerically. However, it is essential to similarly acknowledge the context in which both splits took place. In '69/70 the Goulding leadership was at a significantly weak point with respectss to internal and external support. It was perceived that they had failed the northern republican and nationalist communities by not supplying adequate defence for them. During this time the expectations of both the membership and the public was that the Republican Movement was there to take significant armed action in the defence and protection of the Republican communities. Therefore the leadership's push to

---

[79] Interview by the author with Ruairi O'Bradaigh.

change the political policies of the organization was met with contempt by a large proportion of the membership and community. This is in contrast with the situation in the lead up to 1986. In the aftermath of the electoral success of Bobby Sands and others there was a belief within the movement that Sinn Fein could potentially make significant electoral advances. Therefore the context of the early to mid-1980s provided opportunity to successfully implement political reform within the movement. This reform, and the emphasis on gradualism, continues right through to present day Republicanism.

6

The steps into peace

The 1997 split in the Provisional Republican Movement is the final micro-process in the macro-process of republican involvement in the 'Troubles'. However, it does not mark the end of Irish Republican evolution, as will be seen in the closing chapter. This process resulted in a split in the Provisional IRA bringing about the formation of the Real IRA and a split in Sinn Fein which culminated in the formation of the breakaway group the 32 County Sovereignty Committee.[1] Similar to Republican Sinn Fein and the Continuity IRA these two groups publicly deny any official connection to each other. However, it is widely recognized that the '32s' are the political affiliate of the Real IRA. This was supported in the interview with 'Conor', a leading member of the Real IRA at the time of their inception.[2]

> Representatives from the Army who wanted to split met with the political people (32 County Sovereignty Committee) to decide how best to frame the split.[3]

It is this 'framing' that leads us to understand that we need to look beyond the official reasons given by groups and assess what was actually influencing their decision making, and how they wished to portray it to their membership and support. This was illustrated in the analysis of the previous splits and is highlighted again here. The paramilitary side of the 1997 division officially materialized due to a section the IRA leadership, mainly the IRA Executive, showing their disquiet to Sinn Fein signing up to the Mitchell Principles, a set of

---

[1] Now 32-County Sovereignty Movement.
[2] See also Liam Clarke, Maeve Sheehan, John McManus and Chris Ryder, 'Out of Darkness'. In *The Sunday Times*. (23 August 1998).
[3] Interview by the author with 'Conor'.

standards which every party had to agree to before they could enter into peace talks. Among these standards was a commitment to the total disarmament of all paramilitary organizations and to the exclusive use of democratic and peaceful means. Those disgruntled members within the Executive, and especially the Engineering and Quartermaster departments, saw this as 'an infringement of the organization's constitution and the negation of the IRA's claims to be fighting a legitimate "war".'[4] However, 'Conor' goes further and more in-depth to describe the true rationale and justification, in his eyes, for the split at that time.

> The Army split on practical issues . . . prior to the split certain weapons were not being used, not allowed to be used. If weapons were there prior to the split, why couldn't we use them? We had new weapons coming from Libya that were never used, or even announced.[5]

In his eyes it was not just the fact that the leadership was declaring their commitment to decommissioning and peaceful politics, but that they were doing so at a time of considerable paramilitary strength, or at least that it what they wished to portray. This may give support to one explanation as to why it was those close to the Quartermaster and Engineering Departments who wished to continue the armed struggle. They were keenly aware of the organization's paramilitary strength at the time. However, this compulsion to maintain paramilitary activity was significantly distant from the desire of the majority of the Republican community. Theirs was a desire to maintain a cessation of violence and to engage in peaceful negotiations.

As has been previously detailed 1997 was not a major split in Republicanism. Only a small minority of individuals left either the IRA or Sinn Fein. The majority of these left from the Army Executive, with very few political members exiting. This is resonant of the split in the IRA in 1986 where the founding members of the CIRA were predominantly from the Army Executive. The ability of the Provisional leadership to maintain the support of the majority of the membership and fend off a major split allowed for the continued success of the peace process. They successfully maintained the support of those within the middle-ground of Republicanism. These were neither politicizers nor pure advocates of a continued armed campaign. Therefore by convincing the majority the leadership maintained their power within Republicanism. For

---

[4] Martyn Frampton, *Legion of the Rearguard: Dissident Irish Republicanism.* (Dublin: Irish Academic Press, 2011), 91.
[5] Interview by the author with 'Conor'.

them they not only fended off a *major* split, but they fended off a split in its entirety.

In terms of the situation in the aftermath of the Good Friday Agreement, even lesser so again, with probably only less than five percent of people deciding that this was not the way to go. So I wouldn't have regarded that as a split, so if you like those people tried to cause a split and it was fended off, it was defeated by the strategy put in place by the leadership of Republicanism of Sinn Fein, and indeed the leadership of the IRA were hugely supportive of the process of drawing the Unionists in, and the British government into peace negotiations. So I think that it took considerable skill, dialogue and debate and management to insure that what happened then didn't turn out to be a re-split, which is what the Real IRA people and the 32 County Sovereignty Movement were trying to bring about. So it was fended off then.[6]

This is a net result of the gradualism of change applied by the Adams/McGuinness leadership throughout the process. They eased the membership into the transition.[7] As in the previous splits this was accomplished by gaining the support of influential individuals across the movement, individuals such as Brian Keenan. The process in the lead-up to 1997 should be regarded as the continued politicization of the Irish Republican Movement culminating in the signing of the historic Good Friday Agreement in 1998. Paragraph 25 of the Agreement states that 'those who hold office should use only democratic, non-violent means, and those who do not should be excluded or removed from office under these provisions'.[8] Without the gradual political groundwork within the movement in the years leading up to the signing it would have been inconceivable that the leadership of Sinn Fein could ever have signed up to this.

It is my belief that the lead-up to the 1997 split in the Provisionals should, like the other three, be regarded as a micro-process within the macro-process of Republican involvement in the Troubles. However, as many participants were unwilling to talk in detail or on the record about this split there was not enough data collected to test the process models presented in Chapter 2. There were significant difficulties in gaining interviews with members of either

---

[6] Interview by the author with Martin McGuinness.
[7] Frederick D. Miller, 'The End of SDS and the Emergence of Weathermen: Demise Through Success', in Jo Freeman and Victoria Johnson eds, *Waves of Protest: Social Movement Since the Sixties*. (Oxford: Rowman & Littlefield Publishers INC, 1983), 312.
[8] Multi-party Agreement (10 April 1998) *The Northern Ireland Peace Agreement*, 9.

the Real IRA or the 32 County Sovereignty Movement. Only three individuals from this side of the split were willing to talk. However, the micro-process of the 1997 split is not only notable for the exit of the Real IRA and 32CSC. Throughout the process a number of individuals left the movement on their own rather than with a group due to their disagreement with a specific action, policy or strategy by the Provisionals. Four of the participants interviewed became freelance republican dissidents during this process.[9] They therefore give an alternative perspective to the process than either the Provisionals or 32CSC/RIRA.

While there were nine participants who were either ordinary members or leadership figures within the Provisionals during this process a number of them were dismissive of the 1997 split and were unwilling to talk about the actual process in any great detail. However, they were more willing to talk about the general politicization process within the Provisional Movement. Therefore the present chapter will not be presented as a stage-based micro-process. It is instead presented by first of all detailing a historical analysis of the 1997 split. This is then followed by the analysis of a number of the dominant themes which influenced the outcome and the continued politicization of the Provisionals between 1986 and 1997. Four specific themes are focused on in the analysis, two of which are considered major factors in why and how the split took place. These two themes have been identified as *Change in Strategy* and *Factionalism.* The final two themes have been deemed significant in the result of the split, why the Provisionals were significantly stronger in the aftermath of the split. These themes are *Preparation for Change* and *Gradualism.* As with the previous chapters these are supported with the utilization of quotes gathered during the interview process.

Historical analysis of 1997 split

The aftermath of the '86 split saw the continued politicization of the Provisionals. In 1987 Sinn Fein published 'Scenario for Peace' a document which called for an all-Ireland constitutional conference while also replacing the central Republican demand of 'Brits out' with one of national self-determination.[10] The concept of peace became purposively dominant within the mainstream Republican discourse. However, it was tragically juxtaposed

---

[9] For an analysis of the reasons why people become freelance dissidents and what this entails see, John Morrison, 'Why Do People Become Dissident Irish Republicans?', in P. M. Currie and Max Taylor eds, *Dissident Irish Republicanism.* (New York: Continuum, 2011).
[10] Frampton, 59.

with the Provisionals' on-going paramilitary campaign. Below Mitchell McLaughlin presents the Provisonal development of their concept of peace.

I suppose in the late '80s Sinn Fein began to develop this concept of peace, which started with a debate about 'why do we allow our opponents to take the word peace and use it as a weapon against us? Because that's actually open to whatever you want.' So a discussion started, which actually ended up with a very powerful slogan that was used in much of the Sinn Fein publicity at the time which was 'Freedom, Justice and Peace.' And that was the start if you like of claiming the word peace back. It was more than just a propaganda argument; it was about forcing republicans to start to think about freedom, justice and peace. How do you achieve that? A number of discussion documents emerged 'The Scenario for Peace', 'Peace in Ireland', two key documents were produced in I think '89 and '91. The argument there was that we had first of all demonstrated that the Republican struggle couldn't be defeated, in fact if anything we were at a moment of growth and expansion electorally, and the IRA on the other hand also was perhaps at its best equipped, most militarily proficient, but the question was whether the sacrifices involved and the death and the imprisonment involved, the causalities innocent and combatant casualties, all justified the political outcomes, or whether there was another way of dealing with it. That opened up tensions within republicanism because then you were into this question, which I believe all republicans subscribed to, as long as they didn't need to do anything about it, was 'well there will come a point when the fighting stops and the talking starts'. And that is what this debate was about. We arrived at this moment, because implicit in that is it is time to stop the war.[11]

The year after the publication of 'Scenario for Peace' one of the major advances on the road to a peace process took place with the initiation of talks between Gerry Adams and John Hume, the leader of the constitutional nationalist SDLP.[12] While there was an IRA denial of the possibility of a ceasefire coming from the talks, the meetings clearly showed the intent of the Republican leadership to look beyond the exclusive use of force. These talks were to prove important as it revealed to republicans and nationalists the possibility of a pan-nationalist front,[13] a concept the Adams leadership wished to expand on. Throughout the late 1980s and early 1990s there

---

[11] Interview by the author with Mitchell McLaughlin.
[12] Ed Moloney, *A Secret History of the IRA*. (London: Penguin Books, 2002), 279–81.
[13] Frampton, 91.

were significant advances made within the Provisional IRA and Sinn Fein on the move away from an armed campaign. These advances allowed the leadership to enter into often times secret negotiations with the British and Irish governments. While the Republican Movement put forward their proposals for the advancement of the peace process to the governments in the form of a document developed throughout the process of the Hume-Adams talks[14] Albert Reynolds and John Major[15] in 1993 negotiated a separate document called the Downing Street Declaration.[16] This declaration was seen as a setback in the Republican Movement as it deviated from Hume-Adams but more importantly it saw the Irish government being more willing to negotiate with the British government as opposed to the nationalist and Republican communities,[17] while also being seen to be more favourable to the Unionist communities. The Army Council rejected the Downing Street Declaration. However, Adams convinced the Council not to reveal their rejection immediately and to 'play for time'. They therefore called for clarification on points within the document, while also touring the island to take soundings from their constituencies on their thoughts and aspirations for the movement.[18] This is a tactic which proved highly beneficial for the Republican Movement as the grassroots membership did not feel aggrieved for not being consulted on major decisions. While it has been noted that these years saw the advancement of the politicization of the Movement it must also be observed that parallel to this were some of the most vicious attacks ever committed in the name of Irish Republicanism. Included among these was the unprecedented use of what has been referred to as the 'proxy bomb' in 1990. This is where Catholic civilians were at gunpoint forced to drive explosive laden vehicles to British army checkpoints where they would be remotely exploded by members of the Provisional IRA. So negative was the backlash from all communities to the use of such a tactic that the Provisionals ceased its use, but maintained other forms of paramilitarism.[19]

In 1994 major inroads were made in the burgeoning peace process. In February of that year Gerry Adams was granted a 48 hour visa to the United States by President Bill Clinton, a gesture which showed America's expectation

---

[14] Mallie, E. and McKittrick, D., *The Fight for Peace: The Secret Story Behind the Irish Peace Process*. (London: William Heinemann, 1996), 189–212 and 270–5.

[15] The two national premiers at the time.

[16] Richard English, *Irish Freedom: The History of Nationalism in Ireland*. (London: Pan Books, 2006), 403–7.

[17] Frampton, 91–92.

[18] Moloney, *A Secret History,* 417–8; This shows a continuation of the leadership's embracing of active voice with their membership.

[19] See Mia Bloom and John Horgan, 'Missing the Mark: The IRA's Proxy Bombing Campaign'. *Social Research: An International Quarterly*, 75(2) (2008), 579–614.

that Adams would be able to deliver a move for the Republican Movement away from the armed struggle. Similarly the Irish government removed the broadcasting ban on Sinn Fein members. These actions can be regarded as a show of faith in the possibility of the Sinn Fein leadership bringing about a cessation of violence. From early to mid-94 the possibility of such a ceasefire was being discussed at leadership levels within the Provisional Movement. The topic was first broached in discussions about the possibility for a short exploratory cessation. While talks had collapsed between Republicans and the British they continued between Republicans and the SDLP and the Irish government, and therefore shifted from targeting British withdrawal to the establishment of a pan-nationalist front.[20] These talks developed a blueprint for future Republican strategies and actions. However, what the Republican leadership was telling their membership was different to what they were telling the other negotiators. The membership was being told that the option of the armed struggle was still there while the constitutional nationalists were informed that the leadership wished to move forward with purely political strategies. This is best illustrated through the use and manipulation of the TUAS document, and internal Republican document which can either be interpreted as meaning 'Totally UnArmed Struggle' or alternatively 'Tactical Use of Armed Struggle'.[21]

While negotiations were often times fraught eventually on 31 August 1994 the Army Council of the Provisional IRA announced a four month ceasefire, which was later extended. This announcement was in the acceptance of a 14 point proposal issued by Irish Taoiseach Albert Reynolds.[22] This cessation was greeted with celebrations across the whole island of Ireland as well as in Great Britain.[23] However, while there were celebrations outside of the Republican Movement, throughout this period there was growing unease among a number of members of the IRA and Sinn Fein that the leadership were moving away from their ultimate goal, Irish unity. This discontent was at rank and file level but more worryingly for the Army Council it was most prominent within the Army Executive, which had largely been excluded from the negotiation process to that date. They felt that little or no progress was being made on behalf of Republicans and this was being held back by the British government's refusal to sit down with Sinn Fein officials while also standing firm on the need for a significant move by the Republicans on the

[20] Ibid., 418–22.
[21] Ibid., 423; Kevin Bean, *The New Politics of Sinn Fein*. (Liverpool: Liverpool University Press, 2007), 118–20.
[22] Moloney, *A Secret History*, 424–5.
[23] Henry McDonald, *Gunsmoke and Mirrors: How Sinn Fein Dressed Up Defeat as Victory*. (Dublin: Gill and MacMillan, 2008), 149–51.

issue of decommissioning. For them it was not this temporary cessation of violence which was causing problems, it was what this was leading to which made them uneasy, as is emphasized by 'Una', a member of the 32 County Sovereignty Movement.

> You see because within Republicanism there is never a problem with a ceasefire, because if the war is going nowhere you have to call a ceasefire, morally. You can't have volunteers going out risking their lives to be killed, or kill, if it's not having an effect. So the problem isn't with the ceasefire, the problem is with what came after the ceasefire, and that is why there wasn't a split in 94. It's when people signed up to the Mitchell principles and went on to sign up to the Good Friday Agreement that there had to be a split because they signed up to things which were completely the opposite to what Republicanism stands for.[24]

Within the Executive the discontent was led by the Quartermaster General Michael McKevitt and the IRA Director of Engineering Frank McGuinness. However, these were not the only strong voices of discontent as high ranking members, such as Brian Keenan, also voiced their disapproval. In January 1996 the Executive called an extraordinary General Army Convention. It was clear to the Army Council that the intention of the Executive was to bring an end to the ceasefire and end the Adams leadership of the Movement. In a move to prevent this, the Army Council met in the same month and called an end to the 15 month ceasefire. This culmination was dramatically demonstrated with a bomb in Canary Wharf in London on 9 February 1996.[25]

When the Convention eventually took place in October 1996 the Adams leadership had regained some of the faith of the membership due to a number of 'successful' IRA attacks on British security targets. However, they still faced considerable dissent among certain members of the Executive and other delegates. The majority of the motions tabled at the convention were critical of the peace process and sought to weaken the power of the Army Council to call extended ceasefires and decommission weapons.[26] One of the most important votes came with the election of the new Army Council by the new Executive. While it initially seemed that the newly elected Executive would be able to fill the seven man Council with dissident voices alongside Gerry Adams the last minute vote of confidence for the peace process from

---

[24] Interview by the author with 'Una'.

[25] Moloney, *A Secret History*, 433–41.

[26] George Mitchell issued six principles of non-violence which would govern political talks. Deaglan De Breadun, *The Far Side of Revenge: Making Peace in Northern Ireland*. (Cork: The Collins Press, 2008), 15–16.

newly elected Executive member Brian Keenan[27] and the inability of Frank McGuinness to attend the Convention[28] the new Council was elected and consisted of a majority of members loyal to the Adams-McGuinness leadership and therefore the peace process.[29] It was in the aftermath of this convention that the tense atmosphere continued within the leadership and membership of Sinn Fein and the IRA. In the months following the Convention both Adams and Martin McGuinness issued statements about the possibility of another unequivocal ceasefire and Sinn Fein entering into talks parallel to beginning the process of decommissioning.[30]

The importance of Brian Keenan here must not be underestimated. Soon after his release from prison in 1993 Keenan, a veteran Republican leader, became one of the most vocal critics of the Adams leadership and their handling of the 1994 ceasefire. Similar to those influential individuals from previous splits, such as John Joe McGirl in 1986, the leadership as well as the rank and file membership of the IRA paid a lot of respect to Keenan's position. For them he was one of their most respected leaders. This was belief shared by both Adams and McGuinness and for them the support of Keenan was a priority. In the eyes of Sean O'Callaghan Keenan was the key to their success in '97. He emphatically endorsed this point of view when asked what would have happened if Keenan had not gone with them. He emphasized the power that Keenan had to influence not only rank and file members but some key leadership figures as well.

[Adams and McGuinness would have been] crushed, different ball game. If Kennan goes that was straight forward. That was South Armagh [gone with him]. Absolutely crucial. Belfast what would have happened there? You can take individuals. [Bobby] Storey, [Brian] Gillen, [Martin] Ferris, [Thomas] 'Slab' [Murphy] all of them. Ah you're gone then. Things have moved away then . . . it [the support of Keenan] was key.

For the IRA membership in key areas such as South Armagh, a region which only in the mid-'90s Keenan had resituated himself, his late patronage of the leadership's position was key. While he proved to be their most valuable ally in the end, in his early opposition he was their most dangerous adversary.

---

[27] This is supportive of Dyck and Starke stating that the power of the influential individual endorsement is most significant at a time when they were not previously aligned with that position. Bruno Dyck and Frederick A. Starke, 'The Formation of Breakaway Organisations: Observations and a Process Model', *Administrative Science Quarterly*, 44(4) (1999), 807.
[28] McGuinness missed one of his connecting pick-ups to the Convention.
[29] Ed Moloney, *A Secret History*, 445–54 and John Mooney and Michael O'Toole, *Black Operations: The Secret War Against the Real IRA*. (Meath: Maverick House, 2003), 22–3.
[30] Moloney, *A Secret History*, 454–7.

External from the wranglings within the IRA one of the major breakthroughs for the entire peace process came with a change of government in Britain. The Conservative government of John Major was replaced with the electorate voting Tony Blair's Labour Party into power in May 1997. One of Blair's most significant cabinet appointments was that of Mo Mowlam to the position of Secretary of State for Northern Ireland. Within weeks of her appointment Mowlam gave the Republican Movement the assurance that if they declared a ceasefire that they would be admitted to all-party talks. This removed the obstacle of decommissioning for the leadership. However one of her most impressive achievements at this time was simultaneously convincing the Ulster Unionists to participate in these talks.[31] In response to this in July 1997 the Army Council voted to call another ceasefire. This ceasefire was justified to the Executive on tactical grounds and with the rising electoral popularity of the Sinn Fein party and the combined pressure of the British and Irish governments the British had set a firm date of 15 September for the start of talks which would be concluded in May 1998. However, there was still distrust of the Adams leadership from the Executive especially from McKevitt, Frank McGuinness and Brian Gillen. They believed that another ceasefire would only succeed in weakening the IRA. The ceasefire was therefore called without the full support of the Executive.[32]

While the issue of the ceasefire was strengthening the divisions between the Army Council and the Executive it was the Mitchell Principles[33] which heightened the tension to the point of split. The Executive detailed that signing up to the principles would be denouncing the purpose of the IRA and therefore would be unconstitutional. With members of the Sinn Fein negotiating team such as Gerry Adams, Martin McGuinness and Pat Doherty not only members of the political party but also reportedly the Army Council they were faced with a dilemma. With the Council and the Executive in deadlock over whether this was unconstitutional or not another General Army Convention was convened to decide on the matter. It was clear that the Army Council had prepared well for the Convention[34] and had assured that they were surrounded by supporters of their standpoint on the matter of the Principles, their leadership and the relationship between the Executive and the Council.

---

[31] Peter Taylor, *Provos*, 354.

[32] Ed Moloney, *A Secret History of the IRA*, 464–73.

[33] Adrian Guelke. 'Political Violence and Paramilitaries', in Paul Mitchell and Rick Wilford eds, *Politics in Northern Ireland*. (Oxford: Westview Press, 1999), 29–53 (44–5).

[34] A Republican source informed that the Convention was 'for Sinn Fein to get the Green Light from the IRA to stick with the peace process, but really it was more about keeping the republican movement together.' Emily O'Reilly 'Mickey McKevitt: Life and Times of a Quartermaster.' In *The Sunday Business Post*. (23 August 1998).

However, one of the key factors which swung in their favour was the Belfast Commander Brian Gillen changing his affiliation to support Adams' position at the last minute, similar to what Brian Keenan had done the year previously. The entire Convention went in favour of the Adams faction, with support being given to them to enter Stormont talks. The new Executive, while still dissident to the Adams leadership was only so by a margin of two votes. At their first meeting however five key members resigned from the Executive led by the Quartermaster General Michael McKevitt and the head of the Engineering Department Frank McGuinness. Along with them came the majority of the engineering department and all the Southern Command's quartermasters. They went on to set up a group they titled Oglaigh na hEireann (the Irish for *Volunteers of Ireland*) a name used by every manifestation of the IRA as well as the legitimate army of the Republic of Ireland. However they are constantly referred to as the Real IRA. The official reasoning for the split was given as the acceptance of the Mitchell Principles.[35] The armed group was aligned with the political dissidents the 32-County Sovereignty Committee who were led by figures such as Francie Mackey and Bernadette Sands-McKevitt, the wife of Michael McKevitt and sister of Bobby Sands. This group formed from dissident members of Sinn Fein in December 1997 in opposition to the signing of the Mitchell Principles and in support of the right for Irish Republicans to use armed struggle in the pursuit of national sovereignty.[36] The Sovereignty Committee set itself up as a political pressure group, and under the leadership of Mackey and Sands-McKevitt went about drafting a paper to present to the United Nations accusing the British of denying Ireland of its right to national sovereignty.[37]

In the aftermath of the split the Real IRA became the most dangerous of all the dissident groups. They wished to set themselves apart from the PIRA.

We urged members that they must kill a British soldier face to face, no sniper, with a gun as the Provos hadn't done that in years and this would prove that they were different.[38]

Their desire to be different was a way to announce their arrival but also to legitimize the perceived necessity for yet another IRA.

---

[35] Ed Moloney, *A Secret History of the IRA*, 468–79.

[36] Peter Taylor, *Provos*, 358–9.

[37] John Mooney and Michael O'Toole, *Black Operations*, 47–9; See *Submission by 32 County Sovereignty Committee to United Nations*. www.32csm.net/p/32csm-policy-documents.html (Last accessed, 30 August, 2013).

[38] Interview by the author with 'Conor'.

As with the aftermath of the other three splits the actions and statements of the dissidents in the aftermath of the split can be perceived less as a method of targeting British presence in Northern Ireland and more as a way to set themselves apart from the Provisional IRA and Sinn Fein. Once again the concept of enemy had changed. Under this guise the possibility of a violent feud was always a possibility. In an unverifiable claim 'Conor', a leading Real IRA member, claims that there was initial support among the dissidents to target members of the Provisional leadership in assassination attempts. However, with these supposed assassination attempts deflected, it was deemed more of an imperative to prevent significant violent feuds from escalating. However, even in presenting the possibility of feud prevention he used it as an opportunity to undermine his former comrades.

> Early on many members of the Real IRA wanted to kill Doherty and McGuinness, but what would that gain? . . . In order to prevent a feud I met with five old Republicans and asked them to act as independent intermediaries if a feud took place. These Republicans would call an end to a feud and you would have to listen to them, especially if they were calling for an end to Republicans killing Republicans. News of this was passed along to Adams so that he was aware of what was in place. Adams wanted to meet with me, but when you meet with Adams it is always on his agenda. He talks at you then afterwards he says 'well I sat down and talked with them about it, I tried my best.'[39]

While the aftermath of an individual split is normally defined by the competition between the dividing groups, in a case such as this where there had been a number of divisions preceding it one must also consider the new group's relationship with already existing dissidents. Although they organizationally stand apart their immediate and purposive goals are close to identical, as is their frustration with the parent organization, in this case the Provisionals. In the immediate aftermath of the '97 split representatives of Republican Sinn Fein, and supposedly the Continuity IRA, attempted to meet with McKevitt to discuss the possibilities of working together and possibly even forming a united dissident movement. While Des Long was not able to form the united front he desired at this stage it was an idea which both he and the Real IRA would separately return to over a decade later.

> I set up a meeting with a fella in Dundalk, to meet McKevitt and Sands on the Thursday and then I went to Ruairi O'Bradaigh and convinced him to

---

[39] Interview by the author with 'Conor'.

go to it, and when we got there McKevitt wouldn't meet us. This was after they had split from Adams and company. I figured that there should be one united movement, but he wouldn't meet us.[40]

Even though this meeting never materialized it is clear that some members of the Continuity IRA managed to co-ordinate with the Real IRA, a co-ordination with tragic circumstances. On 15 August 1998 the Real IRA was responsible for one of the worst atrocities throughout the whole history of the Northern Irish Troubles. In collaboration with the increasingly active Continuity IRA they detonated a bomb in the Co. Tyrone town of Omagh. This bomb killed 29 people in total, as well as two unborn babies and injured 310 others.[41] In the years after Omagh although they continued their campaign they were decimated with arrests and departures, and it proved close to impossible to recruit new members.

The Omagh bombing stopped the influx of new recruits and support, and made people leave who were loyal before. . . . Omagh was a mistake, not the way things should have been done on a mission.[42]

Among the most high profile arrests were those of McKevitt and Liam Campbell, the Director of Operations and Colm Murphy[43] who was arrested for conspiring to cause the Omagh bombing.

The Omagh bombing was in reaction to the signing of the Good Friday Agreement. For many observers the Good Friday/Belfast Agreement is characterized as being the end of the Northern Irish peace process. While this is correct it would be somewhat misguided to promote it as the beginning of the peace. However, it did provide the foundations on which the peace was to be built. The Agreement, ratified by overwhelming majorities in referenda both north and south of the border, was the culmination of a long and arduous negotiation process between the governments of the Republic of Ireland and the United Kingdom and political and societal representatives of the people of Northern Ireland. The Agreement set in place the structure under which the devolved legislature in Northern Ireland now operates, while also affirming the modern day relationship between the Republic of Ireland and Northern Ireland. In doing so the people of the Republic of Ireland voted to remove the country's claim to Northern Ireland contained

---

[40] Interview by the author with Des Long.
[41] Deaglan De Breadun, *The Far Side of Revenge*, 168–72.
[42] Interview by the author with 'Conor'.
[43] Murphy was acquitted on 24 February 2010.

within Articles 2 and 3 of the Irish Constitution. The Agreement reaffirmed that Northern Ireland would remain part of the United Kingdom until the majority of the people of Northern Ireland voted otherwise. However, with respect to bringing an end to paramilitarism the Agreement called for a commitment of all participants to 'exclusively democratic and peaceful means'. All signatories of the Agreement committed themselves to using every influence they may have to bring about the full decommissioning of paramilitary arms within two years of the ratification of the Agreement, and in turn the British Government gave a commitment to the normalization of security in the region. As an incentive to follow through with these pledges the UK and Irish Governments gave an assurance that they would give early release to all to prisoners serving sentences relating to paramilitary activity as long as the groups they are affiliated to maintain a 'complete and unequivocal ceasefire'. The Agreement was signed in April 1998 and ratified by referenda on the 22 May of that year.

While the majority of Ireland rejoiced at the signing of the Agreement for the dissidents this amounted to no more than a sell-out. In their eyes the Sinn Fein leadership had sold the Irish people short by approving such an agreement. With British presence still in Northern Ireland, and a claim to the region they could not countenance such commitments. In the pre-Good Friday Agreement 1990s the breadth of violent dissident Republicanism was gradually increasing. It began with the escalation of Continuity IRA activities in the mid-1990s. However, it did not solidify until the emergence of the Real IRA towards the end of the decade. It was their appearance which significantly threatened Northern Irish security more than any other dissident organization. These groups rejected the Good Friday Agreement and everything it represented and it was with this justification that they bombed Omagh. In their words it was 'part of an on-going war against the Brits'.[44] The attack was condemned by all sides, including Sinn Fein. For them the war was over.

Change in strategy: Armed and political to political

As the historical analysis of the split illustrates the major change in the Provisional Republican Movement in the process of the '97 split was a change from an armed and political strategy to a predominantly political strategy. As will

---

[44] Real IRA Statement, 18 August 1998.

be described in the sections outlining the importance of gradualism and pre-split preparation this continuation of the politicization process was successful for the Provisional leadership due to their continuation of only making significant changes one step at a time and ensuring that they had significant levels of internal support prior to attempting these changes. However, as with the previous splits the leadership was unable to convince all the membership of the importance of the change and a minority deemed this move away from the armed strategy as significantly damaging to the organizational identity. For as long as there was a British presence in Ireland the armed strategy was seen by the dissidents as central to the Irish Republican strategy.

For those who moved away from the Provisionals to form the Real IRA in particular the rejection of the armed strategy which came with the acceptance of the Mitchell Principles proved too significant a change for them to countenance. While there had been cessations throughout Republican history the agreement amounted to a final step towards the permanent move away from any form of armed strategy by the Provisional Republican Movement, and the acceptance of a devolved Stormont Assembly. For a minority of the movement this proved to be too significant a change.

> It's when people signed up to the Mitchell Principles and went on to sign up to the Good Friday Agreement that there had to be a split because they signed up to things which were completely the opposite to what Republicanism stands for.[45]

As noted earlier there was a view within sections of the Provisional Movement that the PIRA was at its strongest point in history, both in manpower and in its arsenal. For some of those aware of the significance of the armed faction's strength there was a belief that the armed campaign should therefore be continued, and possibly even intensified.

> The Army were stronger than ever in the lead up to 1997. If weapons were there, prior to split, why couldn't we use them?[46]

However, this was not a view shared by the majority of the movement. While the PIRA was significantly strong in both regards it was not believed that an accentuated armed campaign would benefit the pursuit of a united Ireland. The belief among the leadership and their supporters was that the context of the situation had changed and that there were no longer any benefits in, or support for, an armed campaign. Their retrospective analysis of the situation

---

[45] Interview by the author with 'Una'.
[46] Interview by the author with 'Conor'.

outlines that, as with the abstentionists who moved away in 1986, the 1997 dissidents had confused a tactic with a principle.[47] To the dissidents the armed campaign was, for as long as there was a British presence in Ireland, a principle of the Movement. However, for the politicizers this was a tactic that was utilized within a specific context to serve the perceived purpose of that time. In their eyes its employment no longer had a purpose.

> I think it is mixing up principles with tactics or strategy. Whatever you think of the armed struggle people went into it because they thought that that was the only choice. An armed struggle, in my opinion, always has to be the last choice, the choice that you had no choice but to make.[48]

For the dissidents it was not just the ending of the armed campaign, it was everything that came with this which provoked their exit. In their minds this was analogous to the failure of the armed strategy and therefore the pointlessness of over 30-years of what they constituted as 'war'. They could not be convinced of the acceptance of political participation in a Northern Irish state which they failed to recognize. In essence they saw the politicization of the movement as a betrayal to what they held as their republican principles. This was the net threat of the proposed changes. However, for those internal advocates of politicization they regarded the context to have made the need for political participation as pertinent and as a strategy from which they could achieve much more than through armed action.

> I think politics was relevant, and again we were in a new phase in the developing peace process. The view that politics equalled betrayal was still strong among some of those people, and we couldn't bring them around to the various challenges that the peace process threw up. They saw that as moving away from the fundamentals of Republicanism. They never really proved the case they just. . . . I suppose the Mitchell Principles gave them a bit of a challenge and that is where they made their stand. But again they weren't a major. . . . The vast, vast majority of the movement stayed together.[49]

With this change in strategy came internal factionalism and conflict. This mainly took place within the PIRA.

---

[47] See Brendan Lynn, 'Tactic or Principle? The Evolution of Republican Thinking on Anstentionism in Ireland, 1970–1998'. *Irish Political Studies*, 17(2) (2002), 74–94.
[48] Interview by the author with Gerry Kelly.
[49] Interview by the author with Pat Doherty.

Factionalism

As the previous section suggests the main factionalism within the movement was between those who were committed to the politicization of Republicanism and those who wished to retain the armed campaign. As has been stated earlier the focus of the intra-organizational conflict was within the Provisional IRA's leadership. Similar to both the '86 and '69/70 splits some have looked to define it as a divide between northern and southern republicans, an opinion put forward by six of the participants in this research. However, while the majority of those who moved away to form 32CSC and the RIRA were from the Republic of Ireland; the majority of southern republicans stayed with the Provisionals after the split. Similarly, not all northern republicans stayed with the Provisionals and some left to join 32CSC or the RIRA.

This north/south divide is portrayed very differently by those who left to form the dissident groupings and their former allies who stayed within 'mainstream' Republicanism, as the Provisionals have now become. This points to the power of local influences and regionalism, even among those at leadership levels. Therefore it would seem to counter the assumption that the explanation of allegiance for a member of experienced membership and leadership will be intrinsically tied to the reasoning for the organizational split and suggests an extension to the belief that the explanation of allegiance for a member with a low level of experience will be predominantly tied to local influences and situations. With respect to this split this should also now include leadership members.

In the eyes of the dissidents the regional divide both during and after the process of split was as a result of the northern leadership's failure to focus any significant attention on either the role of the southern membership or the potential for progress within the 26 counties. This led to a sense of alienation among the southern leadership and membership.

> I think that it [the north/south divide] is very true in the Provisional Movement following '86. The northern leadership alienated the south, there is no doubt. It is only in later years that they moved with their southern project. But prior to the more recent electoral successes in the south following '98, prior to that there was no great push in the South for electoral politics.[50]

However, within the Provisional leadership the view of, and explanation for, the north/south divide comes from a different standpoint. For them the reasoning is not due to an abandonment of southern republicanism, in their

---

[50] Interview by the author with Francie Mackey.

eyes, it is best explained by the southern distance from the epicentre of the struggle. For those living in Northern Ireland they had to experience the daily effects of a maintained armed campaign and were critically aware of the lack of support within the Republican communities, or across the wider nationalist population, for a sustained campaign. There was an awareness of the need, and potential, for an alternative strategy. In their eyes the southern members still advocating an armed campaign were able to distance their lives from the daily consequences of an extended armed campaign.

> It was interesting that the shaving off in almost all these incidences was southern based, not entirely, but mostly. . . . People who are affected you will find have a more practical application of their beliefs than people who are sometimes just a couple of hundred yards away, sometimes people who are further away from the epicentre.[51]

This appears to be the reverse of '69 where the northern based republicans were demanding IRA protection, while the Goulding led southern leadership was advocating a political solution. However, this is not comparing like with like. The '97 split was coming at the end of a long-drawn out conflict where there was a perceived willingness among the Republican communities to engage with the possibility of a political solution to the situation. The year 1969 was the dawn of this conflict with the communities feeling the necessity of strengthened protection against sustained attacks.

Looking beyond the north/south divide the core reasoning for the schism, as illustrated earlier, was the debate over the purpose and necessity of a continued armed campaign. For those departing the Provisionals to continue to administer and support an armed strategy they framed their justification as lying in the fact that a united Ireland had not yet been achieved. Therefore they portrayed themselves as 'morally' committed to the continuation of the armed struggle until a stage when this ultimate objective had been achieved. It was only then that they would justify calling for a discontinuation of the violent campaign.

> We didn't pick up guns for this agreement. Morally we couldn't stop as we hadn't gotten what we started out to get.[52]

They were portraying that the conflict at the centre of a split for them was threatening to the organizational identity. However, in contrast those advocating the change regarded the need for an armed campaign to be over

---

[51] Interview by the author with Gerry Kelly.
[52] Interview by the author with 'Conor'.

and the context of the time was providing the need for a different approach to Irish Republicanism.

> It's just he [Michael McKevitt] wouldn't wake up and smell the coffee that the reality is the war was over.[53]

This divergence of positions ultimately caused the split within the movement. However, it did not solely explain the result of the division.

Gradualism: One step at a time

Throughout the process of the '86 split one of the central themes which explained the reasoning for Provisional dominance in the aftermath of the divide was the gradual nature in which changes were made or proposed. This strategy allowed members and supporters to become accustomed to the implications of each individual change prior to the introduction of the next. While this inevitably prolonged the armed campaign it similarly weakened the position of potential dissident groupings. As was demonstrated with the '69/70 split when there are a number of potentially divisive changes made or proposed within a short space of time the position of the dissident grouping is strengthened. When there is only one change made at a time this isolates the potential dissidents who will view this as threatening to the organizational identity of the movement. Due to the positioning of the '97 split at the end of the macro-process of republican involvement in the Troubles one must not only consider the changes being made within the movement at the time of, and in the immediate lead-up to, the split. The '97 split must be seen as a continuation of the macro process of Provisional republicanism and is therefore a continuation of the process began with the '69/70 split. Therefore the politicization of the movement in the lead-up to '97 was a continuation of the politicization process which was identified in the last chapter as having started in 1975. Therefore the gradualism of the '97 process is a continuation of the gradualism which was introduced in the process of the '86 split.

As with '86 the changes implemented by the Provisional leadership in the lead-up to '97 were potentially divisive within the movement and therefore in order to maintain organizational survival, unity and the survival of their politicization process they needed to ensure that the effect of the internal disruption was minimal. Therefore there was the continuation of the application of gradualism which had been largely successful in maintaining

---

[53] Interview by the author with Joe Doherty.

organizational unity in the lead-up to '86. This is a viewpoint accepted by both the Provisionals and the 32CSC/RIRA.

For the dissidents they looked upon this strategy of gradual change as reflective of the 'dishonesty' of the Adams/McGuinness leadership. By changing policies and strategy in this gradual manner they were, in the eyes of the dissidents, betraying the trust of their membership and support network. The view portrayed by the dissenting voices was that the leadership was never fully honest with their members about the direction in which they were taking Provisional republicanism. However, even though they were critical of the use of this strategy of gradualism in implementing desired changes they were similarly complimentary of its effectiveness, even if they did not agree with the overall strategy of change implemented.

> It was broken down to single issue and that was the only issue being dealt with, as if all of the issues weren't co-related. That allowed the leadership the breathing space throughout the whole period to go that one step closer.[54]

As the above quote from Mackey suggests the application of gradualism was necessary for the maintenance of organizational survival and cohesion as well as the successful continuation of the politicization process. This is a view supported by the Provisional leadership who acknowledge that this gradual nature of change was a necessity in order to achieve the successful politicization of the majority of the movement.

> It's a protracted thing. If you look at the situation where in '91 or '92 or whenever it became public that the SDLP and Sinn Fein were in discussions and had been in discussions with the Dublin government, channels had been opened up with the British and all this stuff led in turn to the first cessation and then to the breakdown of that cessation nearly eighteen months later and then to a new cessation in '97 and then to the Good Friday Agreement in '98 and all that has flowed after the Good Friday Agreement. It's all, none of it has been done (clicks fingers twice to indicate quick succession of changes) it's always we're looking for clarification. Obviously we did want that, but there would be other times we did want clarification obviously so that we could have fuller discussion in republicanism to inform people and to try and bring people with you. There is not much point having an organisation if it fractures and if you're not able to try and hold it as a coherent working group.[55]

---

[54] Interview by the author with Francie Mackey.
[55] Interview by the author with Sean McManus.

The final sentence within the above quote from Sean McManus emphasizes the core point at the heart of the gradualism. When an organizational leadership sees the necessity to implement a battery of significant changes to the direction taken by the group they will only be successful if and when they are able to convince the majority of their membership and support of the benefits and necessity of these changes. While it is possible that they may have wished to implement all of the changes which took place over the 23 year period from the beginning of the politicization in 1975 to the signing of the Good Friday Agreement in 1998 it may not have been feasible to convince the majority of the membership of the necessity of all of the changes. Similarly the context of the situation did not always permit or suggest the realistic potential of these changes. Therefore the changes had to be implemented in a gradual manner, one step at a time, in order for the organization to successfully reach a point where the majority of the republican membership was able to accept a series of significant changes. It was these changes which enabled Sinn Fein to successfully engage in the peace of modern day Northern Ireland where they share the office of First Minister and deputy First Minister with the Democratic Unionist Party. Each of the changes successfully implemented by the movement from the mid-'70s right up to today has been part of a process of the politicization of modern day Republicanism. This book posits that the historical changes within Sinn Fein policy could not have been possible without a number of the changes which preceded them both in policy and organizational structure. The mistakes of the Goulding leadership in trying too much too soon were the lessons learned by the Adams/McGuinness leadership in implementing a strategy of gradual change.

There could have been much more disaffection, not necessarily splits, but I think people at each stage became accustomed to what had just happened and then were much more prepared and ready to adopt the next stage. You know if you had said walking around the place in the yard August 1994 'we're going to be supporting the amendment of Articles 2 and 3,[56] ending the Northern abstentionism, supporting a new police service, the IRA is

---

[56] These were articles within the Irish Constitution which were a territorial claim to Northern Ireland as a legitimate part of Ireland. This proved to be one of the most contentious issues in bringing unionists, loyalists, nationalists and republicans to work together. However, these were removed from the Irish constitution with the passing of the Good Friday Agreement in May 1998 and were effectively amended when the agreement came into force in December 1999. For full Irish Constitution including all it's amendments see *Bunreacht na hEireann* (August 2012) www.supremecourt.ie/supremecourt/sclibrary3.nsf/(WebFiles)/B6F8AE45BECA28B080257A8A004 CD65E/$FILE/ConstitutionofIrelandAugust2012.pdf (Last accessed, 30 August 2013).

going to first of all open its dumps, its precious dumps, you know these weapons that had been painstakingly smuggled into the country, open its dumps, then seal its dumps forever, and that Martin McGuinness was going to end up in government with Ian Paisley'. I mean that was so fantastic, and fabulous, if you had said that to me in July 1994 I would have been sending for the men in white coats. But as things progressed you could see that each decision you took had a repercussion or a ramification and I don't think that anybody from either side, I don't think Paisley for example back in July 1994 thought that 'in ten years time I'll be in government with the former Chief of Staff of the IRA', because that would have been again too much for him. I think that once people had it in their hearts that they were going to make peace and they were going to stabilise it and it was the best deal that we could get, even though you cannot do justice to the dead or the sacrifices of the dead, but this is the best shape you can make of it, and you have to go and do it, you have to go in in good faith, even if it means doing unpalatable things, if it means sitting down with former enemies, you know.[57]

Preparation for change: Support

While the success of the politicization of the movement is largely down to the gradual nature of the changes implemented this does not fully explain the situation. Many of the changes implemented throughout the process of the '97 split were potentially divisive in nature. Therefore as with the changes implemented in the '86 process there needed to be significant preparation made by the leadership prior to implementing the amendments. This required the assurance of sufficient support for the changes and as a continuation of the '86 process this was carried out through the application of internal dialogue with the membership. The importance of support had to be viewed as both an immediate aim as well as a longitudinal target. In essence the leadership needed to be sure that they could have specific votes passed without significant levels of divisiveness manifesting in the long-term. The importance of this preparation for change and internal support was seen by the participants among the most decisive factors in the successful implementation of change in the movement, and significant within this was the respect for timing of change. In order to successfully implement potentially divisive changes the context and timing needed to compliment this need for change. It was most receptive to change when the leadership proposing it was in an internally strengthened position and

---

[57] Interview by the author with Danny Morrison.

therefore had the support for their own personal leadership and not just for the changes they were proposing. A strengthened position for them enhanced the trust the membership had in them. Therefore as with the '86 process they implemented the strategy of, where possible, distancing themselves from introducing divisive issues until the point where they were confidant of internal support for both them and the change.

The leadership's preparation for change does not just refer to the immediate lead-up to the ultimately divisive Army Convention of 1997, this preparation includes all the major changes implemented from 1986 onwards. One specific example, six of the participants, including all three of the 32CSC/RIRA members, was the preparation which preceded the August 1994 ceasefire. In order to ensure organizational support for the cessation the leadership had been preparing all levels of membership and support for this possibility for a significant period prior to the actual declaration. This was highlighted both in the external Republican communities and within the Republican prison communities. The leadership met with their communities to discuss the potential for a cessation and to gauge the levels of support and resistance to the proposals, and the entire politicization process. They were also preparing members for what they could realistically expect from the process and how this would benefit the entire process seeking to achieve their ultimate and immediate goals.

> That's what was good about coming up to the ceasefire I think Adams and the people went out into all the Sinn Fein Cumanns. And in the prison [Martin] McGuinness and Gerry Kelly was almost in there every other week, the British allowed them to come in. Everybody went into the canteen, McGuinness was there asking questions and taking questions preparing everybody for 'you know the reality is we're going to enter negotiations, we might not get a united Ireland. Be realistic look at the bigger picture.'[58]

It was this persistent preparation and engagement with all levels of membership which allowed the leadership to gauge the sentiment within the movement and as a result they were aware when the timing for change was right. This preparation prior to each change, not just the '94 ceasefire, allowed for them to gauge the levels of support and the potential for splits within the movement. Therefore they were able to pursue their desired course at the most opportune time when their leadership was not being challenged and also when the opposition to the proposed change was at its weakest point. The more control the leadership had over the context the more potential they had for success.

---

[58] Interview by the author with Joe Doherty.

However, as the violence in the summer of 1969 showed, the leadership does not always have control of the external context. Therefore the most opportune time for change, in order to maintain organizational survival, is when external events have as minimal impact on the internal changes as possible.

As was detailed earlier the modern day Provisional leadership do not regard 1997 as a split in the Movement. They see it more as a split which was fended off by their internal dialogue in the lead-up to the potentially divisive moments.

> So I think that it took considerable skill, dialogue and debate and management to insure that what happened then didn't turn out to be a re-split, which is what the Real IRA people and the 32 County Sovereignty Movement were trying to bring about. So it was fended off then.[59]

This is not a completely accurate depiction of the situation as a split was not fended off. But the dialogue and debate and preparation for change did result in a weakened dissident grouping. With respect to the two divisive Army Conventions, 1996 and 1997, the pre-change preparations were carried out through both 'above board' recruitment of influential individuals to support their position and what the Provisionals in the aftermath of '69/70 referred to as 'internal methods'.

Similar to '86 it was essential for the leadership to have the support of influential individuals both locally and nationally to successfully to maintain the backing of the majority of the movement. These individuals and groupings within the movement provided legitimacy to the position being taken by the leadership. These influential individuals from within the Republican Movement and across Republican history were convinced to lend their support to the proposed actions of the leadership at times of potential conflict. As was stated in the historical examination of the split Brian Keenan,[60] a well-respected senior IRA activist and strategist, moved from being a disapproving voice towards the peace process to one of the most effective proponents of change during the 1990s. His move from dissenter to supporter provided invaluable legitimacy to the leadership's position and proposals.

> At key stages in all of this key people in local areas and at a regional area were wheeled out to say that this was 100% sound. If a key person known

---

[59] Interview by the author with Martin McGuinness.
[60] See interviews with Keenan in An Phoblacht for his account of his Republican past; An Phoblacht (27 March 2008). An IRA leader is Born. In *An Phoblacht*, 4–5; An Phoblacht (3 April 2008). From Civil Rights to Armed Struggle. In *An Phoblacht*, 6–7; An Phoblacht (10 April 2008). Revolutionaries have to be Pragmatic-Wish Lists for Christmas. In *An Phoblacht*, 10–11.

in the locality to be in the IRA, if that person says that something was right well then it was taken as right and that they must have had some reassurances.[61]

The above quote provides further support to the leadership's use of distancing in their advocating of change. The ability of the Sinn Fein leadership to publicly distance themselves from the decision making of the IRA leadership gave them extra time in the external negotiation process as was detailed by Sean McManus in his previous quote where he mentioned the leadership calling for 'clarifications'. However, internally within the organization the support and use of key figures such as Keenan allowed them to distance themselves from the initial suggestion of troublesome proposals such as decommissioning or the dropping of abstentionism to Stormont. It was similarly important for them to acquire the support not only of influential individuals but also influential regional divisions of the movement. Throughout the Troubles the central area of the Provisional IRA was always Belfast. This is where some of the most active units were based and where a significant number of prominent leaders were stationed. In September '69 the significance of the Belfast IRA denouncing of the Goulding leadership is seen by many as one of the most significant moments in the beginning of the Provisional IRA.

That was the beginning of the split; that is where it happened first. In Belfast the IRA split and they set up the Provisional IRA.[62]

Similarly when the politicizing sub-group of the Provisional leadership acquired the support of the Belfast IRA in 1997 it was clear to the dissidents that a dissident majority was impossible and that they would have to leave the movement rather than take it over.

Once the Adams faction had the Belfast members on their side we knew that they couldn't take a majority.[63]

As was suggested earlier this support was not always gained through 'legitimate' means. For the necessary success of Army Convention votes in particular there was the usage of 'internal methods'. This was particularly enforced in the Army Convention of 1996. This is a point referred to by six participants, although it must be noted that none of them were affiliated to the Provisionals in the aftermath of the split.[64]

---

[61] Interview by the author with Francie Mackey.
[62] Interview by the author with Tomas MacGiolla.
[63] Interview by the author with 'Conor'.
[64] It would not be expected that the Provisionals would admit to this.

The '96 convention was potentially extremely damaging for the Adams leadership. In light of this they are reported to have organized for influential dissidents such as Frank McGuinness and others not to be picked up for the Convention so as to ensure that the vote to support and re-elect them was passed. This was to ensure the immediate survival of the movement and their leadership. But it was coupled with the maintenance, and regaining, of support throughout the movement so as to ensure the longitudinal survival of the leadership.

> That is actually the Army Convention where people were not brought. They were left on the sides of roads and stuff, so that Adams could get the vote. He had that all planned well in advance.[65]

This is an accusation made by each of the dissident groupings at the times of each split, and it is also an accusation which precedes the '69 birth of the Troubles. However, the ability of a leadership to survive one vote through such means does not guarantee the survival of their process. They additionally require the longitudinal support of the majority of their membership and base. This is what the Provisional leadership have achieved and this is one of the major reasons for their ability to maintain the politicization of the movement, a macro-process which dates back to the end of the Border Campaign and continues to the modern day.

> Clearly you didn't bring all people with you. But one of the accomplishments of the leadership of both Oglaigh na hEireann [Provisional IRA] and Sinn Fein is that they brought by far the majority of their members with them into the process, through the process and out the other side of the process. I don't think it was humanly possible to avoid some of the disaffections.[66]

---

[65] Interview by the author with Dolours Price.
[66] Interview by the author with Mitchell McLaughlin.

7

United in their division, divided in their unity

The leadership of Oglaigh na hEireann has formally ordered an end to the armed campaign . . . . We believe there is now an alternative way to achieve this and to end British rule in our country. It is the responsibility of all Volunteers to show leadership, determination and courage.[1]

The IRA's mandate for armed struggle derives from Britain's denial of the fundamental right of the Irish people to national self-determination and sovereignty – so long as Britain persists in its denial of national and democratic rights in Ireland the IRA will have to continue to assert those rights.[2]

These two statements issued close to seven years apart illustrate the two disparate sides of modern-day republicanism. The first, the historic announcement of the permanent cessation of violence by the Provisional IRA in July 2005 signified the end to one of the longest running, and most brutal, terrorist campaigns the world has ever seen. This illustrated for many that peace was within reach. It was one more step closer to the full politicization of the movement. The gradual process continued and was finally coming to an end. However, the second statement shown above issued in July 2012 drove home the reality that even as the Provisionals left the paramilitary

---

[1] Provisional IRA Statement on Permanent Cessation of Violence. 28 July 2005.
[2] 'New IRA' Statement on Dissident Merger, 26 July 2012.

stage, there were still small groupings of violent dissidents willing to continue the armed struggle in their place. This declaration signalled the merger of two of the most potent dissident forces of the early twenty-first century, the Real IRA and Republican Action Against Drugs with a number of previously unaligned but dangerous dissidents. Their merger formed a new group calling itself simply 'The IRA'. However, for many they are known as 'The New IRA'. This illustrates the parallel results of the splits; the politicization of one side along with the continued, and at times intensified, paramilitarism of the other. This final chapter assesses both sides of this divide. It analyses the continued post-Good Friday Agreement politicization of Sinn Fein and the Provisional IRA while concurrently assessing the fall and rise of the dissident threat in that same period. In turn it asks how both sides of the divided republican family will mark the decade of centenaries that Ireland is now immersed in. While the previous four chapters have each analysed the process of individual splits this final chapter will give a more general assessment of the positioning of modern day Irish republicanism. However, as with the rest of the book this should not be regarded as an anthology of modern day republicanism. This chapter will only focus on some of the major themes and issues emerging from the analysis of both the interview data as well as the primary sources produced by the groups.

The 1997 split had the positive effect, from the viewpoint of the politicizers, of removing the internal detractors from the movement. The Real IRA ultimately left due to the Provisional leadership's acceptance of the potential for a power-sharing political agreement in place of the use of armed force.[3] This is supportive of the assertion by Balser which stated that splits can be used to end intra-organizational conflict and remove any internal threat to the desired path for the organization.[4] This exit allowed the process to continue to the present day with the signing of the Good Friday Agreement, the acceptance of Sinn Fein to take their seats in Stormont, the republican acceptance of the Police Service of Northern Ireland (PSNI), the signing of the St Andrews Agreement, the resultant successful power-sharing of Sinn Fein and the Democratic Unionist Party (DUP) in the devolved Northern Irish Assembly and most recently and most symbolically of all Martin McGuinness, now deputy First Minister of Northern Ireland, shaking hands with Queen Elizabeth II in 2012. While Northern Irish politics and the maintenance of peace continues to be a difficult and highly sensitive process the progress

---

[3] See James Dingley, 'The Bombing of Omagh, 15 August 1998: The Bombers, Their Tactics, Strategy and Purpose Behind the Incident'. *Studies in Conflict and Terrorism*, 24(6) (2001).

[4] Deborah B. Balser, 'The Impact of Environmental Factors on Factionalism and Schism in Social Movement Organisations'. *Social Forces*, 76(1) (1997), 199–228 (226).

made on all sides since 1997 has insured Northern Ireland to be a much safer country.

While the peace process is internationally acknowledged to have been successful it is unmistakable that the Republican threat is still prominent across Ireland and Great Britain.[5] However, in contrast to the 'war' waged by the Provisional IRA these new dissident groups are much smaller groupings, with little to no support. In spite of this they continue to attack. There has been the specific targeting of Catholic members of the PSNI and members of the British Army both based in Northern Ireland and the Republic. Most recently their attention has also focused on the targeting Northern Irish prison officers. This has been highlighted by the tragic murder of prison officer David Black on 1 November 2012. While each of these may be classified as political targets the reach of violent dissident republicanism extends beyond the political. In spite of nominating themselves as the legitimate protectors of the people of Ireland they are carrying on the long traditions of criminality, vigilantism and violent feuds. Stories mount about involvement in extortion, drug dealing, smuggling and targeted assassinations. Not all of their illegal activities can be labelled as terrorism or paramilitarism. To a large extent the violent dissident Republicans, especially in Dublin and across the Republic of Ireland, are distinctive in their criminality. Before these and other themes can be analysed in depth this chapter will begin by giving a brief overview of the continued evolution of Irish Republicanism, both 'dissident' and 'mainstream' in the aftermath of the Good Friday Agreement.

The continued gradualism

As was alluded to in the previous chapter the Good Friday Agreement while bringing a close to the Troubles, should not be regarded as the dawn of a normalized public and political life in Northern Ireland. Both loyalist and republican groups continued to persist with paramilitary activity, although more sporadically than before. The political structure envisioned within the Good Friday Agreement took a while to hold, and due to a variety of reasons, including the Provisional IRA's inability to reach the decommissioning deadlines set and allegations of them running a 'spy-ring' within the Assembly, the Northern Irish Assembly seemed to be more regularly dissolved than devolved. It was not until March of 2011, 13 years after the signing of the Agreement, that the Assembly managed to sit for a full term.

---

[5] At the time of writing (12 June 2013) the threat levels from Northern Irish terrorism in Great Britain were moderate and in Northern Ireland were severe.

While the Good Friday Agreement should not be seen as the dawn of peace in Northern Ireland it must similarly not be seen as the completion of the politicization of the Provisionals. In the years after the '98 Agreement it is clear that elements of their membership were still involved in illegal activity both internationally and across the island of Ireland. Some of the group's members were accused of training FARC rebels in Columbia. Others were implicated in high profile murders, and the organization was accused of a number of significant robberies. This persistence with illegal activity was most clearly illustrated in the month and a half between 20 December 2004 and 31 January 2005. On 20 December the Northern Bank on Donegall Square West in Belfast was robbed. In total £26.5 million was stolen. The newly established Police Service of Northern Ireland (PSNI) as well as the British and Irish governments claimed that the Provisional IRA was responsible, a claim both the IRA and Sinn Fein deny to this day. Six weeks later in the Markets area of Belfast Robert McCartney, a Roman Catholic from the predominantly nationalist area of the Short Strand in east Belfast, was beaten up and murdered by alleged members of the Provisional IRA. Both of these events took place at a time of impasse in the peace negotiations. The Democratic Unionist Party (DUP), who had refused to sign up to the Good Friday Agreement due to the inclusion of Sinn Fein in the negotiations, had returned to the table. However, their calls for the visible and credible decommissioning of the Provisional IRA, along with their humiliation,[6] brought negotiations to a halt.

At this stage the Provisionals had only partially decommissioned and the DUP, the largest unionist party, was not willing to share power with Sinn Fein. Furthermore, the republicans would still not sit on the policing board of the PSNI, and their communities were advised to go to their solicitor if they had a crime to report. The demonstration of continued illegal activity at the turn of 2005 emphasized to their detractors that the Provisional Movement, and Sinn Fein in particular, could not be trusted. However, what came in the aftermath of the murder of Robert McCartney was an unprecedented series of statements from the IRA and Sinn Fein. In their first two statements in the immediate aftermath the IRA failed to even acknowledge the attack, or the robbery of the Northern Bank. Instead they focused on the impasse in the peace process highlighting how the '[t]he IRA has demonstrated our commitment to the peace process again and again', and how these initiatives 'have been attacked, devalued and dismissed by pro-unionist and anti-republican elements, including the British Government'.[7] It was not until pressure was put on them by politicians in Britain, Ireland and America, but

---

[6] Ian Paisley's speech at North Antrim DUP Association annual dinner, 27 November 2004.
[7] 'IRA Offer Withdrawn: Exclusive Statement from the Leadership of Oglaigh na hEireann'. 3 February 2005.

most importantly by the sisters and fiancé of Robert McCartney and the larger republican and nationalist community that they responded to the event. This response came in the form of a battery of significant statements moving from the complete denial of any Republican's involvement in the murder to the admittance of the involvement of two IRA members and the shocking revelation that they had offered to 'shoot the people involved directly'.[8] For their part Sinn Fein called on witnesses not to go to the police with information but to either meet with 'the family, a solicitor or any authoritative or reputable person or body'.[9]

This emphasized the long road left to travel in the protracted peace process. For the Provisional Republicans they were yet, to completely move away from criminality, to fully decommission their weapons or to acknowledge the legitimacy of the PSNI. However, in spite of this it was them calling on the two government to 'demonstrate their commitment to a lasting peace' stating that '[p]andering to the demands of those who are opposed to change [DUP] is not the way forward'.[10] For their part the DUP were yet to put their full trust in the intent of the Republican Movement to fully commit to peace. Yet it may be that the peace process had to reach the nadir of early 2005, before it could embark on its final journey. Shortly after, in July of that year the Provisional IRA made their historic announcement that they had 'formally ordered an end to the armed campaign'.[11] This was followed on 26 September by a statement by the Independent International Commission on Decommissioning (IICD) stating that in their opinion the Provisional IRA had decommissioned the totality of their arsenal.[12] This full decommission had followed three other partial decommissions between 2001 and 2003.

These historic moves paved the way for the establishment of a new, more inclusive, Northern Irish Executive. They allowed the DUP to enter into negotiations with the British and Irish governments, and all the major political parties of Northern Ireland, including for the first time both them and Sinn Fein. These negotiations came to a fore in late 2006 in St Andrews, Scotland. There over three days of talks the representatives came to an agreement whereby the DUP agreed to power-sharing in the Executive with republicans and nationalists. Sinn Fein committed themselves to the full acceptance of the PSNI, a commitment that was ratified at the party's Ard Fheis in January

---

[8] IRA Statement, 10 March 2005.
[9] 'Adams in Appeal to Catch Killers.' BBC, 14 February 2005. http://news.bbc.co.uk/1/hi/northern_ireland/4263359.stm (Last accessed, 1 March 2013).
[10] IRA Easter Statement, 24 March 2005.
[11] Provisional IRA Statement on Permanent Cessation of Violence. 28 July 2005.
[12] 'IRA has destroyed all its arms.' BBC, 26 September 2005. http://news.bbc.co.uk/1/hi/northern_ireland/4283444.stm (Last accessed, 1 March 2013).

2007. For many this acceptance of the PSNI by Sinn Fein was always deemed improbable. But for the leadership themselves they were fully aware that if the right offer was on the table; there was no way that they could turn around and refuse it. They would have to bring it to a debate, a debate they eventually won.

> We had always said that if we get this right that people knew what we were after, and knew it would be policing with democratic accountability. Then that we were going to have to decide, you can't ask for something and then get it and say 'Oh no I don't want it.' So it was very very clear that if we brought the British government to a point that was acceptable and were genuine to try the new policing then we were going to have to have a debate on that. So there was no secret, no mystery, it was intense, probably the fundamentals of the Good Friday Agreement itself for Republicans because while an awful lot of the peace process and the fine nuances are matters and something they would watch on TV and make up their own mind about the RUC was a living reality and a lot of Republicans would have had bad experiences with the RUC.[13]

On 8 May 2007 Ian Paisley and Martin McGuinness, two historic adversaries who until March of that year had never even had a conversation, took their positions alongside each other in the office of the First Minster and deputy First Minister of Northern Ireland. Even the idea of such a move would have been shocking to both individuals and their parties in the years previous. While the Good Friday Agreement was a structure the region wished one day to achieve the power-sharing of 2007, some nine years later was an illustration of the long-road travelled to get there in the time since.

In the years hence the normalization of Northern Irish political life gathered pace. In April 2010 the Department of Justice was established in the Northern Ireland Executive. This devolution of policing and justice powers came to pass after the Hillsborough Agreement of February of that year, an agreement which also dealt with the eternally contentious issue of parades.[14] This ministry was taken up by the Alliance Party, a non-sectarian party founded at the birth of the Troubles as an alternative to the traditional factionalized political parties. Shortly after the devolution of policing and justice powers to Northern Ireland a moment arrived which will evoke the whole arc of emotions in the nationalist and republican communities across Northern Ireland for many years to come. The British Prime Minister, David

---

[13] Interview by the author with Pat Doherty.
[14] 'Agreement at Hillsborough Castle', 5 February 2010.

Cameron, gave an unequivocal apology for the actions of the paratroopers in Derry on Bloody Sunday in 1972.

> There is no doubt. There is nothing equivocal. There are no ambiguities. What happened on Bloody Sunday was both unjustified and unjustifiable. It was wrong. . . . For that on behalf of the government, indeed on behalf of our country I am deeply sorry.[15]

This apology came in response to the Saville Inquiry which found that it was the paratroopers, and not any marchers or Republican paramilitaries, that fired the first shot, that each of the deceased was innocent of any crime and that some were even shot while fleeing the gunfire.[16] For the families of the victims, the people of Derry and the nationalist community as a whole this was a moment they had been waiting decades for. Although it would not heal their hurt it provided them with an indication that the British government was now willing to take account of their own role in the Troubles. This was one step closer towards gaining their trust.

For their part the evolution of Sinn Fein continued. With political life normalizing in Northern Ireland it seems that from 2010 onwards, and even slightly beforehand, the main focus of the party has been in gaining a foothold in the Republic of Ireland. Although they consistently take great pride in being the only all-Ireland party, during the peace-process the majority of their attention, and success, was in the six counties of Northern Ireland. With the economy in the Republic imploding, proving the once lauded Celtic Tiger to be but an apparition, the left-wing Republican ideals of Sinn Fein were taking hold. With their growing influence their two most recognizable Northern figures, Gerry Adams and Martin McGuinness, attempted to bring their influence south of the border. In 2010 Adams announced that he would be resigning his secure West Belfast Assembly seat to seek election in the constituency of Louth in the 2011 Irish general election, a seat he duly won easily surpassing the quota. While many may view this move south as an attempt to gain greater influence in the Republic for others it could be interpreted as Adams' attempts to avoid an electoral embarrassment at the hands of the dissidents. While his West Belfast seat was surely safe there were murmurings that a dissident republican candidate may prove a thorn in his side. For Adams anything but his customary vast majority of the vote could have been painted as a moral victory for the anti-Good Friday Agreement republicans. For his part McGuinness was nominated as the Sinn

---

[15] David Cameron 'Apology for Bloody Sunday'. House of Commons, 15 June 2010.
[16] 'Report of the Bloody Sunday Inquiry'. 15 June 2010.

Fein candidate in the 2011 presidential election, their first ever candidate. Although he came third in an election won by Michael D. Higgins of the Labour Party his nomination and candidature may well have paved the way for a Sinn Fein candidate being a normality, rather than a news story in itself. While the presidential election may have been the focus of his electoral politics for 2011 and 2012 it was his interactions, and sometimes lack of interactions, with Queen Elizabeth II which would prove to be the most significant issues of his political year.

In May 2011 Queen Elizabeth II, accompanied by her husband Prince Phillip the Duke of Edinburgh, became the first British monarch to visit the Republic of Ireland. A visit only made possible by the advances made the years previous. Hers was also the first visit by a monarch to the geographical area since her grandfather, King George V, visited one hundred years previous in 1911. However, at that stage the entire island of Ireland was still part of the United Kingdom. The Queen's visit was under the invitation of the President of Ireland Mary McAleese, a woman whose role alongside her husband in the normalization of Anglo-Irish as well as Irish-Loyalist relations warrants a book of its own. Although security was tight the visit was deemed a hugely symbolic success. The Queen visited many historic as well as cultural sites. In one of the most significant moments she laid a wreath at the Garden of Remembrance to honour those who had fought for Irish freedom from Great Britain. However, the one act that was noticeable in its absence was that of a meeting with any Sinn Fein representatives. The party issued a statement saying that they believed her visit to be

> . . . premature and will cause great offence to many Irish citizens, particularly to those who have lost loved ones at the hands of the British state forces in Ireland.[17]

While the opposition they took may have been due to their Republican ideals, it could easily be argued that the visit was opposed in order to quell the rising tide of dissent within the party. As will be shown in the next section there was a growing disquiet within Sinn Fein at the lack of progress being made in a post-Good Friday Agreement Northern Ireland. The threat was present that those on the fringes of party were liable to move over to the dissidents, and in some cases were already doing so. Therefore at the time of the Queen's visit in 2011 the Sinn Fein leadership may not have had sufficient support from their base to meet with the monarch, let alone shake her hand. However, while the

---

[17] 'Sinn Fein Oppose Visit by English Queen.' www.sinnfein.ie/contents/20657 (Last accessed, 2 March 2013).

timing was not right in May 2011 the overwhelming goodwill shown towards the visit by the Irish people allowed for Martin McGuinness to meet with her the very next year. In an event as symbolic as they come McGuinness met with, and shook the hand of, the Queen on a visit to Northern Ireland to mark her Diamond Jubilee. For many this was an affirmation that after all of those years the peace process had worked. However, for the resurgent dissidents it was affirmation of their long held beliefs about Sinn Fein.

> He [McGuinness] is part and parcel of British rule here and administering British rule here . . . They are no longer Republicans. Every step you see they are falling further and further into that. Sure why shouldn't Martin McGuinness shake hands with his commander and chief. That's the way it is. That is just how true Republicans see it. Once that handshake took place it was a step too far and they backed off.[18]

In the eyes of many this handshake marks the end of the politicization of Sinn Fein. However, for one former Provisional there is one more step he sees them taking.

> I think they will drop abstentionism [to Westminster] if they can. I'm sure of it. I think there are a number of things. One is why miss the opportunity of trying to influence the British government?. . . When the sorts like Adams and McGuinness are gone and the guys going in are essentially nobodies. There won't be iconic figures like Adams or McGuinness going in to Westminster it will be someone like Francie Molloy or Paul Maskey. Most people wouldn't know who they are. But if you saw Adams on the front page it could be looked upon in a different way. Where else do they go to maximise more? It probably would result in a revolt from their grassroots.[19]

For most the possibility of Sinn Fein taking their seats in Westminster is unfathomable. However, for a movement who since 1986 has dropped abstentionism to Dail Eireann and Stormont, permanently moved away from armed conflict, took their seat on the policing board of Northern Ireland, shared power with the Democratic Unionist Party and has shaken hands with the Queen of England almost anything should be considered as a possibility. Only time will tell.

---

[18] Interview by the author with 'Kate'.
[19] Interview by the author with Sean O'Callaghan.

The fall and rise of violent dissident republicanism

Analysis of violent dissident Republican activity by John Horgan and his team at the International Center for the Study of Terrorism (ICST) at The Pennsylvania State University suggests that there have been three separate waves of activity.[20] The first came with the active arrival of the Continuity IRA in the mid-90s to coincide with the 1994 ceasefire of the Provisional IRA. This wave saw a slow gradual rise in violent activity. However, it was nowhere near the level of dissident violence we see today. This was marked by sporadic bombings, threats and the permanent distancing of the dissidents from the Provisionals' moves towards peace. The end of this wave saw the arrival of the Real IRA, a dissident game-changer. The initial wave was brought to close with the horrific attack on Omagh in August 1998, an attack which emphasized the capabilities and intentions of this newly emerging threat. With the close of the first wave came the introduction of the second, a more sporadic campaign of violence which saw the dissidents attempt a resurgence. Among other violent acts this included attacks across Britain. However, in a post-Omagh environment their actions, and lack thereof, only succeeded in illustrating that at that stage they were unable to mount a sustained and consistent threat. In light of this a number of the organizations sought to regroup, a marker of the culmination of this second wave. With the historic advances in the Sinn Fein politicization process around 2006/2007 the dissidents saw a resurgence in their membership and support, a fact that was reflected in their sharp rise in violent activity. The analysis shows that this activity has been on the rise ever since. While it has never reached the daily levels of violence displayed by the Provisionals during the Troubles it has reached new heights for the modern day dissidents. This current wave has seen them target symbols of 'British rule' in Northern Ireland, Catholic police officers, MI5 barracks, British soldiers, prison officers, the Northern Irish transport network and most recently of all the symbols and offices of Derry/Londonderry as the UK's City of Culture 2013. For the dissidents these targets are not just symbols of British rule they can also be readily described as symbols of Sinn Fein's continued politicization, and their presence within the British ruling class. This is no longer just a 'Brits out' war. Their struggle is to emphasize that they are not Sinn Fein, they are the real and true republicans, their fight is the continuation of that waged almost one hundred

---

[20] John Horgan, *Divided We Stand: The Strategy and Psychology of Ireland's Dissident Terrorists.* (New York: Oxford University Press, 2013), 49.

years previous by their 1916 forefathers. Their message is clear. They are not Sinn Fein.[21]

In a post-Good Friday Agreement Ireland the dissidents have been consistently clear. They are firm in the contempt they hold the newly normalizing Northern Ireland, and most importantly the role which Sinn Fein now play in it. The Real IRA went into ceasefire in the immediate aftermath of Omagh. However, in January 2000 they announced their return by issuing a statement which acted as a recruitment call roundly condemning the Northern Ireland Executive and Sinn Fein. For them their former comrades were now part of 'an elite clique, or corrupt treacherous administration'.[22] While it did not call an end to their ceasefire it did emphasize their intentions. The end of the ceasefire was not far away though as just over a month later the group was responsible for the bombing of Shackleton Army Barracks in Ballykeely, Co. Derry. Through their January statement they had shown their distrust of Sinn Fein, whereas it was their February attack which re-emphasized their war against 'British occupation'.

This disdain for Provisional politicization has been emphasized by the statements and actions of each of the dissident groups since their inception, a theme which is still dominant today. For them a Sinn Fein leadership sharing power in a devolved Northern Irish Executive is tantamount to accepting British rule in Northern Ireland, tantamount to treachery. The continued existence of the Provisional IRA at the turn of the century in the dissidents eyes was only in name. As they had accepted the political initiatives of the Good Friday Agreement, they could no longer class themselves as republicans. For the Continuity IRA it was time for the Provisional IRA to disband and give up their weapons to those 'prepared to defend the Republic'.[23]

Throughout their paramilitary activity dissidents have aimed to mark positive turning points in the peace process with their contrast of violence, a reminder that they were not going away. When devolution was restored to Stormont on 30 May 2000 this was quickly followed by a small bomb on Hammersmith Bridge in London. While the size of the bomb was small, and it came at a time of intensified dissident activity in Northern Ireland, this attack on its own was still significant. It displayed for the first time that the dissidents were prepared to attack Great Britain. This was followed over the

---

[21] For a full analysis of the three waves of violent dissident activity see John Horgan, *Divided We Stand: The Strategy and Psychology of Ireland's Dissident Terrorists*. (New York: Oxford University Press, 2013), 47–76.

[22] John Mullin, 'Real IRA Ends Silence With a Call to Arms', *The Guardian*, 21 January 2000. www.guardian.co.uk/uk/2000/jan/21/northernireland.johnmullin (Last accessed, 12 March 2013).

[23] 'Provos Should Disband: CIRA' *Irish News*, 11 May 2000.

next year and half by a series of Real IRA attacks across England. Just over two weeks after the Hammersmith Bridge attack they planted a bomb on the railway line at Ealing Broadway Station. Over the months ahead their attacks would go on to target the symbols and centres of British power, institutions such as the BBC and MI6. To their small band of membership and support they were bringing the fight to the 'oppressor'. However, this surge of activity in both Great Britain and Northern Ireland throughout 2000 and 2001 was to be the height of their powers during this second wave. Their insistence on maintaining the armed struggle was failing to gain any traction within the broader republican and nationalist communities, an essential next step if they were to mount a sustained campaign. In the broader republican communities the peace process was worth giving a chance.

However, it was not only their lack of support which was diminishing their capabilities the already small and divided groupings were splintering yet again, a fact compounded by their clear infiltration by informers. Many of these new splits were not taking place on a national level, but were happening more regionally and affecting the groups at a local level. Within the Real IRA itself it was clear that there was significant discontent. A new faction was forming within the organization. This was led by the former Provisional quartermaster Mickey McKevitt and a selection of his fellow prisoners and external supporters. Due to the internal disagreement over the preferable path for the organization to take and accusations from incarcerated members about external 'fraternisation with criminal elements'[24] the group was splitting. McKevitt and his faction went on to establish the New Republican Forum, while the Real IRA continued with their ailing campaign. However, from 2002 to 2006 they were entering what Frampton has perfectly described as 'the nadir of dissident republicanism'.[25] With the Real IRA dividing across accusations and personalities both sides were aiming to justify their position. One leading RIRA member placed the blame for McKevitt's dissension on his own personal grievances, and his attempts to secure release.

> Once McKevitt went into prison both he and [his wife] Bernadette Sands McKevitt muddied the waters with other members by concentrating purely on getting him out.[26]

---

[24] 'Interview with Republican Prisoners', *Forum Magazine*, February 2003; For an overview of this division see Martyn Frampton, *Legion of the Rearguard: Dissident Irish Republicanism*. (Dublin: Irish Academic Press, 2011), 145.
[25] Martyn Frampton, *Legion of the Rearguard*, 157–200.
[26] Interview by the author with 'Conor'.

In reaction to the emerging statement from the McKevitt led faction the external leadership carried out an interview whereby they put forward their own account of the division while also laying out their aims and agenda.

> The statement from Portlaoise should be viewed as absolute treachery . . . . They have manipulated a situation for their own selfish agenda. The days of the Republican Movement following false icons are over and we will be guided by our principles and the views of all our Volunteers. Our Volunteers' position is not reflected in the statement from Portlaoise. The allegations made in that statement are a complete red-herring . . . . There are mechanisms in place to deal with the relationship between Óglaigh na hÉireann and prisoners. Some individuals in Portlaoise have already been dismissed and further investigations are ongoing.[27]

The true effects of this split were not to be seen for another seven years. However, it was not only the Real IRA who were dividing. The age old republican struggle with the splits was similarly affecting the Continuity IRA. In February 2006 the Independent Monitoring Commission (IMC), a body set up under the Good Friday Agreement to monitor paramilitary activity, reported the existence of a Strabane based Continuity IRA splinter group going by the name of Oglaigh na hEireann. In reaction the parent organization ordered the splinter group to leave Northern Ireland.[28] This localized form of Continuity fracturing was reflected once again in 2008 with the emergence of the minor grouping calling themselves the Irish Republican Liberation Army (IRLA), a group based in the Ardoyne area of West Belfast who announced their arrival by threatening members of Sinn Fein who were involved in District Policing Partnerships.[29] However, it was the tensions emerging from within the Real IRA divisions in 2002 which was to result in the most potent of the dissident splinters. It was from this fracturing that 2009 saw the emergence of yet another group claiming the moniker of Oglaigh na hEireann. However, unlike the Continuity splinter of the same name this organization was to become one of the most potent and dangerous groups in modern day Northern Ireland. They have been responsible for brutal attacks on PSNI officers, the Northern Ireland headquarters of MI5 and civilian targets. In March of 2013 they claimed responsibility for an intercepted car bomb intended to attack the Lough Erne Resort in Co. Fermanagh, the June 2013 venue of the G8

---

[27] Damien Okado-Gough, '"Real" Irish Republican Army (rIRA) Statement.' CAIN, http://cain.ulst.ac.uk/othelem/organ/ira/rira280103.htm (Last accessed, 1 June 2013).

[28] Eighth Report of the Independent Monitoring Commission, 14.

[29] Eighteenth Report of the Independent Monitoring Commission, 5.

summit. The excess of dissident factions is marked by their division from the Provisional Movement and Sinn Fein. They have sporadically shown an ability to co-operate. However, without a coherent voice and strategy their campaigns have failed to gain any traction. This is a fact of which the dissidents are all too aware, an issue they are attempting to resolve. Later on in the chapter is an analysis of their attempts to form a united front against the British and the normalization of Northern Irish life.

With the second phase of dissident violence coming to a close with ineffectual or intercepted attacks and minimal support it was time for the dissidents to regroup. In February 2008 members of the Real IRA leadership carried out an interview with the journalist Suzanne Breen. In it they described the reorganization the group was just emerging from, and with it admission that their original mode of operation had been flawed.

> We're emerging from a three-year period of reorganising in preparation for a renewed offensive . . . . In terms of other internal changes, people have been dismissed from the movement in Belfast and elsewhere. Units that weren't up to scratch have been disbanded. Mistakes were made previously but more rigorous vetting of volunteers is now in place.[30]

In the interview they made clear statements of intent to target PSNI officers as well British government ministers. Within this claim there was agreement that Sinn Fein ministers would be considered to be British government ministers. However, there was also an admission that even though they would be deemed as a legitimate target that their targeting may have a negative effect on the dissidents' support network.

It was their stated plan to target PSNI officers and their barracks which was a clear omen of what was to come in this third wave. In this statement of intent they made reference to the Strand Road PSNI station in Derry. They used it as a signal of the steps being taken by the PSNI to protect themselves, a sign of the effect the dissidents were having on them. This station would prove to become one of the most consistent targets of the dissidents over the next five years, and possibly even more.

> In November, the IRA carried out operations within days in three separate locations – attempting to kill RUC/PSNI officers in Derry and Dungannon, and planting a bomb on Remembrance Sunday in Newry. That shows increased confidence. The IRA believed it could kill a cop and take whatever the state threw at it . . . . There was talk of a 'new style' unarmed RUC/

---

[30] Suzanne Breen, 'War Back On-Real IRA'. *The Sunday Tribune*, 4 February 2008.

PSNI in non-combative clothing. Well they're back wearing flak jackets and still carrying guns. Strand Road barracks in Derry is being refortified to make it rocket-proof.[31]

Throughout the Troubles Irish Republicans had been ostensibly fighting to bring an end to the British presence in Northern Ireland. Publicly they wanted to get rid of British army patrols from the streets of the region. However, in reality this provided a visible enemy for them to target and to fight. For them this visible enemy provided them with legitimacy, and with this legitimacy came a means of recruitment and strengthening support. For the dissidents they do not have this recruitment tool. The British Army no longer patrol the streets of Belfast and Derry. The RUC has been replaced by a more representative PSNI. Without a visible enemy this has hampered their ability to recruit. It should therefore come as no surprise the intention of their actions. To sustain their fight and justify their existence, they needed this obvious enemy.

With more attacks on the RUC/PSNI we believe the stage will be reached where British soldiers are brought back onto the streets to bolster the cops. This will shatter the façade that the British presence has gone and normality reigns. People will once again be made visibly aware that we remain occupied.[32]

The dissidents still struggle to find that visible enemy. Although their campaign has intensified it has failed in bringing the British army back on to the streets of Northern Ireland. However, in spite of this the interview with Breen has proven to be prescient. The third wave of dissident activity has been marked by the targeting of PSNI officers, both current and former, as well as their families. Within this there has been particular focus on the targeting of Catholic PSNI officers. Stephen Carroll, Peadar Heffron, Ronan Kerr, were all targets of various dissident groups, all Catholic PSNI officers. For those who simply define Northern Irish paramilitarism as a fight between Catholics and Protestants the targeting of these officers would seem to be irrational. The question would be asked 'why are these groups targeting their own communities?' However, the answer is clear. Similar to the British Army the old Royal Ulster Constabulary provided a visible enemy to fight against. It was, accurately, portrayed as a Protestant police force. It was resultantly, and successfully, painted as a sectarian police force.

---

[31] Ibid.
[32] Ibid.

This in turn provided further legitimacy for the IRA to 'police' the Catholic neighbourhoods. However, with the implementation of the Patten Report on Policing which called on 'an equal number of Protestants and Catholics [to] be drawn from the pool of qualified recruits'[33] this legitimacy was being challenged. Their aim in targeting Catholic police officers therefore has not only been their way of targeting a British police force. It has also been their attempt to deter potential Catholic recruits from joining the PSNI. With success they would have been able to clearly, and effectively, deride the PSNI as an unrepresentative sectarian force. As of March 2011 the PSNI are no longer appointing recruits on this 50/50 basis. However, at the end of this policy in March 2011, just days before the murder of Ronan Kerr, they had succeeded in having a 30% Catholic police force, a huge improvement on before.[34]

By 2007 the Provisional leadership had brought the majority of their membership and support through a large number of substantial changes. For some they had never imagined dropping abstentionism to the Dail or Stormont or to call off the 'war' short of a united Ireland. But they embraced the change by assessing to the context of the time and the opportunities it provided. However, along the way certain change was seen by some as a step too far. It was deemed detrimental to the organizational identity. The Sinn Fein support for the PSNI was one such issue. As always the leadership of the party made sure that they canvassed their members before bringing it to a vote. They understood that it was as important, if not more so, to enter into internal talks as it was to partake in external negotiations.

> I think one of the things that we learned earlier on in negotiations is that there are two levels of negotiations. There is your external and your internal. You negotiate at two ends of the spectrum, if you try and you negotiate externally and forget about your internal then you are in trouble, the other way about likewise.[35]

However, even after a careful negotiation process the group is always prone to losing some members at such a significant turning point. It is apparent that as with '86 and '97 this was also the case in 2007. For many the acceptance of the PSNI, the heirs to the RUC, was a step too far, a step which forced their exit.

---

[33] *The Patten Report on Policing: Summary of Recommendations.* Paragraph 15.10.

[34] 'PSNI 50/50 Recruitment Policy Ends', *The Belfast Telegraph*, 22 March 2011. www. belfasttelegraph.co.uk/news/local-national/northern-ireland/psni-5050-recruitment-policy-ends-28600138.html (Last accessed, 3 June 2013).

[35] Interview by the author with Tom Hartley.

What really upset people was the joining of the police service and that became a defining moment for many people who have left. We would see a sea change in attitude across the Republican base even people who stayed with Sinn Fein up until quite recently would be more prepared to stand and have a conversation, I suppose lamely acknowledge the legitimacy of your position, things like that that wouldn't have happened ten years ago.[36]

While their exit was minimal in size, it was significant in effect. When Ronan Kerr was murdered by a mercury tilt switch car bomb a claim of responsibility shortly followed from the newly formed 'IRA', a grouping of former Provisionals based largely in Tyrone. Although small in number the group was significant due to the former seniority and experience of their members. This was an experienced group who had given the peace process a chance. They had waited to see if 'a peaceful route toward independence and national liberation would emerge'[37] claiming 'minimum reforms proposed by Patten'[38] had not reformed the RUC, even if it was now operating under a different name. Resultantly they were exiting to return to armed republicanism. Within their claim they vowed to 'bring our struggle to a successful conclusion through military operations'.[39]

This is a new form of dissident, one with the opportunity to tap into the sentiment of a wider republican community. By acknowledging that they had given the peace process a chance they are able to portray themselves as a more reasonable group, one with the willingness to give peace a chance. They are utilizing this to justify their return to violence. Their attacks are not violence for the sake of violence. They have returned to bring 'a successful conclusion' and finally achieve a united Ireland. They were also showing their willingness to work with other dissident groups with the same goal. In doing so they are saying to their potential membership and support that they are not interested in petty grievances and personal credit, their focus is purely on the final goal. They are therefore attempting to tap in to the 'true' republican psyche.

At the birth of a new group, or the move into a new phase of paramilitary violence, the groups want to do something different. They want to distinguish themselves from the parent group which they had emerged from, or their

---

[36] Interview by the author with Francie Mackey.
[37] Suzanne Breen 'Former Provos Claim Kerr Murder and Vow More Attacks'. *The Belfast Telegraph*, 22 April 2011. www.belfasttelegraph.co.uk/news/local-national/northern-ireland/former-provos-claim-kerr-murder-and-vow-more-attacks-28610456.html (Last accessed, 1 April 2013).
[38] Ibid.
[39] Ibid.

previous wave of violence. This has been highlighted in the paragraphs above but was also referred to in the previous chapter. 'Conor' a leading member of the Real IRA stated that with the emergence of the new group they had:

> . . . urged members that they must kill a British soldier face to face, no sniper, with a gun as the Provos hadn't done that in years and this would prove that they were different.[40]

This quote comes from an interview carried out on 12 January 2009. On 7 March of that same year, two days before the Continuity IRA murder of Stephen Carroll, the Real IRA murdered two off-duty British soldiers, Sappers Mark Quinsey and Patrick Azimkar, as they were collecting a delivery pizza at the Massereene Barracks in Co. Antrim. The assailants first shot at the soldiers from their car from distance. However, with the ensuing gun battle over a gunman exited the car and shot the bodies lying on the ground. They had succeeded in doing what the 'Provos hadn't done in years'. They had shot a British soldier face to face.

The targeting of PSNI officers and British soldiers is very different to the civilian tragedies of Omagh. While they cause outrage and revulsion in the wider community they have more potential to improve support within the small sections of the nationalist and republican communities. For them it is easier to paint these victims as symbols of British oppression. It legitimizes their war and their very existence. By deliberately targeting PSNI officers with greater intensity post-2007 they are continuously emphasizing not only their hostility towards this 'British police force' but they are re-emphasizing their opposition to the position taken by mainstream republicanism to support the PSNI.

While the dissidents may not have achieved a terrorist 'spectacular' in recent years the question remains 'do they want to?' The effects of Omagh demonstrated that theirs is a weak support, a support which can be easily dispersed. For some groups such as the weakening Continuity IRA this may prove to be a phase of recruitment rather than sustained paramilitary activity.

> Over the next few years we will just work on recruiting and getting our voice heard around the place. It is still a long slog but we will get there eventually . . . . I can't see any military operations [from the Continuity IRA] in the near future. I feel they will stand back and they will do their job, is what they want to do, their recruitment and training and everything else. I would agree with that 100%.[41]

---

[40] Interview by the author with 'Conor'.
[41] Interview by the author with 'Kate'.

However, for other groups they may be biding their time. This phase of their struggle may be more about strengthening that base rather than losing it with one miscalculated attack. Their rebuilding phase continues until they can sustain the inevitable backlash a spectacular would bring. The continuous weapons finds have shown that they have the capability to mount such an attack.[42] However, having the capability to physically mount an attack and survive the backlash are two very different things. They may be biding their time to mark the centenary of 1916.

Coirpigh na hEireann: Criminals of Ireland

Since the dawn of the Troubles Irish republicans, in their various guises, have been rightly classified as terrorist groups. Their predominant strategy has been one of sustained political violence, and threatened violence, aiming to bring fear to a wider audience with the goal of achieving a political effect. However, this does not accurately describe the full scope of their illegal activity. Alongside their terrorist and paramilitary violence they have similarly been involved in vigilantism, organized crime and violent feuds with fellow paramilitaries and criminal gangs. They have even been seen to bring in known criminals to bolster their ranks at certain periods.

> They [the INLA] started bringing in criminals off the lower Falls, car thieves and this that and the other. They dropped the criteria as they needed numbers and they found themselves immediately in this defensive war against the Officials.[43]

The modern day dissidents are no different. Across the island, but most visibly in Dublin, these groups have been involved in sustained levels of criminality. There have been various reports of dissident involvement in extortion rackets,[44] drug trafficking,[45] cigarette smuggling,[46] and arms trades with

---

[42] 'Northern Ireland Police Find Huge Unexploded Bomb'. *CNN*, 28 April 2012. http://edition.cnn.com/2012/04/28/world/europe/northern-ireland-bomb (Last accessed, 1 June 2013).

[43] Interview by the author with Sean O'Callaghan.

[44] Tom Brady and Fergus Black 'Irish Police Swoop on Suspected Extortion Rackets by Dissidents'. *The Belfast Telegraph*, 30 March 2013. www.belfasttelegraph.co.uk/news/local-national/republic-of-ireland/irish-police-swoop-on-suspected-extortion-racket-by-dissidents-29164097.html (Last accessed, 1 April 2013).

[45] Tom Brady 'Dissidents Move Into Drug Trade to Raise Cash', *Irish Independent*, 28 January 2013. www.independent.ie/irish-news/dissidents-move-in-to-drug-trade-to-raise-cash-29023595.html (Last accessed, 1 April 2013).

[46] Stephen Wright 'IRA's Cigarette Smuggling Millionaires'. *The Daily Mail*, 6 June 2013. www.dailymail.co.uk/news/article-2336865/IRAs-cigarette-smuggling-millionaires-Former-terrorists-flooding-UK-potentially-lethal-fakes-cheating-taxpayers-billions.html (Last accessed, 6 June 2013).

known criminals.[47] In 2002 the Northern Ireland Affairs Committee stated that the running cost of the Real IRA was approximately £500,000 but that it makes £1.5 million from criminality.[48]

On 3 September 2013 Alan Ryan, a leading member of the Dublin branch of the Real IRA was murdered. The Gardai believed that his killing was as a result of an on-going feud with a Dublin crime gang.[49] Ryan, his brothers and other leading members of the Dublin paramilitaries were widely believed to be involved in extortion rackets and various forms of intimidation and organized crime.[50] While he is revered by his comrades as a political paramilitary his actions were more reminiscent of a criminal enforcer. The case of Ryan is a clear example that just because an individual or organization uses the moniker of republicanism this does not automatically mean that all of their actions are with the aim of achieving a united Ireland. In the aftermath of Ryan's death talk of internal feuds within the Dublin branch have abounded, especially since the murder of fellow Real IRA member Peter Butterly in Gormanston Co. Meath in March of 2013.[51]

For Sinn Fein, in competition for membership and support with the dissidents, they have consistently grasped on to the opportunity to dwell on this criminal connection. In their eyes this represents an opening to bring into question the republicanism of these groups, and to reveal their true nature to potential supporters.

> Whatever else about those groups responsible it is obvious that they have now been swamped by ruthless criminal elements with an island-wide network.[52]

However, this opportunity has also been exploited by rival dissident organizations to isolate and demean their rivals. Similar to Sinn Fein it allows

---

[47] Rosie Cowan 'Irish Terrorists Blamed for Illegal Gun Trade with UK', *The Guardian*, 15 October 2003. www.guardian.co.uk/uk/2003/oct/15/northernireland.ireland (Last accessed, 1 April 2013).

[48] Martyn Frampton, *Legion of the Rearguard*, 299.

[49] Conor Lally 'A Dangerous and Determined Organisation'. *The Irish Times,* 28 September 2012. www.irishtimes.com/news/a-dangerous-and-determined-organisation-1.539710 (Last accessed, 1 April 2013).

[50] 'Funeral of Real IRA Member'. *The Irish Times*, 8 September 2012. www.irishtimes.com/news/funeral-for-real-ira-member-1.735408 (Last accessed, 1 April 2013).

[51] Ken Foy 'IRA Man Was Betrayed By Pal in Car Park Feud Killing'. *The Evening Herald*, 8 March 2013. www.herald.ie/news/ira-man-was-betrayed-by-pal-in-car-park-feud-killing-29117825.html (Last accessed, 8 April 2013).

[52] Gerry Moriarty, Mary Minihan and Marie O'Halloran 'McGuinness Admits Lack of Cohesion'. *The Irish Times*, 13 April 2013. www.irishtimes.com/news/politics/mcguinness-admits-lack-of-cohesion-1.1358842 (Last accessed, 14 April 2013).

them the chance to bring into focus their grievances about their competitors and resultantly paint themselves as the only true Republicans.

> The only difference between the Continuity IRA and the Real IRA with the Real IRA all the top men all they were doing all their life was smuggling diesel and cigarettes.[53]

While dissidents' engagement with the Dublin crime scene has engulfed the headlines south of the border one of the most sustained criminal activities north of the border is organized vigilantism. Groups such as Republican Action Against Drugs (RAAD), a Derry based organization believed to be made up of former Provisionals, have become one of the most persistently violent of the dissident groups.[54] Within the most Republican areas of Derry and north Donegal they have become the self-appointed guardians of morality. While other groups have targeted symbols of British occupation RAAD's almost total concentration has been on the targeting of alleged drug dealers. They have utilized the Provisional tactics of kneecappings and expulsion, while also attacking the homes of suspected criminals with pipe bombs and giving them the 'ultimate sanction' of assassination.[55] While other groups have left some of their attacks unclaimed RAAD have proven to be one of the most consistent to release statements of responsibility.[56] Coupled with their violence these statements serve a clear purpose. They allow the group the opportunity to portray themselves as the protectors of the communities. In their minds theirs is a job that the PSNI, and the Provisionals, are unwilling, unable or are unentitled to carry out. This violence allows them the chance to put themselves forward as the indispensable guardians of the peace.

The merging threat

Expanding on Horgan's thesis I believe that we may be entering a fourth wave of violent dissident republicanism. Recent years have seen a number of these disparate groups show their awareness that if they are to gain any ground in their armed campaign, or credibility among supporters, that they need to be displaying a more united dissident movement. Across the groups they are

---

[53] Interview by the author with 'Frank'.
[54] Horgan, *Divided We Stand*, 39–40.
[55] 'RAAD Issues Chilling Warning'. *Inishowen Independent*, 23 February 2012. www.inishowennews.com/012RADDwarn085.htm (Last accessed, 1 April 2013).
[56] John Horgan and John F. Morrison, 'Here to Stay? The Rising Threat of Violent Dissident Republicanism in Northern Ireland', *Terrorism and Political Violence*, 23(4) (2011), 642–69 (648).

united in their aim to continue the armed campaign and their contempt for Sinn Fein and the peace process. However, in this unity of ideas they are divided by personality, regionalism and petty feuds. But in recent times in the lead up to 2016 there has been a concerted effort to unite under one banner in order to sustain and intensify the armed campaign. Historically they had shown a willingness to work together on individual operations, a co-operation which up until recently they had always stopped short of formally aligning. This was admitted in the 2008 interview with Suzanne Breen.

> The IRA will work with the Continuity IRA and INLA on issues where there is common ground. But there are no organisational links and there will be no joint operations. We are not seeking to amalgamate three armies into a 'super republican group'.[57]

As we have already seen with the case of 'the IRA' after the death of Ronan Kerr they are willing to put aside petty rivalries and personal feuds in order to achieve the end goal of a united Ireland. Just a year later it appears that this has come to pass with the July 2012 announcement of a merger between the Real IRA, RAAD and previously unaligned Republicans including those responsible for the death of Kerr. They claim to have formed a united organization under a 'unified structure, under a single leadership'.[58] Their aim is to appeal to a wider population and to put forward a united Republican Movement in opposition not only to British occupation but also to Sinn Fein and the peace process. In this opening statement they also ventured to portray themselves as victims purely due to their non-conformity with the Good Friday Agreement.

> Non-conformist republicans are being subjected to harassment, arrest and violence by the forces of the British crown; others have been interned on the direction of an English overlord. It is Britain, not the IRA, which has chosen provocation and conflict.[59]

It is this message of prisoner victimization which may prove to be the most powerful tool they have. It is a topic which each of the dissident factions has grasped on to in the past few years. There have been mounting

---

[57] Suzanne Breen, 'War Back On – Real IRA'. *The Sunday Tribune,* 4 February 2008. www.nuzhound.com/articles/Sunday_Tribune/arts2008/feb3_RIRA_interview__SBreen.php (Last accessed, 31 August 2013).

[58] 'New IRA' Statement on Dissident Merger, 26 July 2012.

[59] 'New IRA' Statement on Dissident Merger.

demonstrations, both within and outside of the prison over the use of strip searching, 'internment without trial'[60] and the use of ineligible evidence.[61] The prisoners have gone on intermittent hunger strikes and dirty protests, and their external supporters have mounted consistent protests and campaigns in their name. For their part the paramilitary conglomerate chose to announce the birth of their new armed campaign off the back of this, with the murder of prison officer David Black. While the murder of PSNI officers was to highlight disquiet with the new police and Sinn Fein's support of it, by targeting a prison officer their aim was not only to bring the story of the prisoners' struggle to the masses but also, like other new groups before them, to do something that has not been done for a long time.

One of the ironies of this current push for Republican unity is that it has caused yet another split within Irish Republicanism. In 2010 the Continuity IRA and Republican Sinn Fein went through yet another division in their membership. Led by the Limerick faction, including the likes of Des Long and Joe 'Tiny' Lynch, a split took place at the leadership levels of both the paramilitary and political groups. The organizations seem to have split on strategic as well as personal grounds. The newly formed faction, still maintaining the name of the Continuity IRA, claimed in their opening statement that

> . . . delegates [at a General Army Convention] expressed serious dissatisfaction with the former Leadership who were attempting to subvert the military campaign and had allowed elements within the Republican Movement to engage in corruption over an extended period of time.[62]

Similar to that of the 'New IRA' they have called for the unity of the 'true Republican Movement' a movement they admit to be widely splintered. They believe that 'broad front' republicanism is the only way to overthrow British rule, a point emphasized by Joe Lynch in his 2011 speech at Bodenstown.

> Whereas those who still adhere to traditional Republican principles are fragmented, broken into various groupings, engage in verbal warfare over minor issues and fail to present a coherent effective strategy for tackling the British presence. Today we are the continuity of that tradition of [Theobald] Wolfe Tone and it is up to us to urge the unity of all true Republicans who support the principles of the Movement he founded.[63]

---

[60] See the cases of Martin Corey and Marian Price.

[61] See the case of Brian Shivers and Colin Duffy for the Massereene Barracks attack.

[62] 'New Army Leadership Elected by Continuity IRA', *Saoirse Nua*, Issue 1 October 2010.

[63] 'Call for a Unity of Republicans'. *Saoirse Nua,* Issue 5 September/October 2011, 4.

However, even with their similar calls for unity with the 'New IRA', and attempts of contact, they are yet to embrace this organization into their merger, a point validated by one of the Limerick faction's leading members.

> I am hoping they work out . . . but unfortunately I haven't heard any word of it since. I haven't been approached.[64]

For the membership of the movement they left behind this exit comes as no surprise. In their minds it had been coming for a number of years. However, it was only at the 2010 Ard Fheis where there was a vote on who should replace the ailing Ruairi O'Bradaigh that it really came to a head.

> Some of the people wanted, really I suppose, to form a broad front again. People from Fermanagh and people from Limerick really would have been the strongest instigators of it. Also when Ruairi O'Bradaigh stepped down as president and Des Dalton was vote in as president Des Long from Limerick was quite upset that he wasn't elected. He stood for election but he was quite upset that Des Dalton beat him. After that there was a kind of a whispering campaign that the vote was rigged, the count was rigged and all that kind of rubbish.[65]

These two groups are now in immediate competition for both membership and support. They are in the final stage of the process of split. They are therefore simultaneously trying to promote the legitimacy of their group while dismissing the actions and claims of the others. For their part the parent organization, the original Continuity IRA and Republican Sinn Fein, are claiming the splinter group's links with criminality. In doing so they are attempting to dispel their republican claims.

> No matter what they do they're not Republicans, they're only criminals and that's what happened. They went further down that criminal road and there is no way that they will ever be affiliated with us or use our name.[66]

In response the splinter group is similarly attempting to denigrate their former comrades. They are questioning the ability of the organization to progress under the control of a 'clique of elderly women', a reference to prominent women in the organization such as Geraldine Taylor and Josephine Hayden.

---

[64] Interview by the author with 'Peter'.
[65] Interview by the author with 'Barbara'.
[66] Interview by the author with 'Kate'.

Well the most recent one was that a number of people were completely dissatisfied with what they call 223 [Parnell Street]. It's being run by a clique of women. Kind of a Cumann na mBan clique are running it and [Ruairi] O'Bradaigh had tolerated this, very much so. There was never going to be expansion.[67]

While there will be continuing calls for a united or broad dissident front the organizations have many struggles ahead. A number of these groups have been divided for a significant period of time. They have formed their own leaderships within their autonomous organizations, positions they will unlikely wish to give up freely, thus causing the possibility of further factionalism. It is rare within Irish Republicanism that fractures are healed. A number of these groups have been bitter rivals in the past, and have left 'mainstream' Republicanism on contentious issues while their new comrades stayed behind on a politicizing platform. For the moment they are united but it is unclear how long that will last, but even with this unity they are unlikely to bring down the peace process they so vehemently oppose.

Towards 2016

The historic splits, and recent mergers, within Irish Republicanism have provided the setting for a tense, and potentially violent, journey towards the centenary of the 1916 Rising. The observed rise in violent dissident activity has illustrated their intent to mark this with a sustained armed campaign. In their eyes without a united Ireland the armed campaign must be maintained, continuing the struggle of Connolly and Pearse. For the dissidents this will provide an opportunity to gain an upturn in their support, an opportunity they are already attempting to manipulate in the development of their united front. In analysing how the dissidents may attempt to capitalize on 2016 Sean O'Callaghan outlines a potential strategy to be employed by the groups in order to portray a united front. It is likely that they will continue to draw on the perception that the Sinn Fein leadership, as well as the Irish government, has 'sold out' on the ideals of 1916.

The general sense that the Irish state has sold out on 1916, the Provos have sold out on 1916 will be accepted I think. I think if some of them were clever enough. They don't really need to focus too much on the points of potential dissension . . . . So let's agree that the 1916 ideals have been

---

[67] Interview by the author with 'Derek'.

sold out by successive Irish governments and now by the Provos. Let's agree we've got an opportunity there to begin to undermine the Provos, get some traction there. We have got the potential to rattle Loyalists and see what that provokes in terms of street reaction.[68]

In reaction to this the leadership Sinn Fein will more than likely continue to claim themselves as the heirs to 1916. They will claim that it is now only through political means that a united Ireland will be achieved. It is important in order to properly counter the dissident threat that the reality of the groups is continuously re-emphasized. The leadership of Sinn Fein, the SDLP and the Irish government need to be continuously reacting to dissidents with the emphasis on their criminality. This counter-narrative needs to also spread beyond these traditional bases. While the key job for the Sinn Fein leadership is to conserve its existing membership and support their voice does not carry must weight in the predominantly dissident stomping grounds. For many there the sentiments and ideals of Martin McGuinness and Gerry Adams are held in the same level of contempt as those of David Cameron or Peter Robinson.[69] They are now seen as traitors to their forefathers and servants of British rule. There needs to be an alternative influential voice within the communities, one non-aligned to mainstream Republicanism but willing to speak out against the dissident threat, while also listening to the concerns of the potential and current dissidents.

While these groups are small now history has shown that there is persistent potential for recruitment to Irish Republican paramilitary organizations. This is not a threat which should be taken lightly. Both the Irish state and Sinn Fein need to be careful and sensitive in how they are to mark the centenary of the Rising, a wrong step either way brings the potential of problems.

I think you have got a number of things. You have got how the south is going to deal with 2016 is very, very crucial. I suspect what they will try to do is a kind of muted celebrations and be very careful about it. But that might be easier said than done. They've got to be careful of attaching that to the Republicans, ultra-nationalists and the left.[70]

For the time being we have a manageable threat, one which the PSNI and the Gardai have proven time and again that they are able to deal with. The question now is how should this threat be reduced? By assessing the history of the

---

[68] Interview by the author with Sean O'Callaghan.
[69] The leader of the DUP.
[70] Interview by the author with Sean O'Callaghan.

Troubles the greatest success has come when influential actors on all sides are willing to take brave steps. Whether this be John Hume, Ian Paisley, Gerry Adams, John Major or others peace has been reached when a bold move has been made, often times against their better judgement. The politicization of the Provisional Movement detailed across this book has emphasized this on a number of occasions. Northern Ireland would be a very different place without the brave moves by all communities and governments. In 2010 Martin McGuinness revealed that both the British and Irish governments were in on-going talks with the violent dissident groups.[71] It is this kind of brave move that must be sustained to maintain peace across Northern Ireland. While the threat of a return to the Troubles is not alive the steady increase in paramilitary activity we are seeing today must not be tolerated. The police on both sides of the border can only do so much to alleviate the immediate threats. It is only dialogue that will bring about a cessation. In the words of the former head of MI5 Lady Eliza Manningham-Buller

> Dialogue, even with terrorists, is necessary . . . . Talking doesn't mean approval. It's a way of exploring peaceful options, what compromises, if any, can be reached.[72]

---

[71] Henry McDonald 'Irish Dissidents "in talks with British government," says Martin McGuinness'. *The Guardian*, 12 August 2010. www.guardian.co.uk/uk/2010/aug/12/uk-government-contact-republican-dissidents (Last accessed, 12 June 2013).

[72] Richard Norton-Taylor 'Former MI5 Chief Urges Terrorist Talks', *The Guardian*, 13 September 2011. www.guardian.co.uk/uk/2011/sep/13/former-mi5-chief-urges-terrorist-talks (Last accessed, 12 June 2013).

Appendix A:
Table of interviews

Participant	Date
Geraldine Taylor	15 October 2007 and 23 January 2009
Roy Johnston	29 November 2007, 19 December 2007, 17 January 2008, 3 February 2008 and 21 February 2009
Danny Morrison	21 January 2008
Mitchell McLaughlin	24 January 2008
Gerry Adams	30 January 2008
Joe Doherty	1 February 2008
Fra Halligan	6 February 2008
Ruairi O'Bradaigh	20 February 2008
'Denis'	29 February 2008
Harry Donaghy	6 March 2008
Sean O'Hare	6 March 2008
Anthony McIntyre	8 March 2008
Richard O'Rawe	9 April 2008
Dolours Price	21 April 2008
Cathleen Knowles McGurk	13 May 2008
'Una'	14 May 2008
Pat Doherty	19 May 2008
Sean McManus	29 May 2008
Des Long	7 June 2008
Joe O'Neill	10 June 2008 and 13 August 2008

Participant	Date
Martin McGuinness	23 June 2008
Francie Mackey	25 June 2008
'Paul'	10 August 2008
Paddy Woodworth	15 August 2008
Sean O'Bradaigh	17 August 2008
Richard McAuley	12 September 2008
Thomas MacGiolla	15 September 2008
Martin McGonagle	18 December 2008
Tom Hartley	6 January 2009
'Conor'	12 January 2009
Mick Ryan	22 January 2009, 2 February 2009, 16 February 2009, 18 March 2009, 24 March 2009
'Alex'	23 January 2009
James Scullion	23 January 2009
Anthony Coughlan	31 January 2009
Gerry Kelly	4 February 2009
Patrick Kennelly	10 March 2009
'Frank'	11 March 2009
Mick Murtagh	11 March 2009
'Kate'	24 August 2012
'Peter'	25 August 2012
'Barbara'	26 August 2012, 25 May 2013
Sean O'Callaghan	19 March 2013

Index

Lightning Source UK Ltd.
Milton Keynes UK
UKHW031259020919
348951UK00002B/109/P